EVOLVE

TABLE OF CONTENTS

BASICS

Evolve is an asymmetrical, multiplayer first-person shooter played by five players—four Hunters against one Monster. In the primary Hunt mode, Hunters are dropped into a wild environment, where they must hunt down and kill the giant before it defeats them. Each player has a unique role in the group, as the team must work together to take down the foe.

The fifth player takes the role of the Monster, feeding on a variety of wildlife as it flees from the pursuers. With enough energy saved up, it evolves into a tougher Stage 2 version, which evens out the fight against the Hunters. Reach the ultimate Stage 3, and the odds turn to the big guy's favor. At any time, though, the beast can employ its skills against the puny humans.

A selection of characters, perks, modes, maps, and map effects offer a nice variety in gameplay. Play alone with computer-controlled bots, or take your skills online and hunt your friends and fellow gamers.

You can play *Evolve* on your own, with friends, and with online players through matchmaking. The game is played with four other players, either human or AI-controlled. Select Solo if you wish to go it alone, or Multiplayer when you want to go online. Either way, you earn XP after each game, which in turn unlocks more characters, perks, skins, and badges.

MENUS

From the main menu, select from the following: Multiplayer, Solo, Switch User (on Xbox One), Profile, Extras, Options, and Store.

MULTIPLAYER

Multiplayer connects you to the game servers, allowing you to participate in a game online with other players or hook up with friends in a Custom game. Selecting Skirmish or Evacuation for the first time gives you an opportunity to set up your role preference. Rank the four Hunter positions and Monster in the order that you would prefer to play. It will attempt to place you in a game starting with your first option, then your second, etc. You may also select No Preference to randomly be placed in a role.

SKIRMISH	Play one round at a time, matchmaking and cycling maps in Hunt mode.
EVACUATION	Play five missions in a dynamic campaign where all game modes are played. Players affect the environment by winning and losing.
CUSTOM	Play a private game with one or more of your friends using modified rules.
INVITE FRIENDS	Invite friends to join your game.

Skirmish matches you with four other players in a game of Hunt. It cycles through the maps as you continue to play in the same mode.

Evacuation is a game of five rounds, which take place in any of the four modes. For more information on Evacuation, refer to the Game Modes chapter. At the Evacuation menu, you can select to play Co-op, where 2-4 player-controlled Hunters take on an AI-controlled Monster, or PVP, where all five characters are player-controlled.

Custom gives you full control of the setup, with only friends involved. From there, you can select from all of the modes, maps, and map effects. You also have a number of extras that can be modified to change the way the game is played. These are listed in the following table:

In each of these modes, you can select Invite Friends to bring a friend into your game. These players will follow you into whichever mode you select until you return to the main menu.

DIFFICULTY	Increase the damage output of one team.	Favors Hunters, Balanced, Favors Monster
WILDLIFE POPULATION	Adjust the amount of wildlife found in the map.	Low, Normal, High
ROUND LENGTH	Set the duration of the round. The default length varies depending on the game mode chosen.	Default or 5:00–40:00
ROUND ROBIN	Enable/disable cycling the Monster role from one player to the next.	On or Off
REINFORCEMENT TIME	The amount of time for dropship reinforcements to arrive. The default length varies depending on the game mode chosen.	Default or 0:15–2:00
STRIKES	The number of times Hunters can be incapacitated before dying. The default is 2.	0, 2, Infinite
CHARACTER PERKS	Enable/disable character Perk selection before the match begins. Elite wildlife Buffs are still available.	On or Off
MASTERY BONUSES	Enable/disable all item, weapon, and ability mastery bonuses.	On or Off
ELITE WILDLIFE	Enable/Disable elite wildlife spawning.	On or Off
VOICE CHAT	Switch between team and open chat.	Team Only, Open Chat

SOLO

Select Solo to only play with computer-controlled bots. The options here are very similar to Multiplayer, except for Quick Play and Replay Tutorial. Quick Play selects a random mode and map. Replay Tutorial allows you to try the Goliath and Markov tutorials again to better your time or perhaps refresh your memory on the basics.

Another difference in Solo from Multiplayer is that you can customize the other characters. After selecting your character, you can choose which Monster and/or Hunters you play with and against.

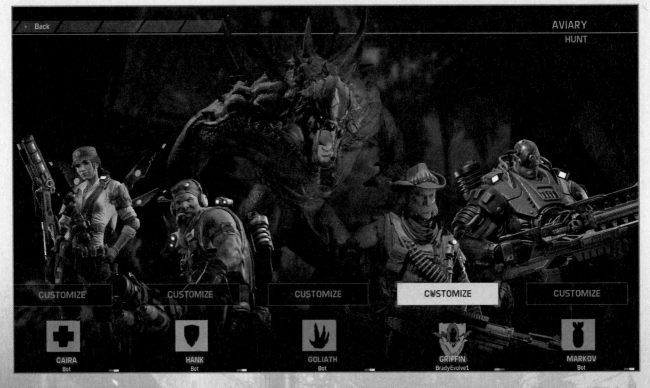

PROFILE

Profile allows you to see how you are doing in the game and create a custom Badge. Three tabs along the top grant access to your Profile, Accolades, and Badges. You can also access this information from most menus by clicking the button shown along the top of the screen.

The Profile tab allows you to check your progress and the leaderboards. See how you rank with the rest of the world or just your friends. Select the Monster or one of the Hunters to get more specific leaderboards, as well as progress toward Character Mastery and Awards earned.

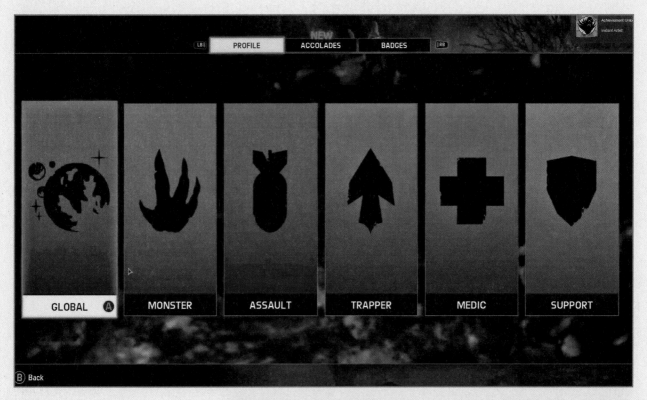

Accolades are earned as you complete specific objectives. These Accolades have five stars that increase in difficulty as you proceed, earning you XP for each one. Refer to the Accolades chapter for full details.

Select the Badges tab to customize your emblem to your liking. As you level up, you unlock foregrounds and backgrounds. The colors in these pieces can all be altered and saved once you are happy with your design.

EXTRAS

The Extras menu gives you access to the Credits, my2K, the Video Gallery, and Help (on Xbox One, also accessible from the Pause menu in a Solo game). The Video Gallery has many basic and advanced tutorials that are worth checking out to get the most out of the game.

OPTIONS

Select Options from the main menu or pause menu to make adjustments in Gameplay, Video, Controller Settings, Audio, and Language.

GAMEPLAY

In Gameplay, four options allow you to adjust the way you play.

HEAD BOBBING	Toggles up and down motion of the camera as the Hunter moves.	Normal or Minimal
AIM TOGGLE	Toggle iron sights with a button press instead of a hold.	On or Off
AUTOMATIC SPRINT	Automatic Sprint allows you to sprint without needing to press the button.	On or Off
RESET HELP TEXT	Reset Help Text so that it goes through the original lessons.	N/A

VIDEO

On PC, a few options allow you to adjust the graphical detail of the game. You can modify these settings if your game is not performing well enough.

DISPLAY MODE (PC)	Change how the game is displayed, either using up the entire screen or played within a window. Note that Windowed modes may decrease performance.	Fullscreen, Windowed, Windowed [Fullscreen]
RESOLUTION (PC)	Change the screen resolution that the game is played in. Available settings depend on your monitor and GPU. Higher resolutions may affect performance.	800 x 600 up to 1920 x 1080
GRAPHICS QUALITY (PC)	This sets advanced graphic options. Note that this greatly affects how well the game plays. If the game is not playing smoothly enough, lower this setting.	Low, Medium, High, Very High
ADJUST GAMMA	Set the overall brightness of the game.	Adjustment slider ranging from .08-1w.25
ADVANCED GRAPHICS (PC)	Select this to configure several advanced graphic options: Texture Detail, Shader Detail, Model Detail, Shadow Quality, Particle Quality, Anti-aliasing, Tessellation, and VSYNC. Each of these options can have an effect on game performance.	Various options, Low, Medium, High, Very High
APPLY CHANGES	Apply any video changes. If you have made any changes in the Video Settings, click this to accept them.	N/A
ADJUST SCREEN EDGES (XBOX ONE)	This brings up the option to adjust the edge of the screen so no HUD elements are hidden from view.	N/A

KEYBOARD/MOUSE SETTINGS

These settings allow you to modify the controls when using a keyboard and mouse.

MOUSE SENSITIVITY	Higher mouse sensitivity increases mouse movement. Increase this setting to the highest that you can handle, as this allows you to turn around quicker, giving you an edge against other players.	0–100
LOOK INVERSION	Reverses the up/down directional mouse look. Toggle this on if you prefer to look up when you pull the mouse down and vice versa.	On or Off
KEY BINDINGS	Modify which keyboard/mouse buttons the listed actions are bound to. Change any of the controls if you do not like the defaults.	See the Controls section in this chapter for default key bindings.
MONSTER ABILITY TRIGGER	Choose between releasing the button/trigger to fire an ability or priming an ability before firing it with a second press.	Release to Fire or Toggle to Fire

AUDIO

SUBTITLES	Control how subtitles are displayed. Turn on if you want text to appear when characters talk.	On or Off
PUSH TO TALK (PC)	Enable to manually transmit your voice by pushing down a key, or disable to have an open mic. You can rebind this command in the Keyboard/Mouse Settings menu.	On or Off
MUSIC VOLUME	Adjust overall in-game music.	—
EFFECTS AND CINEMATICS VOLUME	Adjust volume of sound effects and cinematic movies.	—
DIALOG VOLUME	Adjust volume of characters' speech.	—
VOICE CHAT VOLUME (PC)	Adjust volume of in-game chat.	—

LANGUAGE

There are several languages that you can select for the spoken audio and written text.

CONTROLLER SETTINGS

This allows you to select from a few controller layouts, as well as modify some options specific to the game controller.

CONTROLLER ICONS (PC)	Replaces the current bullet icons with an image of the corresponding controller button.	On or Off
HUNTER CONTROLS	Modify the Hunter controller layout. Allows you to choose between five layouts.	Default, Undead, Aftershock, Radioactive, or Sprocket
MONSTER CONTROLS	Modify the Monster controller layout. Allows you to choose between four layouts.	Default, Joyous, Division, or Bumped
LEFT STICK/RIGHT STICK LAYOUT	Modify the Left Stick/Right Stick layout.	Default, Southpaw, Legacy, or Legacy Southpaw
LOOK SENSITIVITY	A higher look sensitivity will rotate the view more quickly. Increase this setting to the highest that you can handle, as this allows you to turn around quicker, giving you an edge against other players.	0-100
LOOK INVERSION	Look inversion will invert look up and look down on the controller.	On or Off
VIBRATION	Enable the controller vibration.	On or Off
AIM ASSIST	Adjust whether your weapon soft-locks on to targets you aim at.	On or Off

PAUSE MENU

During a Solo game, press the Pause button to bring up the following options:

RESUME	Continue the game.
RESTART	Restart the game.
OPTIONS	Modify Gameplay, Video, Controller, and Audio settings.
DIFFICULTY	Change difficulty to Favors Hunters, Balanced, or Favors Monster.
LEAVE GAME	Quit the game.

STORE

Select the Store when you are ready to purchase downloadable content. New Hunters, Monsters, and skins will be available down the road.

CONTROLS

The following tables list the default controls for PC, Xbox One, and PlayStation 4. You can change button layouts and key bindings in the Options.

PC

These are the default controls when using the keyboard and mouse. You can also hook up a controller if preferred.

GLOBAL INPUTS

PUSH TO TALK	G

SHARED INPUTS

MOVE FORWARD	W
MOVE BACKWARD	S
MOVE LEFT	A
MOVE RIGHT	D
TOGGLE MINIMAP	Tab
PLAYER LIST	T

HUNTER INPUTS

SPRINT	Left Shift	SECONDARY	2
USE	E	EQUIPMENT	3
JUMP	Space	ABILITY	4
FIRE	Mouse Button 1	MARK WAYPOINT	Q
ZOOM	Mouse Button 2	HOTSWAP ASSAULT	5
RELOAD/USE	R	HOTSWAP TRAPPER	6
NEXT WEAPON	Mouse Wheel Up	HOTSWAP MEDIC	7
PREVIOUS WEAPON	Mouse Wheel Down	HOTSWAP SUPPORT	8
PRIMARY	1	RESPAWN	B

MONSTER INPUTS

EAT	E	SNEAK	Left Ctrl	ABILITY 4	4
CLIMB	Left Shift	ABILITY 1	1	EVOLVE	V
HIT	Mouse Button 1	ABILITY 2	2	SMELL	Mouse Button 2
SPECIAL MOBILITY	Space	ABILITY 3	3		

XBOX ONE AND PLAYSTATION 4 CONTROLS

The default controller layouts for both the Monster and Hunters.

MONSTER CONTROLS

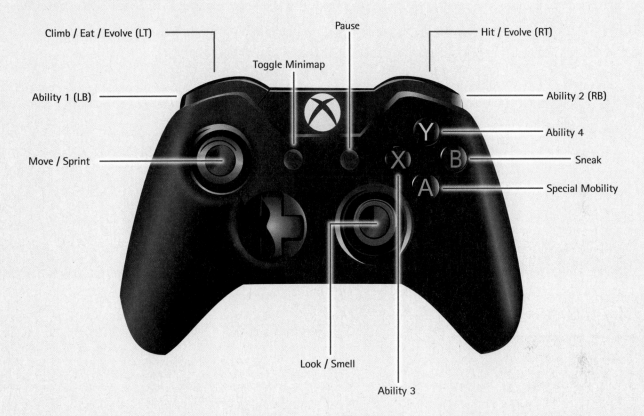

Climb / Eat / Evolve (LT)

Pause

Hit / Evolve (RT)

Toggle Minimap

Ability 1 (LB)

Ability 2 (RB)

Ability 4

Move / Sprint

Sneak

Special Mobility

Look / Smell

Ability 3

Climb / Eat / Evolve (L2)

Hit / Evolve (R2)

Toggle Minimap

Pause

Ability 1 (L1)

Ability 2 (R1)

Ability 4

Sneak

Special Mobility

Look / Smell

Move

Ability 3

HUNTER CONTROLS

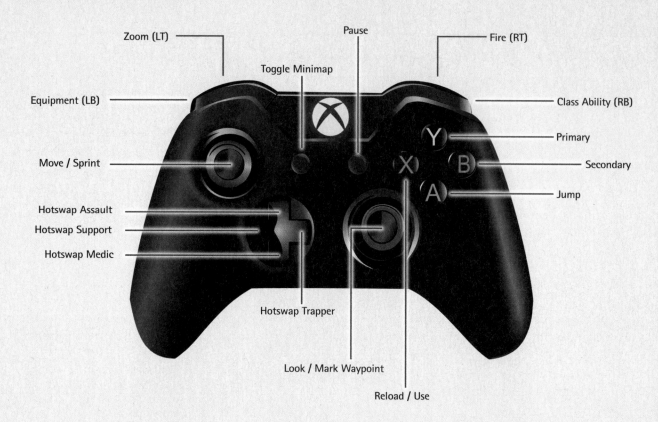

Zoom (LT)

Pause

Fire (RT)

Toggle Minimap

Equipment (LB)

Class Ability (RB)

Primary

Move / Sprint

Secondary

Jump

Hotswap Assault

Hotswap Support

Hotswap Medic

Hotswap Trapper

Look / Mark Waypoint

Reload / Use

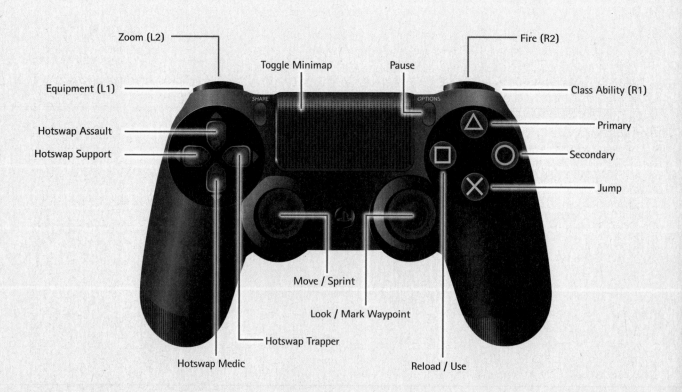

Zoom (L2)

Fire (R2)

Toggle Minimap

Pause

Equipment (L1)

Class Ability (R1)

Primary

Hotswap Assault

Secondary

Hotswap Support

Jump

Move / Sprint

Look / Mark Waypoint

Hotswap Trapper

Hotswap Medic

Reload / Use

SELECTING A CHARACTER AND PERK

After selecting your role, you are given the chance to select your character. For Hunters, simply choose whom you wish to play. If you have unlocked extra weapon skins, you can change that at this time. Skins are purely cosmetic; they provide no extra benefits. For Monsters, you must pick your Monster and then put three points into the four available abilities.

At this point, a Perk is selected to assist in your gameplay. To start out, only Level 3 Jump Height for Hunters and Level 3 Climb Speed for Monsters are available. As you level up, eight more Perks unlock for both sides. Once all nine are open, the second and third levels are unlocked for each.

Select a Perk that complements your play style, although you may occasionally want to select one that goes best with the mode or map you are playing next.

MAP EFFECTS

The following are examples of map effects, and they can be added when you set up a Custom game. They also appear during rounds of Evacuation. Nearly all of these effects favor either the Hunters or the Monster, so it provides a strategic advantage to either side. For additional details, refer to the Map Effects chapter.

FAVORS HUNTERS

ARMORED TURRETS	Adds armor to turrets in Defend mode.
ATTACK DRONES	Attack drones patrol the map and attack the Monster.
BIRDS	More birds make it easier to find the Monster.
CARGO SHIP	A cargo ship patrols the skies, helping to spot the Monster.
CLEAR SKIES	Clear skies force predators into hiding.
COLONISTS	Two colonists joint the Hunters.
EBONSTAR ALLY	A soldier joins the Hunters.
FAIR WEATHER	Experience natural lighting.
FORCEFIELD	Limits the available space for the Monster.
MEDBAYS	Heals the Hunters and removes strikes.
SCENT MASKING	Inhibits the Monster's ability to smell.
SENTRY GUNS	Turrets defend areas against the Monster.
SPACE LASER	A laser periodically fires at the Monster.
TELEPORT GATES	Allow Hunters to teleport to a central location.

FAVORS MONSTER

ARMORED MINIONS	Minions are given extra armor in Defend mode.
CANYON STRIDERS	Additional Canyon Striders provide more food for the Monster.
CARNIVOROUS PLANTS	Additional carnivorous plants make it more dangerous for Hunters.
EBONSTAR CORPSES	Corpses provide more food for the Monster.
EMP	An occasional EMP blast disables Hunters' class abilities temporarily.
FALLING SATELLITE	Pieces from a satellite fall to the ground and damage Hunters who are caught.
HOSTILE WILDLIFE	Wildlife becomes more hostile toward Hunters.
MAN-EATING EELS	Man-eating eels are added to flooded areas, making the environment more dangerous for Hunters.
MUTATED PLANTS	Carnivorous plants can be eaten by the Monster to restore health.
PHANTOMS	Phantoms are added to environment, making it more dangerous for Hunters.
RADIOACTIVE CLOUDS	These clouds damage Hunters in their vicinity.
SECOND MONSTER	Adds a minion to the fight.
STORMS	Weather becomes stormy.
TELEPORT RIFTS	Allows Monster to teleport to different locations.

THE HUD

You can gather a lot of information from your HUD. The HUD differs greatly between the Hunters and Monster.
The following images show many of the elements that can be displayed onscreen.

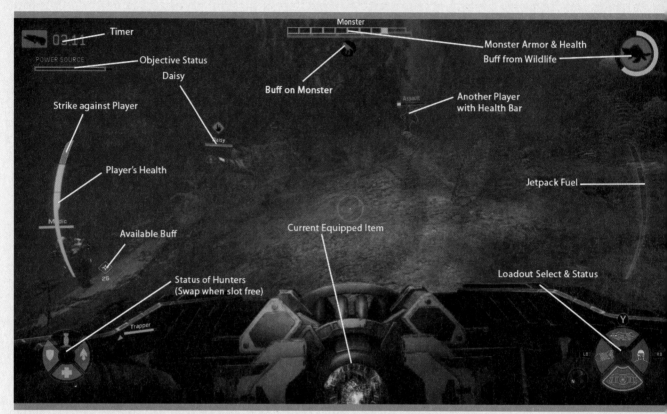

Timer
Objective Status
Daisy
Strike against Player
Player's Health
Available Buff
Status of Hunters
(Swap when slot free)

Monster
Buff on Monster
Monster Armor & Health
Buff from Wildlife
Another Player
with Health Bar
Jetpack Fuel
Current Equipped Item
Loadout Select & Status

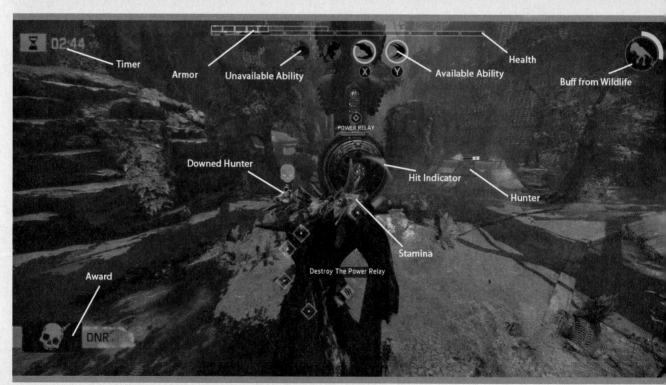

Timer
Armor
Unavailable Ability
Downed Hunter
Award

Health
Available Ability
Buff from Wildlife
Hit Indicator
Hunter
Stamina

USING THE MAP

Press the Toggle Minimap button to bring up the map during a game, along with your current objective and buff. Your coordinates are shown just to the left of the map in case you need to give a more accurate location.

The bright big white dot is your character, with a cone showing the direction you are facing. Similar yellow dots show the rest of your team, and a Trapjaw icon shows Daisy's location (if applicable). More icons appear as you spot the Monster and the birds are spooked. Objectives are also shown on the map. The following table lists possible icons:

ICON	REPRESENTS
[WHITE DOT WITH CONE]	Player
[YELLOW DOT WITH CONE]	Other Hunters
[TRAPJAW ICON]	Daisy
[RED DIAMOND]	Monster Sighting
[RELOAD BUTTON ICON]	Buff
[BIRD INSIDE RED CIRCLE]	Birds Reveal Monster Location
[BLUE DIAMOND INSIDE BLUE CIRCLE]	Power Relay
	Egg in Nest Mode

ICON	REPRESENTS
	Survivor
	Extraction Point
	Generator
	Attack Drone
	Teleport Gate
	Teleport Rift
	Medbay
	Ally
	Minion

Learning your way around each map is a huge help when hunting down the Monster. Knowing where the edges of the map and inaccessible areas are allows you to better guess the beast's next movement. Similarly, the Monster can lose the Hunters more easily with knowledge of the map.

THE ENVIRONMENT

The environment plays a huge part in the game during both the hunt and the fight. Wildlife and carnivorous plants are both ready to snatch a Hunter up, while birds give away a Monster's location if it isn't careful. Always be aware of your surroundings, and be ready to help a teammate out.

WILDLIFE

Various species of wildlife roam the planet Shear. From the tiny Spotter to the big Tyrant, these creatures come in all sizes and manners. Some are completely aggressive, while others need some provoking to take you on.

As a Hunter, you mostly want to avoid them, though sometimes you have no choice—such as when one snatches a teammate. Taking down the wildlife gives the Monster a free meal. They are good target practice when you are trying to progress through a Character Mastery.

A Monster depends on the wildlife. After taking one down, eat the entire corpse to gain energy and progress toward the next evolution stage.

Keep an eye out for elite wildlife, which are marked by a star icon. Once taken down, these guys give the Hunters and Monster a five-minute Buff, which is like having a second Perk.

SCARED BIRDS AND CARRION BIRDS

You can find groups of birds all throughout Shear. They don't pose a threat to anyone, but if a Monster passes close enough, they fly off. This alerts the Hunters to their target's location.

If you are playing as a Monster and feeding on the wildlife, Carrion Birds are drawn to you at random. The more you eat in a small time frame, the more likely they appear. Just like with the Scared Birds, Hunters are alerted to your position.

PLANT LIFE

Regular plant life is not a threat to anyone either, but plants can also alert the Hunters to the Monster's position. An attentive player will notice fallen trees and broken limbs, which can give clues to where the beast is heading.

CARNIVOROUS PLANTS

Watch out for the occasional carnivorous plant. They look harmless from afar, but they will snatch a Hunter if one gets too close. A teammate can free you from its grasp by attacking.

WATER

The water on Shear can be a hazardous place, or it can save your life. Dangerous wildlife makes these locations their habitat, and a Hunter is unable to fire while moving through it. It also slows the player down as he or she swims through the muck.

The water can be useful, though, as it does remove fire. A Hunter who has been hit with the Goliath's Fire Breath or a Monster burning from the Flamethrower or a Napalm Grenade simply needs to find water to put out the flame.

Goliath often uses Fire Breath to reveal cloaked Hunters, so being near a body of water can be useful. The Hunter still splashes in the water, but it is less noticeable than being on fire.

GAME MODES

Evolve features four basic game modes: Hunt, Nest, Rescue, and Defend. These offer a variety of gameplay options for the Monsters and Hunters. Simply hunt each other in Hunt mode, or fight over objectives in the others.

Evacuation mode is another option where the Hunters go up against the Monster in five days, or rounds, of varying modes. The first day is always a Hunt. Rounds two through four are voted on and are fought in Hunt, Nest, or Rescue mode. The fifth and final day is a game of Defend, where the Hunters defend three objectives against the Monster and its minions. A game of Evacuation is a bigger time commitment, but the exciting back and forth between the two sides makes for an intense game.

AI OR HUMAN

Five players participate in a game of *Evolve*, but it is possible to play alone, with AI bots controlling the other characters. You can also play with a team of friends and AI bots together. Be careful, though, as gameplay against and with humans differs greatly from playing with computer-controlled players.

Playing Solo is great for getting used to the game and learning the various equipment and abilities. Figuring out how to use each character and the best combinations is invaluable when you take your game online. No matter which way you play, you still level up and unlock characters and Perks.

You may have figured out the computer's tendencies and learned how to defeat it consistently, but going up against real people is a whole new ballgame. With gameplay that is much more unpredictable and the ability to communicate, a team of four Hunters presents many more challenges to the Monster.

When playing as a Hunter with a computer-controlled team, the group tends to stick with the player and waits for him or her to make a move. Play with one friend and two AI teammates, and the computer characters split up and follow each player. Team up with three human Hunters, though, and everyone may go their own way (which can be a worthwhile tactic under certain circumstances).

The game is best played with the ability to communicate. Using headsets to talk amongst your teammates is crucial when going up against a skilled Monster. Tag and call out everything you encounter, and be sure to speak up when you need assistance.

POST GAME

After each game, the players are awarded with experience based on any completed Awards and Accolades. Earn enough XP, and the player moves up to the next level and unlocks a Perk.

Progress toward your Character Mastery is displayed next. For Hunters, this involves using your three non-class specific skills or weapons. Monsters must use all four abilities to complete their mastery. Every time a star, or tier, is completed, you are rewarded with an improvement to that weapon or ability. New characters, badge pieces, and skins are also unlocked as you do so.

A big part of playing as one of the Hunters is knowing your role in the group, but first, you must learn how to get around and how to best use each character's loadout. This chapter covers everything you need to take on the beastly Monster, including moving around the environment, surviving the environment, playing your part on the team, and taking on the Monster itself.

GETTING AROUND

DROPSHIP

The Monster always gets a 30-second head start before the Hunters are released from the dropship. This gives it time to get away from the drop zone and start feeding. The team drops in and immediately prepares to track the beast. Quickly look for tracks, or if Daisy is present, follow her lead.

After a Hunter dies, he or she must wait for the next dropship, which by default arrives every two minutes. In Defend mode, dropships arrive more often. Reviving a player gives a strike penalty to the maximum health. Lazarus can keep teammates from having strikes by using his Lazarus Device, which will keep them off the dropship. Once a Hunter has strikes, only the Medbay map effect can remove them.

RUN/SPRINT

Moving your character in **Evolve** is similar to any other first-person game. By default, the Left Stick or the W, A, S, D keys on the keyboard are used to run. The Right Stick or mouse movement causes the Hunter to look around.

 TIP

SPRINTING

In Gameplay in the Options menu, Automatic Sprint can be toggled on or off. By default, this is on, so your character sprints automatically. Turn it off to require a button press to sprint.

TIP

LOOK SENSITIVITY

You can adjust the speed at which your character spins around with the Right Stick or mouse by selecting Controller Settings in the Options menu. It is a good idea to crank this up as high as you can handle. The quicker you can turn around and target the Monster, the better you perform in combat.

JUMP

With a press of the Jump button, the Hunter bounds into the air. This is great for clearing short distances or hopping over an obstacle.

JET PACK

Each Hunter is equipped with a Jet Pack that allows them to move higher and farther through the air. However, any use depletes the Jet Pack fuel,

as the meter on the right side of the screen indicates. It is best to conserve fuel when hunting the Monster and go into a fight with as close to a full meter as possible.

Press the Jump button a second time while in the air to use the Jet Pack and travel even farther. Hold the button down to reach greater heights.

JET CLIMB

Even with an empty Jet Pack, you can still climb up a vertical surface, albeit very slowly. Move in close to the wall, and hold down the Jump button to rise to the top. Be sure to hold in the direction you want to climb.

JET DODGE, JET THRUST

Double tap the Jump button while pressing left, right, or down to perform a Jet Dodge in that direction. This is very helpful in combat, allowing you to avoid incoming attacks. It's especially helpful against slower attacks, like Goliath's Rock Throw.

Performing this maneuver while pressing forward is called a Jet Thrust. This allows you to cover more ground when moving to a location. This is best used when the Monster is far away. Conserve fuel as you approach your target so that you go into a fight better prepared to dodge any attacks.

CONSERVING FUEL

Learning when to use your Jet Pack and when to conserve your fuel is very crucial for both the hunt and for battling the Monster. When in pursuit of the beast, it is good to always have some fuel in reserve to avoid getting stranded at the base of a cliff and forced to ascend via a slow Jet Climb.

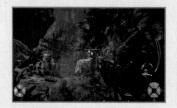

When hunting the Monster, combine regular jumps with Jet Pack use to conserve your fuel. For example, to cross a big gap, jump off the cliff, and just as you start to drop, use a little Jet Pack. Repeat this process until you reach the other side.

Jet Pack fuel in battle is even more important than in the hunt. If you are unable to dodge a Kraken's Lightning Strike, you are a sitting duck; unless you have a shield ready, you are immediately struggling to stay upright. Watch for the Monster to ready an ability, and use the Jet Pack to dodge out of the line of attack.

MARK WAYPOINT

By pressing the Mark Waypoint button, a location can be noted for the rest of the group. Depending on what you mark, a specific colored dot is placed that the other Hunters can see. There are three possible markings, as noted by the following table.

YELLOW	General
ORANGE	Wildlife
RED	Monster

Whenever you spot wildlife or the Monster, mark them so your team knows what to expect. Only a few dots can be placed at a time, so be careful in populated areas.

TRACKING

It is incredibly intense as you hunt down the Monster. You must remain confident in your team role, as you could be jumped at any moment. But, if things go well for the group, the Monster will be the one surprised.

The easiest time to lose a game of Hunt is during this hunt itself. When a team has trouble tracking the Monster down, they may not face the foe until it has reached its full potential, which means a much tougher fight for the Hunters.

Once the team is dropped into the environment, use everything at your disposal, along with keen eyesight, to track the Monster down. As soon as you touch down, look around for Monster tracks and follow them. These blue markings light up in the direction the beast is moving. Note that a flying Kraken leaves a different print than when it walks.

 TIP

DO NOT RELY ON TRACKS ALONE

Monsters cover more ground than the Hunters in the same amount of time. Therefore, you will never catch up if you simply run behind. Learn the maps and use other clues to reach the boss more quickly.

Tracks are not always available, though. As the beast sneaks, climbs, or wades through water, nothing is left behind. Avoid getting fooled by misdirection, where the Monster takes one route before sneaking back and following another. Sometimes, it is best to split the team up for a better chance at finding it. Be sure to divide into groups of

two so that everyone can be saved from wildlife or plants.

You can glean more clues from the environment. Toppled trees, corpses,

and birds give away a Monster's location (or at least whether it came through your location). Scared Birds and Carrion Birds are especially useful, as they give the exact location at that time.

TRACKING EQUIPMENT

Various Hunter skills help the group with the tracking. Each of the Trappers has their own tracking equipment. Maggie has her Pet Trapjaw, Daisy, Griffin has Sound Spikes, and Abe uses a Tracking Dart Pistol. Bucket's UAV and Cabot's Dust Tagging add to your chances of finding the foe.

With Maggie on the team, it is as simple as following the Trapjaw. Daisy attempts to guide you straight to the Monster's location. As you close in, you must anticipate the enemy's movement and cut it off. Combine Maggie with Caira's Adrenaline Field to speed the pet up and reach your target quicker.

Griffin can strategically place his Sound Spikes around in the hopes of tagging the Monster. Use the map to see where the spikes have been placed. As long as the Monster is in the Sound Spike area, it will be tracked.

Abe's Tracking Dart Pistol can be used on the Monster itself or on the wildlife. He must be within sight to hit them with the dart. If a tagged creature is eaten, then the Monster is marked.

By using Bucket's UAV skill, his head can be moved throughout the environment to spot the Monster. Bucket remains in his original location, so there may be some catch-up time once found. Cabot drops his tagging dust in an area to mark all nearby life forms. This acts similar to the Dart Pistol.

As you can see, the selected Trapper greatly changes the way the team hunts the Monster. Use this equipment often to track it down. The sooner you find your target, the more of its health you deplete, and the easier it is to take down later on.

TRACKING STRATEGIES

There are many strategies that you can implement as you hunt down your target. The simplest tactic is to follow the footprints, but a good Monster uses this to their advantage by sneaking and mixing things up.

Try splitting the team up to cover more ground and find the Monster more quickly. Divide into groups of two, putting the Medic and Support into opposite parties. If the Medic duo runs into trouble, a Healing Burst keeps them going. Support's Cloaking Field helps the other two to ease past any trouble areas, or at least gives them time to sit and wait if they find their objective. The Monster typically moves in circles or straight out, so have the two teams move outward and flank from both sides.

Once the Monster is found, the first decision is whether to engage it immediately or wait until the group is together. Slowing it down with Harpoon Traps, Harpoon Gun, Stasis Grenades, and/or Val's Tranquilizer Gun makes it easier to remain with the giant. Next, the Trapper must decide to deploy the Mobile Arena or not.

It is easy to get tunnel vision as you hunt for the Monster, but you must stay alert of everything around you. If you are focused on the distance, wildlife or a carnivorous plant can attack when you least expect it. If your full attention is on the nearby area, you may miss a glimpse of your target on the horizon.

 TIP

THE MONSTER GLOWS

When the Monster gains armor, it begins to glow. The glow's intensity is proportional to the Monster's armor level; full armor produces a full glow. This makes it a little easier for the Hunters to spot the beast.

HUNTER'S LOADOUT

Each Hunter has a selection of gear to deal damage, help out teammates, or trap the Monster. Learning how to best use each character's equipment while playing your role in the group goes a long way in taking down the Monster.

Four buttons select each of the four abilities. Some, such as the Personal Shield, are instantly used, while others require a second button press to deploy.

The circular graphic in the lower-right corner displays your four skills, as well as the button that uses each. As one is used, the blue background is depleted. Some weapons can be reloaded to top them off, while the rest of the skills regenerate as they cool down. This allows you to quickly see when each ability is available.

For complete information on using each character's skills, refer to the Hunters chapter.

CLASS-SPECIFIC SKILL

CLASS	CLASS SKILL
ASSAULT	Personal Shield
TRAPPER	Mobile Arena
MEDIC	Healing Burst
SUPPORT	Cloaking Field

While the characters have their own unique selection of equipment, each class shares a skill between them. This is the only skill that does not attribute to Character Mastery.

PERKS

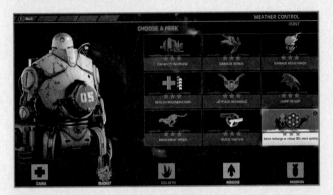

After selecting your class and character, a Perk is chosen to assist in your gameplay. Only Jump Height is available from the start. As you level up, eight more Perks are unlocked. Which Perk you select is primarily based on your preference or one that complements your play style. Sometimes, you may want to select one that goes best with the mode or map you are playing next. For full details on each Perk, refer to the Perks section.

WILDLIFE

Many species of wildlife live on Shear, each with its own characteristics. Some ignore you, while others attack any time you get too close. Some go down fairly easily, whereas the big ones take several hits to kill.

For Hunters, unless a teammate is in trouble, it is not necessary to take these creatures down. In fact, by killing wildlife, you are basically giving the Monster easy food. (However, their corpses do decay and eventually disappear so that your nemesis cannot devour them.) Using your equipment on the wildlife is also an easy way to work toward your Character Mastery.

Use the corpses lying around to help track the Monster. If a corpse is intact, it has not been eaten. Since some wildlife kill others, this doesn't necessarily mean the Monster did it. A bloody-looking corpse has been eaten, so it is possible that your target has been through the area. However, some wildlife will eat their prey. Some Monsters pass the corpses up to either put more distance from the Hunters or to throw you off.

ELITE WILDLIFE

Occasionally, you may encounter an elite wildlife. Approach the corpse, and press the Reload button to gain the Perk. Now an icon appears in the top-right corner of the screen, with a circular timer around the outside. After five minutes, the Buff is lost.

Each member of the team can grab the Buff if desired. Usually, you should partake in the Perk. But if you already have one that you like better, perhaps you should pass it up. Sometimes, you may want to save it for later, but note that it will not be there forever. A Monster can also grab that Buff if it gets there quickly enough.

Buffs are associated with specific wildlife. It can often benefit the team to go after a certain Perk if you know where one can be found. Removing a particularly beneficial one to the Monster is another great tactic. As a bonus, the enemy might be thinking the same thing, and you may end up battling before it gets the opportunity to power up.

REVIVING TEAMMATES

When a Hunter's health is fully depleted, he or she is knocked to the ground and begins to bleed out. A player who is down but not out is represented by a skull icon with red filling draining out. Once it is empty, the Hunter is dead and must wait for a dropship to show up so they can reenter the game. However, Lazarus can bring a dead Hunter back to life.

During this time, a teammate can revive this player by holding down the Reload/Revive/Use button while standing nearby. Be careful, as the Monster can continue attacking the downed Hunter until he or she is dead. A Monster may also use the body as bait so that it can get an easy second kill.

Any Hunter (as well as Daisy) can revive a teammate with this slow method, but Medics revive faster than other classes by healing the downed player until he or she is back up.

When you are down but not out, you are equipped with a handgun that you can use to continue the fight. This is really weak and only good for firing at wildlife or a Monster that has a sliver of health left.

A downed Hunter can still use a cloak or shield. Use the cloak if you don't want to attract any attention from the Monster while you wait to be revived. The shield allows you to prolong your life a little while longer. Be careful, as shooting while cloaked reveals your location. Healing a hidden Hunter also gives players away.

STRIKES

Each time a Hunter is knocked down and revived, they return with a strike, which lowers the player's maximum health by 25%. A second strike reduces it to 50%. For the third knock out, there is no bleeding out. The Hunter goes straight to death and then on to the dropship. Strikes are permanent, unless removed by a Medbay map effect. Or, in Defend, if you take the dropship and are not revived, you will not get a strike; if you are revived, you get a strike.

Lazarus has the unique ability to revive a dead human without a strike. This

means that if he is on your team, refrain from reviving anyone, unless Lazarus himself goes down.

SWAPPING BETWEEN HUNTERS

When playing with computer-controlled teammates, or if a player drops out of your game, you can switch to an open class by pressing one of the directional-pad buttons. A graphic representing these buttons is shown in the lower-left corner of the screen. Press the following buttons to switch to the corresponding Hunter.

UP	Assault
RIGHT	Trapper
DOWN	Medic
LEFT	Support

The blue background on the swap graphic shows the Hunter's health. Once it is depleted, a skull icon appears to indicate that he or she is dead and no longer available to be swapped to.

TEAM PLAY

When playing on the Hunter side, it is best to work as a team. Keep track of your teammates' locations, and be cognizant of what is going on around you. Certain combinations go well together, but it is often best to go in with the character you are most comfortable with.

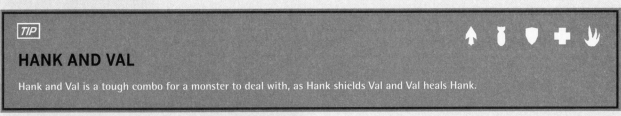

TIP

HANK AND VAL

Hank and Val is a tough combo for a monster to deal with, as Hank shields Val and Val heals Hank.

Become familiar with all of the Hunters and their loadouts. This way, you can anticipate other players' moves and know when and where to use your own. For example, if Lazarus is on your team, you should refrain from reviving another player—unless, of course, it is Lazarus who needs saving.

Avoid straying away from the group. Monsters can easily take you out with a Sneak Pounce. Plus, if a creature or carnivorous plant swallows you, there is no one around to save you.

Splitting up in groups of two is a great strategy when looking for your target, but be sure that the other half of the team isn't too far away, or a Monster may take care of your half before help arrives.

COMMUNICATION

Communication is extremely important. Calling out any sightings and needs goes a long way in taking down the Monster. For example, letting the team know when Assault's Personal Shield is used lets Hank know that he doesn't need to waste his Shield Projector on him.

Speak up when helpful skills are available, such as healing, speed boost, or cloaking. As Hank, announcing an Orbital Barrage keeps teammates from being surprised when they are knocked away from the fight.

MARKING WILDLIFE AND THE MONSTER

Use the Mark Waypoint skill often to alert the team to nearby wildlife and the Monster. Similarly, take advantage of equipment such as Abe's Tracking Darts and Cabot's Dust Tagging whenever available to spot any creatures.

GROUP ROLES

Each Hunter has a role to play within the group. Assault is about getting in the Monster's face and dealing out damage. The Trapper leads the team in tracking the Monster and (as the title implies) pins it down when the Hunters are within range. The Medic keeps the group alive while staying out of harm's way. Support assists the rest of the team while dealing his own share of damage.

Forgetting to throw the Mobile Arena or losing track of a teammate as the Medic can be the difference in winning and losing. Know your part, and stick to it whenever possible.

MINIONS

Defend mode presents a unique challenge for the Hunters, as two minions join the Monster in the fight. They are smaller versions of the Goliath with the same selection of moves. They do have lower health, making them easier for the team to kill. In Nest mode, the Monster can hatch a minion from one of the eggs, though there is a limit of one at a time. The second Monster map effect also adds a minion to the battle.

FIGHTING GOLIATH

The Goliath is big, slow, and extremely powerful. He has a lot of armor and health, which takes a while to get through. Hit him with Val or Lazarus' Sniper Rifle to create weak spots for the other Hunters to aim for.

You can dodge Goliath's Rock Throw and Leap Smash, but you must be ready for them. Keep Jet Pack fuel in reserve in case you need to make a quick dodge. If possible, fight from a higher point or behind some cover.

Stay in the open against Goliath. If he pins you in a cave or a corner, his melee attacks and Fire Breath are deadly, and it is tougher for a teammate to get to you when you need a heal or shield.

Keep some distance between the Hunters. All of Goliath's abilities can hit multiple targets. If everyone is in a tight pack, you can all take serious damage in little time. Watch out for Goliath's Charge ability, which can clear out your group fairly easily. Dodge out of the way and use this opportunity, as Goliath passes by, to hit it with a big attack.

He is the least stealthy of the three Monsters, though a Goliath that hides behind a building or brush can still get a Pounce attack on an unsuspecting Hunter.

FIGHTING KRAKEN

The Kraken has the unique ability to fly and stay out of reach of close-combat attacks. He does gradually fall when hovering in combat, but he is able to stay up for a long time. However, he must drop to the ground to make his Aftershock ability effective.

Kraken is at his best when in the air. Val's Tranquilizer Gun, Maggie's Harpoon Traps, and Griffin's Harpoon Gun are great for knocking him down. Place the Harpoon Traps on surrounding cliffs to grab him.

Stay alert for Kraken's Banshee Mines as you hunt the foe, especially hidden in the foliage and at choke points. Destroying them as soon as they are spotted is good for the rest of the team, but you can also avoid them altogether. Watch out, as they will move toward you as you near their position.

Kraken's Lightning Strike is his most devastating attack. When fully upgraded, it can almost kill any Hunter in one shot. It is easily avoided when you see it coming, but be sure that you have an escape route. A good Monster unleashes the move when his enemies are backed into a tight space.

The Aftershock ability has a big area of effect, which chains a lightning attack to anyone caught inside. Move out of this space to minimize the damage taken.

Vortex has an incredibly long range, so always be ready for it. Dodge to the side to avoid getting knocked back. This deals little damage compared to Kraken's other abilities, but it is very effective in creating distance, which is what the Kraken always wants.

FIGHTING WRAITH

The Wraith is all about stealth and trickery. She excels against lone Hunters, so travel near your comrades. With very little armor, she is relatively easy to defeat against the full group.

Her Decoy ability can be extremely deadly if you are not careful. The Wraith can send out a Decoy to turn a lone Hunter around. Then, while invisible, she pounces on the unsuspecting player, who lacks any way to escape without a teammate nearby.

The Warp Blast and Supernova moves can inflict some serious harm. The Warp Blast has an area of effect, but it can be avoided by dodging out of the area. If she deploys the Supernova Aura, move out of its range, and avoid her Abduction ability as she tries to bring you back in. She deals her greatest damage inside this zone.

Keep in mind that the Wraith cannot fight for too long with her small amount of armor and health. Be ready with the Mobile Arena if she engages the group. This Monster sticks around for a much shorter time than the others.

When the Wraith charges or attacks, or a decoy is suspected, immediately unload your weapons on it. The faster it's destroyed, the faster it's revealed as the decoy. If it's not the decoy, then you are are immediately inflicting damage, which is crucial against the Wraith.

Wraith's Abduction has a very long range, which means a Hunter can be picked away from the group at almost any time. Keep your eyes peeled for the Monster, and watch your teammates' backs.

CHARACTER MASTERY

Characters, Badge pieces, and skins are unlocked by progressing through each Hunter's Character Mastery. For the most part, using all of your skills will get you to the next unlock, but it is good to check what is needed every once in awhile. This can be seen for your current character after each match, or by selecting Profile from many of the menus. Just make sure that you do not get caught up in completing a star when you should be helping your team out. Tables listing all of the requirements for Character Mastery can be found with each Hunter in the next chapter.

MASTERY REWARD

Every time a star is completed for each skill, you receive a mastery reward. This is always a stat boost for that skill, such as increased range, damage, or duration.

EVOLVE: HUNTERS QUEST

The *Evolve* companion app allows you to continue your Character Mastery away from the game. It's a match-3 style puzzle game in which you select your Hunters and go up against wildlife and Monsters. Match 3 tokens of the same color to unleash devastating attacks on your enemies, and fill up energy bars to activate Hunters' special abilities. Earn Mastery Points to rank up your character in both the PC and console games. Explore the planet of Shear in search of new wildlife. Discover and complete your collection of exotic wildlife in the Bestiary, and earn unique Badge art for the *Evolve* game. Enhance your *Evolve* skills by watching your multiplayer match replays from a strategic top-down view, and devouring intel in the Game Changer. *Evolve: Hunters Quest* is available for iOS, Android, and Windows mobile devices.

Full functionality requires a my2K account and a supported copy of *Evolve* game. See www.2k.com and www.evolvegame.com/territories for details.

ASSAULT TUTORIAL: MARKOV

GOAL TIME	MEDAL	XP	UNLOCKS
15:00	Hunter Bronze	50	
8:00	Hunter Silver	100	
6:00	Hunter Gold	150	

Complete the Markov tutorial within these goal times to earn XP and the corresponding Badge pieces.

MOVING AROUND THE ENVIRONMENT

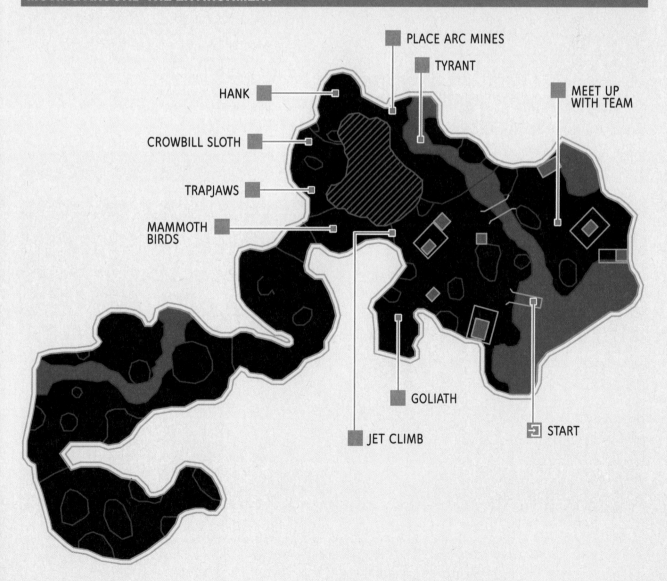

The Hunter tutorial uses Markov to learn the ropes. Most of the basics are shared between the 12 Hunters, though their equipment and skills vary greatly. The Assault Hunter is the damage dealer of the group.

Move across the bridge to the first waypoint, and then use your Jet Pack to get on top of the rock platform on the right. Pressing the Jump button causes your character to hop. Holding it down uses the Jet Pack to rise into the air, allowing the Hunter to reach higher levels.

Watch your Jet Pack meter on the right side of the screen. Any time you use the Jet Pack, this meter is depleted (though it does recharge over time). Glide over to another rock structure, drop to the ground, and continue around to the left.

JET DODGE, THRUST, AND CLIMB

Double-tapping the button while moving gives you a burst of speed in the direction you are going. This also uses your Jet Pack, so watch the meter. Dodge left, right, and then back when instructed to do so.

Follow the waypoints along the dirt road ahead, using a forward Jet Dodge, or Jet Thrust, to move quickly. Move up the right path, and then use a Jet Climb to ascend the tall wall. By moving into a vertical surface and holding down the Jump button, you can slowly climb any distance regardless of fuel.

USING YOUR LOADOUT

ASSAULT RIFLE

Use the Assault Rifle to kill hostile wildlife. Always dependable, the Assault Rifle is the go to weapon when other gear is recharging.

ASSAULT RIFLE KILLS: 2/4

Use Markov's Assault Rifle to take down the four mammoth birds ahead. The weapon is already selected, so aim down the sights, or simply fire from the hip. The Assault Rifle is good for long-distance fighting or when the Lightning Gun is recharging. Once you have taken care of the birds, Jet Climb up the nearby cliff to reach the next waypoint.

Press the Primary button to equip the Lightning Gun and use it on the pack of Trapjaws ahead. This weapon has a relatively close range and is great for quickly eliminating a group of enemies, as it chains between nearby foes.

Each class has a unique special ability, such as the Assault class' Personal Shield. This allows the character to absorb damage for a short period of time. It is best used just before taking a beating from the Monster or big wildlife.

Just around the rock ahead is a bigger, tougher wildlife creature. Fire at it with your Lightning Gun, using the Personal Shield as it attacks.

REVIVING A FALLEN ALLY

Jump up to the landing ahead and approach Hank, who has been taken down. He has fallen and is slowly bleeding out. A skull icon represents the time you have to revive him. Get to him before the red drains out of it. Quickly use the Lightning Gun to eliminate the wildlife that surrounds your teammate. With them out of the way, hold the Reload/Revive/Use

button to revive Hank. Taking damage interrupts the reviving process, forcing you to begin again.

USING THE ARC MINES

Press the Equipment button to select the Arc Mines, and place one near each of the three green circles near the water ahead. These are great for planting around an objective or battlefield. Once they are in place, fire at the elite wildlife in the water to draw him your way. Approach the corpse, and pick up the temporary Buff. This time, it is Health Regeneration.

Follow the shore to the right toward the drop zone, where Hank and Markov are to meet Val and Maggie. Fallen Hunters return on a dropship every two minutes by default. Drop down the waterfall, and head to the waypoint.

TRACKING THE MONSTER

Blue footprints lead into the water. These tracks fade over time, so follow them quickly. No tracks are made when the Monster climbs, so glide up the rock to pick the trail back up again. Continue along the path until you find Goliath.

DEFEATING THE MONSTER

Use your Personal Shield, and hit him with your Lightning Gun. Retreat when the shield is used up, and use the Assault Rifle to continue damaging the beast. Deplete Goliath's health to complete the tutorial.

Playing as the Monster isn't for the faint of heart. Monsters must move quickly while maintaining a fair amount of stealth to prevent the Hunters from tracking them down early. A good Monster is an opportunistic predator, taking down packs of animals or eating dead carcasses while still maintaining a good speed around the map.

GETTING AROUND

Each Monster has a distinct pair of footprints that it leaves around the map when using the standard movement options. Although the Monster cannot passively see its own tracks, activating Smell will not only show the Monster's prints, but also the Hunters'. Keep in mind that some Monsters leave bigger prints than others. For example, Goliath leaves a full footprint on the ground, while Wraith leaves a small slice in the ground when not sneaking.

CLIMBING

Unlike the Hunters, the Monsters can climb tall objects quickly, with no need for Jet Packs. To climb, press the Climb button, and send your Monster in the direction of the tall cliff or building. If the object is climbable, your Monster ascends to the top of the object. Special movement abilities like Goliath's Leap become more effective when activated from higher ground.

MAINTAINING STEALTH

Keeping a low profile is the key to success in the early game, as the Hunters will try to end the game as quickly as possible to prevent the Monster from gaining any sort of advantage. Walking in water prevents the Monster from leaving tracks. However, water is not always available, so the Monster is forced to use its ability to sneak.

SNEAKING

Sneaking prevents the Monster from leaving tracks at the cost of movement speed. Make sure to put some distance in between yourself and the Hunters before attempting to sneak. If you're too close, the Hunters can quickly catch up to you near the end of your tracks. Use Sneak to misdirect the Hunters by moving one way, such as into a cave or around a corner, and then activating Sneak and choosing a different direction to progress in. If you pounce an animal from Sneak, this leaves one footprint near the creature you pounced. Remember to reactivate Sneak before moving on. Sneaking also prevents birds from being spooked when the Monster comes within the standard alerting range.

POUNCING

When sneaking, sometimes the Monster will see a target get highlighted with a red circle. This means that the Monster is within Pounce range. Activate Pounce by pressing the Melee button, and the Monster will immediately jump at the target. It then pins its prey to the ground, unleashing attack after attack until the target has been incapacitated. This not only works against creatures, but it is also extremely effective against the Hunters.

A single Pounce can take down a lone Hunter. The only way to break a Pounce is to either press the Sneak button again, or be shot off by another Hunter. Downed Hunters cannot use their pistol to break a Pounce.

Pouncing is effective even in team battles. Set quick traps by waiting around corners or on top of tall objects, where only one Hunter typically comes at a time. Use Smell to look for a Hunter who may be trying to run or flank you. Even if you cannot complete a full Pounce attack, you leave the Hunter with a small amount of health, making a follow-up attack lethal in most cases.

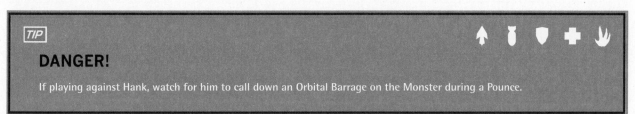

TIP

DANGER!

If playing against Hank, watch for him to call down an Orbital Barrage on the Monster during a Pounce.

SPECIAL MOVEMENT

Each Monster has a different special movement ability that affects both the way it moves around the map and how it reacts when in combat.

STAMINA

Much like a Hunter's Jet Pack, which relies on fuel, a Monster's special movement uses stamina to activate. Each Monster has three stamina bars, which regenerate over time. If you find yourself using the special ability often, consider bringing the Stamina Increase Perk. This allows you to use your Monster's special ability more frequently. Stamina regenerates faster while in combat.

GOLIATH

LEAP

Goliath uses his strong legs to leap toward the direction in which the player aims, covering a good distance quickly. Effective Leaps are based on the angle where the player aims, and aiming a little above center covers the greatest distance. Aiming high before leaping causes Goliath to jump vertically, which you can use to gain high ground quickly.

KRAKEN

AIRBURST

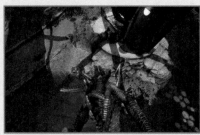

Airburst enables Kraken to fly into the air. Once in the air, Kraken can use successive Airbursts to gain more altitude or move laterally while flying. To quickly descend from the sky, use the Sneak button.

WRAITH

WARP

Wraith's ability to open wormholes allows her to travel quickly between two points. Much like Goliath's Leap, Wraith's Warp is best used from high ground. When activated, Warp goes in the direction where the player is aiming. This gives Wraith the ability to gain altitude from a Warp. Wraith descends slowly when falling from ledges or coming down from a Warp, so consider using a Warp that directs her toward the ground.

TRACKING THE HUNTERS

The Hunters aren't the only ones that need to watch for footprints. Although the Monster cannot actively see footprints without using Smell, there are a few signs you should look out for.

While dead Elite (Albino) animals are a good source of food for the Monster, they are also an accurate sign that the Hunters came through, as no other creature is likely to kill them.

SMELL

By pressing the Smell button, the Monster uses its Smell ability to sniff out the Hunters, creatures, and other potential threats.

When using Smell, you'll see a variety of colors that represent different types of creatures, and other threats to the monster.

COLOR	MEANING
BLUE	Edible Copses
YELLOW	Small and Medium Prey, Incapacitated Hunters and Survivors
ORANGE	Medium and Large Predators, Survivors, Non-Startled Birds
RED	Hunters and Daisy, Scared Birds, Carrion Birds
GREEN	Nest Eggs, Hatched Goliath

Although most creatures that show up yellow in color are non-threatening, some still actively attack a Stage 1 Monster. Elite (Albino) creatures that grant Buffs will not show the Buff symbol through objects, forcing the Monster to obtain a closer look.

Use Smell to set up traps and evade the Hunters. Watch for the moment one Hunter splits off, or catch them recovering from an engagement with other creatures.

The Monster can also detect the footsteps of the Hunters, as well as prints that it has left behind itself. Monster prints show up in green, while Hunters leave small red footprints. Hunter footprints tend to disappear quickly, so if you find them, the Hunters are most likely close by. Smell can also detect the footprints of cloaked Hunters.

MONSTER DIFFERENCES

Although all of the Monsters are extremely dangerous, each is played very differently.

SURVIVAL

Each Monster has a different health and armor value, affecting their ability to survive high-damage encounters.

MONSTER	ARMOR	STAGE 1 HEALTH	STAGE 2 HEALTH	STAGE 3 HEALTH
GOLIATH	10	5	8	11
KRAKEN	8	5	8	10
WRAITH	5	4	6	8

Number values in the above table represent the amount of armor or health bars in the game.

When playing, keep in mind that you cannot regenerate health by eating animals (unless you have picked up the Health Regeneration buff). Begin to leave combat while you still have a small amount of armor left to prevent taking permanent damage.

ABILITIES

Each Monster is granted up to four different abilities in a match. The player determines these using a "pick 3" method. Initially, you start with three points to apply toward the Monster's four main abilities. Gaining three points every time the Monster evolves, you can choose to stack up a few abilities or unlock them all, lowering the damage output of another ability. Choose abilities based on what is most effective for the game mode. Cycling through abilities is the key to taking out Hunters quickly. For an in-depth breakdown of each ability, check out each Monster's specific section.

GOLIATH

ABILITY	DESCRIPTION
CHARGE	Rush forward at high speed, causing damage and knockback.
FIRE BREATH	Spits a jet of liquid flame that does damage to Hunters for a short time.
LEAP SMASH	Devastating jump attack that deals splash damage when Goliath lands.
ROCK THROW	Rip a huge boulder from the ground and launch it at an enemy.

KRAKEN

ABILITY	DESCRIPTION
AFTERSHOCK	Emits an energetic burst that chains electricity to nearby foes.
BANSHEE MINES	Charged orbs that home in on nearby foes and deal explosive damage.
LIGHTNING STRIKE	A devastating ranged blast that never needs to strike twice.
VORTEX	A moving wall of elemental energy that knocks back enemies from afar.

WRAITH

ABILITY	DESCRIPTION
ABDUCTION	Quickly warp to a target, dealing damage before grabbing it and warping back out.
DECOY	Wraith activates a cloak while summoning a Decoy to attack the Hunters.
WARP BLAST	Warp to a point before emitting a blast of energy that deals damage to nearby enemies.
SUPERNOVA	Unleashing a shroud of nebula energy, Wraith does bonus damage while inside the area.

EVOLVING

With the exception of Defend, in every match, the Monster is tasked with evolving from Stage 1. Each level of evolution grants the Monster bonus amounts of health and more ability points. An effective Monster player balances time between combating the Hunters and hunting down creatures to regain armor.

EVOLUTION METER

The evolution meter is only visible when the Monster is consuming a creature. You can raise the evolution meter in two ways.

The easiest way to raise the meter is hunting down different creatures throughout the map. Don't spend too much time in one spot when consuming creatures, as the Hunters are always hot on your trail. Eating creatures also regains some of the Monster's lost armor. When you've gained a little bit of armor, and the Hunters aren't nearby, consider taking on an Elite (Albino) animal to gain a Buff and fill a considerable amount of the evolution meter.

Incapacitating Hunters also contributes to the evolution meter, granting two bars whenever a Hunter is downed. If you find yourself with an evolution meter that is almost full, consider going into combat to fill the rest of the meter.

WHEN TO EVOLVE

Evolving at the wrong time can end the game early for the Monster.

Get distance from the Hunters; not only does evolving force you to stay stationary during the process, but you also lose any armor that was accumulated prior to the start of the evolution. The Monster is most vulnerable during and after the process, so look for an area that helps visually conceal the Monster during evolution, such as high ground or a few bushes.

Always have a way out. Be conscious of the area around you, and have an escape plan if the Hunters catch you mid-evolve.

Because you lose all armor during evolution, don't let it go to waste! Engage in combat with the Hunters, hopefully getting a few strikes on them before evolving. After the fight, gain some distance from the Hunters. If executed correctly, the Hunters will not chase, as they will be focused on recovering and healing each other. Using this tactic improves your advantage by both weakening the Hunters and giving you strength after evolving.

PERKS

A Monster can attain two different types of Perks in the game. There are a few Perks that are the same between Hunters and Monsters, but Perks like Feeding Speed and Smell Range are Monster-specific.

PERMANENT PERKS

You select permanent Perks at the start of the match. These are unlocked and upgraded as you level up. For a full breakdown on the levels required for the different Perks, consult the Player Progression chapter.

A Monster player should select a Perk based off of the current game mode and the style they choose to play. For example, when playing in Rescue mode, Movement Speed or Stamina Increase can help the Monster quickly descend on the survivors and eliminate them before the Hunters even get close.

For a mode like Hunt, choosing Armor Regeneration or Feeding Speed helps a Monster spend less time searching for food and more time searching for the Hunters.

Players seeking to gain an edge in combat should chose Damage Bonus or Cooldown Reduction. Damage Bonus boosts the overall damage output of melee attacks and the Monster's abilities. Cooldown Reduction helps Monsters like Kraken constantly use their abilities, keeping the Hunters on their toes and forced to dodge each attack.

PERK	BONUS	LEVEL 1	LEVEL 2	LEVEL 3
ARMOR REGENERATION	Armor regeneration increase	15%	30%	50%
CLIMB SPEED	Climb speed increase	N/A	N/A	30%
COOLDOWN REDUCTION	Abilities recharge faster	15%	20%	30%
DAMAGE BONUS	Increased damage output	5%	10%	15%
DAMAGE RESISTANCE	Reduce incoming damage	5%	10%	15%
FEEDING SPEED	Increased feeding rate	25%	50%	75%
MOVEMENT SPEED	Top movement speed increase	10%	15%	20%
SMELL RANGE	Increased Smell radius	25%	50%	75%
STAMINA INCREASE	Traversal stamina recharges faster	15%	30%	50%

TEMPORARY BUFFS

You can acquire temporary Buffs by consuming an Elite (Albino) creature. Not all Buffs are available on every map, as some animals only inhabit certain biomes. Partially consuming a creature grants the Buff, but completely consuming the creature takes the Buff away from the Hunters. The Monster can still consume Elite (Albino) creatures that the Hunters have killed for a Buff. The current Buff displays at the top-right area of the Monster's HUD.

ANIMAL	BUFF
ARMADON	35% damage resistance increase
BASKING CEPHALADON	100% feeding speed
BLITZLEOPARD	50% climb speed increase
CROWBILL SLOTH	35% damage increase
MAMMOTH BIRD	50% faster ability cooldown
MARSH STRIDER	35% faster movement speed increase
MEGAMOUTH	Deal stealth damage faster

ANIMAL	BUFF
NOMAD	100% Traversal cooldown
OBSIDIAN GRUB	Armor regenerates over time
REAVER	Scared Birds give Hunters no indicator
SPOTTER	200% increased Smell range
STEAMADON	Melee attacks stun Hunters for one second
TYRANT	Regenerate health over time
VENOMHOUND	Melee attacks deal poison damage

CHOOSING THE BEST MONSTER

Each Monster has advantages and disadvantages in each game mode. However, all of this also relies on a player's knowledge, skill, and confidence with their chosen Monster. If you aren't comfortable with a Monster, try practicing with that Monster offline.

HUNT

Monster players win Hunt by either killing the Hunters or evolving to Stage 3 and destroying a Power Relay.

This mode relies on the player's ability to evade and effectively win combat engagements against the Hunters. There is no clear choice to say which Monster has an edge in Hunt, but there are a few easy choices to match a player's play style.

If playing with Kraken, you can use the Lightning Strike and a few Banshee Mines to perform a rush attack on the freshly landed Hunters. Although unlikely in the first wave of attacks, you can get an early strike in on at least one of the Hunters. However, this style of play is incredibly risky: if the Trapper drops the Mobile Arena quickly, you will have no armor and be forced to fight for survival.

Wraith has the lowest amount of health, so rushing isn't an option. Seek out armor quickly while avoiding any creatures that may do damage to her health early. Stealth is key when playing as Wraith, so if you enjoy sneaking around and striking isolated Hunters when the time is right, she is your choice.

From throwing rocks to getting up close and personal with a burst of Fire Breath, Goliath is the most versatile choice when playing Hunt. Although it may be harder to physically conceal yourself while you stomp the ground and knock down trees, Hunters aren't much of a threat when they find Goliath loaded up with armor. Goliath holds the highest armor and health values in the game. The Hunters will look to drain your health early; make sure to get some good distance using a combination of leaping and sneaking to keep them guessing as you gain armor and work toward evolution.

NEST

Sometimes, playing as the Monster might get lonely. Nest enables the Monster to hatch an egg spawning a minion that quickly finds and attacks the Hunters. Try to hold back on hatching an egg until ready for combat, as a team of Hunters can fairly easily fight a minion in most situations. However, hatching a damaged egg still spawns a full-health minion.

Goliath and Kraken are the two best choices for Nest.

Kraken can use his high-flying ranged attacks to support the minion and down Hunters while protecting the egg. You can use this tactic early on to scare the Hunters off an egg, buying a little extra time to work toward evolution.

With Goliath's high armor, he can fill his armor bar, hatch a minion, and go for a quick attack on the Hunters. With the minion at your side, you can quickly achieve victory at Stage 1. Look to target and pounce Hunters who get tossed away. If they don't communicate with the other Hunters, you'll get a quick incapacitation while the rest of the Hunters work to take down the minion.

RESCUE

In this game mode, winning requires the Monster to kill at least five survivors or eliminate all the Hunters.

The most effective way to eliminate the survivors is to get there quickly, and kill the incapacitated survivors before the other Hunters even get a chance to rescue them.

With her high mobility and damaging melee, Wraith is a very strong choice in Rescue. Quickly move to a downed survivor and eliminate them. Then, consider using Abduction to pull the next survivor to a different position, confusing the Hunters and letting Wraith finish them off safely.

Alternatively, Kraken's ranged attacks can attack survivors from a long distance, keeping away from the Hunters and putting the beast a little bit closer to the next batch of survivors. This is less effective in the early game, but once evolved, Kraken's abilities can deal heavy damage to the survivors.

DEFEND

Defend starts off with a fully loaded Stage 3 Monster of your choosing. The Monster achieves victory by destroying two generators and the Power Source.

Staying high in the sky and attacking the turrets with abilities and ranged attacks makes Kraken an easy choice for Defend mode.

Use the first wave of minions as cover to quickly look for creatures and get Kraken's armor up. If the minions are still alive at the end of this process, sneak in, and try to down a turret with a Lightning Strike and a few ranged attacks from the sky. Focus on taking down the turrets first, then move on to protecting the minions. Distract the Hunters, and let the minions complete the objective for you. Use your abilities to sneak in a few attacks on the generator to speed up the process.

Goliath may not have the ranged advantage of the Kraken, but his high armor allows him to join the minions in the fight. Damage the turrets with a few well-placed Rock Throws before coming in to take down the generators with the minions. Don't get too caught up in battle, as the Hunters still achieve victory if they kill the Monster.

CHARACTER MASTERY

You can unlock badge pieces, characters, and skins by progressing through each Monster's Character Mastery. This forces you to use all of a Monster's unique abilities to progress to the next level. Character Mastery is something that should be completed passively, as actively trying to complete these challenges could cause you to take a few losses. You can find each Monster's specific Character Mastery in its respective section.

MASTERY REWARDS

Whenever the Character Mastery objective is met for a skill, you are automatically granted a small percentage bonus to that skill. To advance the skill again, you must complete the mastery challenge for the three other skills. Doing so unlocks a badge, a new character, or a skin, depending on the level achieved.

MEDALS

There are many Medals that you can only attain while playing as the Monsters. Medals are accumulative totals of all matches, and they grant increasing experience bonuses as each tier is completed.

NAME	REQUIREMENT	TIER 1	TIER 2	TIER 3	TIER 4	TIER 5
ALL MEAT DIET	Eat X wildlife	25	100	250	500	1000
BLOODTHIRSTY	Incapacitate X Hunters	10	25	100	250	500
BULLET SPONGE	Absorb X damage using armor	2500	10000	25000	50000	100000
OSMOLOGIST	Use Smell X times	10	50	100	250	500
STOP WRIGGLING	Eat X Hunters	1	10	50	100	200
SUPER SNEAKY	Sneak X meters	25	100	250	1000	2000
WALL CRAWLER	Climb X meters	100	250	1000	2500	10000

In the Requirement column above, values for X appear in the five Tier columns.

MONSTER TUTORIAL: GOLIATH

GOAL TIME	MEDAL	XP	UNLOCKS
15:00	Monster Bronze	50	
8:00	Monster Silver	100	
6:00	Monster Gold	150	

Complete the Goliath tutorial within these goal times to earn XP and the corresponding Badge pieces.

MOVING AROUND THE ENVIRONMENT

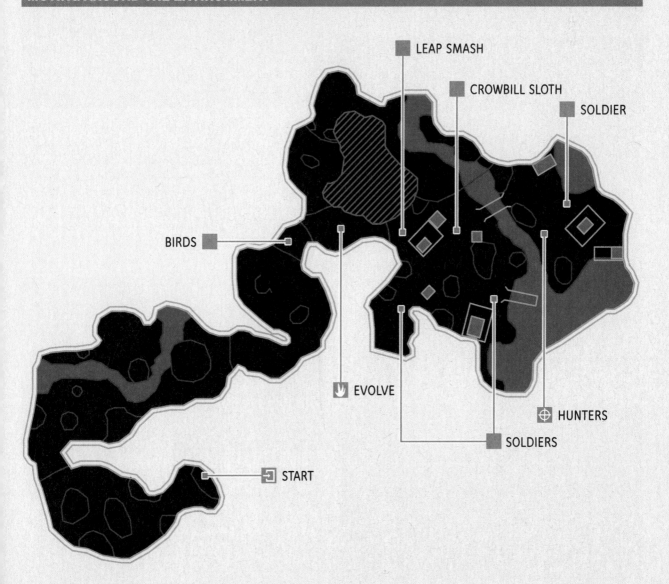

The Goliath tutorial runs you through the basics of playing as the Monster. It teaches you how to move around the environment, along with information about evolving and fighting the Hunters. Finishing it within the goal times and earning the three Medals grants you experience and Badge pieces. To get the Monster Gold Medal, you must swiftly move between the sections, completing the objectives as quickly as you can.

Start out by following the waypoints ahead, using the Climb button to scale the rock formations. Hold the button down as you run into a scalable surface, and Goliath smoothly mantles over obstacles or ascends walls. A crossed-out reticle indicates a wall that you cannot climb.

After ascending the cliff wall, Goliath reaches a big gap. Press the Special Mobility button to leap into the air, and then use your reticle to aim the jump. Along the bottom of the cursor, three red marks represent your stamina. Each leap uses one of these marks, though the marks recharge over time.

It is important to learn how to use your stamina best to flee the Hunters. Be careful using your final bar of stamina, as you don't want to end up having to drop to the ground far below and then climb back up, when a leap to another platform could save valuable time.

HUNTING THE WILDLIFE

After a few more leaps and scaling another cliff wall, drop into an enclosed area. Click the Smell button to reveal the nearby wildlife. Use your melee attack to take them all down. The Smell ability is extremely valuable, so use it often to find the Hunters, wildlife, and corpses.

Before moving on, hold the Eat button to feed on the three corpses. Use the Smell ability when feeding to avoid being snuck up on. Feeding is vital to your success, as it is the only way to build the Monster's energy and evolve to the second and third stages. It is also how you regenerate your armor. This is also very important, as health cannot be recouped. Always remember that it is better to lose armor than health. If possible, you can flee a battle, feed on some wildlife, and return to the fight.

SNEAKING TO AVOID DETECTION

With the next barrier dropped, press the Sneak button to crouch. Sneaking leaves no tracks and reduces noise while you're moving, which makes it tougher for the Hunters to find you. Use this to your advantage to lead them one way as you sneak away in the opposite direction.

Smell to expose more wildlife, and move toward the nearest one. While sneaking, a melee attack performs a Pounce attack on your target. Goliath continues to beat up on the foe until it is dead or until the Monster is hit.

Pounce on two more wildlife to continue the tutorial. Be sure to sneak before attacking, or they will not count toward your objective. This attracts Carrion Birds to your location. These birds appear randomly when feeding and give away your position to the Hunters.

Spin around until you spot the short cliff that leads farther into the map. Climb out of the cavern to startle a group of birds at the top. If you see these birds hanging out in the environment, you should either keep your distance or sneak past them to avoid giving away your location.

EVOLVING THE MONSTER

Drop into another enclosed area, kill the wildlife, and feast on their corpses to fill up your energy meter. Once it is full, hold the Zoom and Hit buttons together to evolve to the next stage. Though you have no worries here, you are incredibly vulnerable during this process. In a typical game, you may want to find a more secure location.

Evolving makes Goliath bigger and stronger, also giving him more health. During each evolve process, you get to select new abilities or upgrade existing ones. Select the three abilities that you want to improve. Make your choices quickly so that you are ready to go once the Monster is done changing.

EVOLVE TO STAGE 3

EVOLVE
Evolve to Stage 3. Your size, strength, and health increase.

USING THE MONSTER'S ABILITIES

Move through the new opening, and look down on the wildlife below. It is now time to learn how to use your abilities. These special attacks allow you to take on bigger creatures, along with the well-armed Hunters. Each Monster has four abilities that you trigger by pressing one of the four Ability buttons.

The four icons below your health bar represent these four moves. If the corresponding icon is lit up, you can perform the ability. Press the Ability 2 button to perform a Leap Smash on the wildlife. Be sure to get one of the creatures with the attack, or you will have to wait and try again.

ESCAPING HARPOON TRAPS

As you move to the next waypoint, Harpoon Traps snare you. Whack them with a melee attack to escape their grasp. Repeat this farther down the bridge, when a couple more grab hold.

MELEE TO BREAK HARPOONS!

HARPOON TRAPS
Harpoon Traps are set by hunters to ensnare and immobilize monsters. Melee attack the beams to free yourself.

DEFEATING THE SOLDIERS

At the next waypoint, you must deal with three soldiers. These are the first humans you face in the game, but they are not nearly as tough as the Hunters themselves. You can use any of your attacks to defeat them, but you must hit them with your Fire Breath at least once. This attack can hit multiple enemies simultaneously and continues to damage them over time. If your target moves, sweep the fire along with him to be sure to catch him on fire. Once you've taken care of these three, continue to the next marker, swiping the Harpoon Trap that can ensnare the Monster.

A second group of soldiers requires at least one hit with the Rock Throw. Aim carefully with the rock, as it can easily miss its target if the soldier flees or the projectile clips an object. Use all of your abilities to eliminate the foes.

Find a third group on a nearby dirt road. Before continuing, you must damage them with at least one Charge move. Use the ability immediately to push them against the nearby barrier, and then bombard them with the rest of your attacks.

With them out of the way, head back down the road, where an Elite (Albino) Crowbill Sloth awaits. Killing an Elite (Albino) wildlife grants a temporary Buff to the Hunters or Monster. The Monster must eat the creature to gain the bonus, while each Hunter simply presses the Reload/Revive/Use button to obtain it. Eat the Crowbill Sloth to gain an increase in damage output.

FIGHTING THE HUNTERS

Proceed to the next waypoint atop a rock formation to reach your final objective. The four Hunters are introduced in a short cinematic.

Start out by performing a Leap Smash into the group, and then continue eliminating them one at a time. Target Val the Medic first, as she will otherwise just heal the rest of the group. Hank, the Support, has a Shield Protector that protects a fellow Hunter, so killing him second is ideal. Use all of Goliath's powerful abilities to defeat the Hunters. This completes the tutorial. Finish it within a target time to earn a Badge piece, a Medal, and XP.

HUNTER

The Hunters have a huge task ahead of them: track down a Monster many times their size, and take it down with teamwork. This task becomes tougher the longer it takes. The playing field evens out when the Monster evolves to Stage 2. At Stage 3, the favor turns to the big guy's side.

The team consists of four classes: Assault, Trapper, Medic, and Support. Each has their unique role, along with a loadout that has been selected to get the job done. Within each of these classes, three different characters offer up unique ways to tackle the job.

The following four sections give you everything you need to get started with the Assault, Trapper, Medic, and Support classes: listings of all unlockables, detailed information about each piece of equipment and skill, and strategies for fighting as each character.

TEAM COMPOSITIONS

Combine the various characters to take full advantage of their loadouts. Certain combinations can gain an edge in specific modes or against one of the three Monsters. Here are some suggestions for fighting each Monster and for each mode. Bear in mind that these are merely suggestions.

AGAINST EACH MONSTER

MONSTER	TEAM
GOLIATH	Hyde, Griffin, Bucket, Caira
KRAKEN	Markov, Abe, Cabot, Val
WRAITH	Parnell, Maggie, Hank, Lazarus

IN EACH GAME MODE

GAME MODE	TEAM
HUNT	Hyde, Griffin, Lazarus, Bucket
NEST	Parnell, Abe, Caira, Cabot
RESCUE	Markov, Maggie, Caira, Hank
DEFEND	Markov, Abe, Val, Bucket

HUNTER AWARDS

	AWARD	MODE	DESCRIPTION	XP EARNED
	CRYPTOZOOLOGIST	Any	Kill 10 wildlife	50
	LIBERATOR	Any	Rescue a grappled Hunter	100
	EGG BEATER	Nest	Deal 300 damage to eggs	50
	MINION MASHER	Defend, Nest, or with Second Monster map effect	Deal 4000 damage to minions	50
	EVACUATION AWARD	Evacuation	Complete an Evacuation campaign	Variable, based on campaign outcome
	HELPING HAND	Rescue	Pick up two survivors	50

HUNTER ACCOLADES

ACCOLADE	REQUIREMENT	TIER 1 #/XP	TIER 2 #/XP	TIER 3 #/XP	TIER 4 #/XP	TIER 5 #/XP
10 Miles High	Jet Pack for # meters	1000/1000	2500/2000	5000/3000	10000/4000	16093/5000
Boom, Headshot!	Get # headshots	10/100	50/300	100/500	250/700	500/900
Cradle to Grave	Deal # damage to evolving Monsters	250/250	500/500	1000/1000	2500/2500	5000/5000
Freestyle Champion	Swim # meters	25/500	100/1000	250/1500	750/2000	1500/2500
Go, Go, Go!	Deploy # times	10/100	25/200	50/300	100/400	250/500
Stay Classy	Use a class ability # times	10/100	50/300	100/500	250/700	500/900
The Assault	Get # Assault Awards	25/100	100/200	250/300	500/400	1000/500
The Medic	Get # Medic Awards	25/100	100/200	250/300	500/400	1000/500
The Support	Get # Support Awards	25/100	100/200	250/300	500/400	1000/500
The Trapper	Get # Trapper Awards	25/100	100/200	250/300	500/400	1000/500
Waypoint Wizard	Mark # Monsters using the Waypoint tool	5/100	25/300	50/500	100/700	250/900

ASSAULT

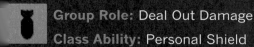

Group Role: Deal Out Damage

Class Ability: Personal Shield

Above all else, the Assault class excels at dealing damage. This guy is your front line offense, equipped with a Personal Shield to lessen the Monster's blows. This protection is only temporary, so it is wise to get out before being pummeled to death.

If possible, let this guy take the beating while the Medic keeps him alive. All three Assault Hunters are equipped with powerful weaponry and ultimately deal the most damage. The more time they can spend hitting the Monster, the quicker the team gets the job done.

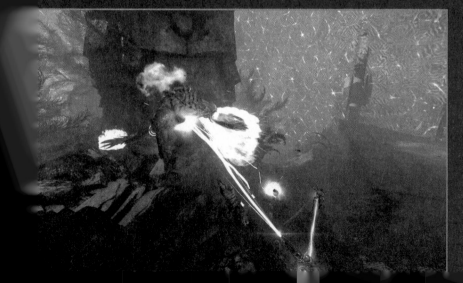

Most of your time is spent firing one of the Hunter's two guns, but don't forget about each character's third skill: Markov's Arc Mines, Hyde's Toxic Grenade, and Parnell's Super Soldier. With proper use, these skills make Assault an even deadlier class.

"HAH! YOU WORRY TOO MUCH, VALERIE. BE LIKE MARKOV! BE WITHOUT WORRY!"

Use Markov's Arc Mines to defend objectives or line them up at choke points to deal some initial damage as you confront the Monster. Tossing a few around the battlefield allows teammates a place to retreat when they get in trouble.

Hyde's Toxic Grenade excels at flushing the Monster out from an advantageous position. Knock it off of a high perch, or save an ally when a teammate is in trouble.

Super Soldier gives Parnell faster movement and a quicker fire rate temporarily. When you face the Monster, combine this with the powerful Combat Shotgun to unload even more buckshot into your target.

PERSONAL SHIELD

Duration: 10 seconds

Cooldown: 30 seconds

An Assault Hunter's Personal Shield gives him temporary protection against his foes. When available, press the Ability button to deploy your shield. This puts a blue aura around the character and health bar, which makes it easy for other players to see that the Assault character is protected.

The shield's duration is very short, so popping it just as a Monster attacks is key to obtaining the most benefit. It is okay to take a small amount of damage before deploying it; you can rely on your Medic to heal you. Learn to use the shield efficiently, and don't waste it if you don't need it.

When playing online, always call out your use of this skill so other players know you are shielded. This is especially true if Hank is on the team. Otherwise, he may waste his Shield Protector on an already protected Hunter.

Assault characters must get up close and personal with the Monster, so the Personal Shield becomes invaluable in battle. Rely on your team to keep you alive,

but don't be afraid to flee if you get into trouble.

You can deploy the Personal Shield after being knocked down. It will protect you from being finished off and give other players a chance to revive you—or (at the least) waste more of the Monster's time.

MARKOV

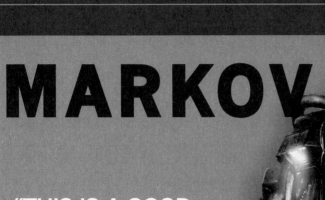

> "THIS IS A GOOD
> PLAN. THIS IS
> THE BEST PLAN."
>
> — MARKOV

We all have dreams.
Markov's just happens
to be dying in glorious
battle. This explains his
desire to go toe-to-toe
with giant Monsters.
But his deadly arsenal
consisting of a Lightning
Gun, Arc Mines, and an
impenetrable Personal
Shield means that dream
may never come true—
and that's just fine with
his fellow Hunters.

SKINS

SKIN	HOW TO UNLOCK
DEFAULT	Unlocked from start.
MARKOV ELITE SKIN	Earn 3 stars in all items in Character Mastery.

LOADOUT

	ITEM	DESCRIPTION
	LIGHTNING GUN	Energy weapon that deals substantial damage and chain-attacks nearby foes.
	ASSAULT RIFLE	Deal damage at longer range with this powerful automatic rifle.
	ARC MINES	Explosive mines that can be used for damage, crowd control, or defense.
	PERSONAL SHIELD	Temporarily soaks up damage.

CHARACTER MASTERY

	TIER 1 REQUIREMENTS		TIER 2 REQUIREMENTS		TIER 3 REQUIREMENTS	
	REQUIREMENT	BUFF	REQUIREMENT	BUFF	REQUIREMENT	BUFF
LIGHTNING GUN	Do 24,000 damage	Range increase	Do 84,000 damage to the Monster	Range increase	Do 23,000 chained damage	Range increase
ASSAULT RIFLE	Do 4,000 damage	Accuracy increase	Do 18,000 damage to the Monster	Accuracy increase	Do 10,000 headshot damage to the Monster	Accuracy increase
ARC MINES	Do 8,000 damage	Damage increase	Do 50,000 damage to the Monster	Damage increase	Damage the Monster with two Arc Mines without taking damage 60 times	Damage increase

MASTERY UNLOCKS

You must complete all mastery challenges within the same tier set before moving on to the next set. Progress toward the next challenges will not be accrued before being unlocked.

TIER 1: Hyde

TIER 2: Badge Foreground

TIER 3: Badge Foreground, Markov Elite Skin

AWARDS

AWARD	DESCRIPTION	XP EARNED
LIGHTEN UP	Dish out 2,000 damage to the Monster with the Lightning Gun.	50
BULLET TIME	Deal 2,000 damage to the Monster with the Assault Rifle.	150
TESLA COILED	Deal 1,000 damage to the Monster with the Arc Mine.	75
SELF-DEFENSE	Absorb 800 damage with the Personal Shield.	50

"IT WILL RUN AT FIRST ... BECAUSE IT KNOWS WE ARE STRONGER!"

— MARKOV

LOADOUT

Markov's two guns are the powerful Lightning Gun and the longer-range Assault Rifle. Switch between the two while the other cools down. Combine these with his Arc Mines, and he can deal some serious damage. Don't forget about the Personal Shield, as it can save the day while fighting the Monster.

LIGHTNING GUN

Mastery Reward: Increased Range

Damage: 150/sec

Max fire duration: 5 seconds

Maximum Range: 22.5 meters

The Lightning Gun is an energy weapon that does substantial damage and chain-attacks nearby foes. Press the Primary button to select the gun, and then squeeze the Fire button to let the bolt fly. Use this weapon as much as possible, as it inflicts the greatest damage.

Because the lightning chains between nearby foes, the gun is extremely useful against packs of wildlife such as the Blitzleopards and Trapjaws. This also makes it great in Defend mode when facing the Monster and its two minions.

The Lightning Gun deals out a good amount of damage, but it is also great for finding a hidden Monster. The trigger can be held down as you run around, and as long as nothing is nearby, it does not fire. Once you get within range of a creature or the Monster, it targets the foe, though it significantly slows the Hunter down.

ASSAULT RIFLE

Mastery Reward: Increased Accuracy

Damage per Bullet: 20

Fire Rate: 480 Rounds per Minute

Ammo capacity: 48 Rounds

The Assault Rifle is the long-range weapon of choice for Markov. Press the Secondary button to equip the gun, and then squeeze the Fire button to shoot bullets at a high rate of speed. Press the Reload button to top off the ammo whenever possible.

Use the Assault Rifle as you move into range of the Lightning Gun or while you're waiting for it to cool down. This weapon is ideal at long range when the Monster is first spotted or as it flees the Hunters.

ARC MINES

Mastery Reward: Increased Damage

Damage: 630

Trigger Radius: 4 Meters

Maximum Toss Distance: 7 Meters

Arc Mines are powerful explosives that can be used for damage, crowd control, or defense. Press the Equipment button to equip the mines, and then tap the Fire button to lay the explosive down. You can emplace five mines at once. Blue dashes under your reticle indicate how many have been placed so far. Place a sixth mine, and the first one disappears. Small red domes over each one indicate their blast radius. When the Monster, a minion, or wildlife gets too close, they are hit with the explosion.

There are a number of uses for the Arc Mines, but note that there is a short delay before it is set. Don't expect to throw one at the Monster and have it explode on contact.

Toss these down at choke points and around objectives to get easy damage on the Monster and minions. Note that the Monster can destroy the mines, though. Hide them near walls, in the foliage, or on the cliffs above. Put some distance between them. With all five in a small area, the Goliath can eliminate them all with one shot of his Fire Breath.

Arc Mines can be very effective in combat. Throw them down in the open, and call them out to your team. Players can move behind them when in trouble, luring the Monster into the explosives.

When you're roaming the environment on your own, the Arc Mine can be a great defense against the Monster's Pounce. Equip the explosive when an ambush may be expected. As soon as you notice the move, drop it, and the explosion releases you from the grasp.

FIGHTING THE MONSTER

Markov's primary role is to deal out as much damage as he can against the Monster, but there is more to this tough guy. During the hunt, while the Trapper sniffs out the target, you should be handling most of the creatures that you encounter. No need to go though too much trouble for the normal wildlife: just keep the rest of the team clear of any trouble. Try to keep up with the team so that you can start depleting the foe's health as soon as possible.

Markov has the longest range of the Assault Hunters, so he is a good choice against the Kraken. His Arc Mines aren't the greatest threat against the flying enemy, but they are still effective around objectives or on cliff edges.

Whenever there is an objective for the Monster, such as the Power Relay or Generators, lay Arc Mines nearby to get some easy damage. You should also throw mines at choke points or on bridges.

Once the Mobile Arena has been thrown, it is time to get down to business. Get up close to the Monster, and try to keep its attention. Rely on the others to keep you healthy. Use your Personal Shield after taking a little damage, and continue unloading everything you got on the foe. Keep the attacks coming until the Monster is out of your sight.

HYDE

"FIRE'S ALL THE PLAN I NEED. WORKS EVERY TIME"

—HYDE

Sadistic. Sociopathic. Deeply disturbed. These are but a few of the compliments Hyde has received from those who've seen his handiwork. What bothers Hyde most about this job isn't the sheer amount of death and destruction the Monster has caused—it's that even with his Minigun, Toxic Grenades, and Flamethrower, it makes Hyde only the second most frightening thing on the planet.

SKINS

SKIN	HOW TO UNLOCK
DEFAULT	Unlocked with Hyde.
HYDE ELITE SKIN	Earn 3 stars in all items in Character Mastery.

LOADOUT

	ITEM	DESCRIPTION
	FLAMETHROWER	Makes close-up extermination of vermin a thing of joy.
	MINIGUN	A mid-range solution for chewing through just about anything.
	TOXIC GRENADE	This grenade keeps the hurt on long after it explodes.
	PERSONAL SHIELD	Temporarily soaks up damage.

CHARACTER MASTERY

	TIER 1 REQUIREMENTS		TIER 2 REQUIREMENTS		TIER 3 REQUIREMENTS	
	REQUIREMENT	BUFF	REQUIREMENT	BUFF	REQUIREMENT	BUFF
FLAMETHROWER	Do 20,000 damage	Range increase	Do 50,000 damage to the Monster	Range increase	Do 50,000 residual burn damage	Range increase
MINIGUN	Do 4,500 damage	Accuracy increase	Do 15,000 damage to the Monster	Accuracy increase	Do 3,000 headshot damage to the Monster	Accuracy increase
TOXIC GRENADES	Do 11,000 damage	Damage increase	Do 32,000 damage to the Monster	Damage increase	Do 100 damage to Monster with a single grenade 250 times	Damage increase

MASTERY UNLOCKS

You must complete all mastery challenges within the same tier set before moving on to the next set. Progress toward the next challenges will not be accrued before being unlocked.

TIER 1: Parnell

TIER 2: Badge Foreground

TIER 3: Badge Foreground, Hyde Elite Skin

AWARDS

AWARD	DESCRIPTION	XP EARNED
FLAME BROILED	Deal 2,000 damage to the Monster with the Flamethrower.	50
RPS BEAST	Deal 2,000 damage to the Monster with the Minigun.	50
NOXIOUS	Deal 1,000 damage with the Toxic Grenade.	50
SELF-DEFENSE	Absorb 800 damage with the Personal Shield.	50

LOADOUT

Hyde can deal out some serious hurt on the Monster with his selection of weapons. The Flamethrower has the highest damage output among the Hunters, but its range is very short. Therefore, it is necessary to get up close in the Monster's grill as you set it on fire. Toxic Grenades grant the ability to flush your target out from an advantageous position, while the Minigun rips through your foe from a longer distance.

> "OI, BUCKET. I DON'T TELL YOU HOW TO ROBOT, YOU DON'T TELL ME HOW TO BURN THINGS."
>
> – HYDE

FLAMETHROWER

Mastery Reward: Increased Range

Damage per Second: 170 plus Residual Burn Damage

Maximum range: 15 Meters

Max fire duration: 10 Seconds

The Flamethrower is an incendiary device that deals a lot of damage at close range. Press the Primary button to equip the weapon, and squeeze the Fire button to spray fire onto your foes. The weapon can be reloaded any time there is a lull in the action.

Enemies hit with the flame continue to burn and take damage for some time. This weapon is great for spraying across several enemies simultaneously, such as packs of wildlife. Be sure to hit the Monster early and often with it to keep it burning.

The range of the Flamethrower is its weakness. Hyde must get in close to do damage with it. Backpedal as you spray an approaching foe to remain out of reach.

Once the Monster is out of the Flamethrower's range, switch to the Minigun or Toxic Grenades to keep the hurt on your foe. Whenever you are close to your target, pull this weapon out to maximize the fire damage.

Use the Flamethrower to help out an ally in trouble. If you spot a teammate struggling against the Monster, immediately spray the foe. More than likely, this onslaught gets the foe's attention and forces it to retreat.

You can also use the Flamethrower to reveal the Wraith's location. Sweep the flame in the area you believe she hides, and the Monster gets set aflame. This makes her more visible for the entire team, where she is at her worst.

MINIGUN

Mastery Reward:

Increased Accuracy

Damage per Bullet: 21

Fire Rate:

400 Rounds per Minute

Ammo Capacity:

80 rounds

The mid-range Minigun has a very high rate of fire, allowing it to chew through just about anything. Press the Secondary button to equip the gun, and squeeze the Fire button to shoot. Press the Reload button to top off the ammo when necessary.

> ## "OH. BUT I LIKE MELTING FACES."
> — HYDE

The damage that the Minigun deals is much lower than the Flamethrower, but it possesses a longer range. Use this gun while you get close enough to use the more powerful weapon, or employ it as the Monster moves away.

Exploit weak spots created by Val or Lazarus to deal out even more damage. Grab the Poison Damage Buff to make this firearm even more deadly.

TOXIC GRENADE

Mastery Reward: Increased Damage

Damage: 90 per Second

Duration: 7 Seconds

Effective Radius: 10 Meters

The Toxic Grenade leaves a damaging gas cloud after detonation. Press the Equipment button to equip the grenade. The Fire button tosses it toward your reticle. Hold the Fire button down to get an arc for more precise aiming. After using one grenade, a number on the side of the device counts up to 100 to easily indicate when another is ready.

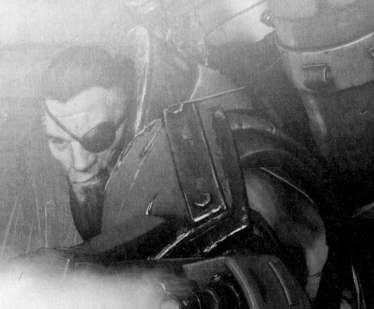

You can use this explosive to simply damage the Monster, but it is ideal at flushing it out from an advantageous position. Is the Goliath pummeling teammates in a corner? Toss the Toxic Grenade in to make him retreat. The Kraken causing havoc from a cliff above? Use this explosive to move him to a better position for your team.

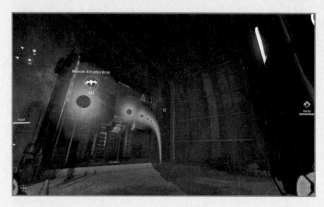

Be careful, as the explosives cloud slows down your group as they pass through. Don't try to hit a fleeing Monster with one, or you will likely lose the beast quicker than normal. Instead, pull out the Minigun, and deplete more of the Monster's health as it moves away.

"C'MON, JUST ONE LITTLE SHOT OF LIQUID COURAGE."

— HYDE

FIGHTING THE MONSTER

Hyde must foremost put the hurt on the Monster once it is found. Before finding the target, Hyde can still be extremely useful.

The Flamethrower is great against hostile packs of wildlife. Spray the fire out ahead of the group to take care of the weaker creatures.

Hyde's Flamethrower is extra useful against the Wraith, as it can reveal the stealthy foe if she decides to hide nearby. The flame is also very effective against a Goliath. Keep the fire going by using this weapon early and often.

Hyde's Toxic Grenades are extremely valuable when a Monster holds an beneficial position. Toss one into tight spaces or onto high cliffs to flush the beast out. Be careful, though: as the Monster attempts to flee, the grenade also slows your group down.

Hyde has the shortest range of the Assault Hunters, so it is important to get up close and personal with the Monster. Deploy the Personal Shield wisely, and use the full canister of fuel on the enemy. Switch to another weapon when the Flamethrower is unavailable, but immediately pull it back out to deal the most damage possible.

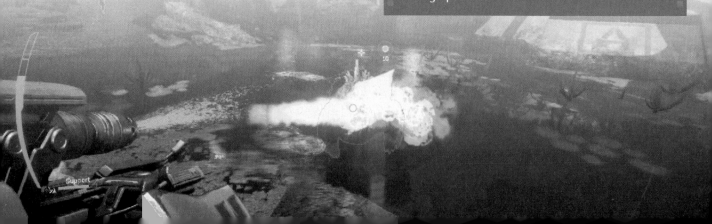

PARNELL

**"JUST GLAD I'M
NOT IN CHARGE
OF THIS BUNCH
OF LUNATICS."**
— PARNELL

The fact that Parnell packs a Combat
Shotgun and Rocket Launcher proves
how committed he is to obliterating
uncooperative wildlife. His Super
Soldier ability cranks up the violence
by vastly amplifying his damage output.
If you need to kill something, you call
on Parnell.

SKINS

SKIN	HOW TO UNLOCK
DEFAULT	Unlocked with Parnell.
PARNELL ELITE SKIN	Earn 3 stars in all items in Character Mastery.

LOADOUT

ITEM	DESCRIPTION
COMBAT SHOTGUN	High damage, close-range destruction.
MULTIFIRE ROCKET LAUNCHER	Long-range firepower to crush your prey.
SUPER SOLDIER	Fire and move faster than humanly possible, dealing significantly more damage at a small cost to your own health.
PERSONAL SHIELD	Temporarily soaks up damage.

CHARACTER MASTERY

	TIER 1 REQUIREMENTS		TIER 2 REQUIREMENTS		TIER 3 REQUIREMENTS	
	REQUIREMENT	BUFF	REQUIREMENT	BUFF	REQUIREMENT	BUFF
COMBAT SHOTGUN	Do 19,000 damage	Damage increase	Do 75,000 damage to the Monster	Damage increase	Do 31,000 headshot damage to the Monster	Damage increase
MULTIFIRE ROCKET LAUNCHER	Do 32,000 damage	Damage increase	Do 64,000 damage to the Monster	Damage increase	Get 900 direct hits to the Monster	Damage increase
SUPER SOLDIER	Do 17,000 damage using Super Soldier	Duration increase	Do 58,000 damage to the Monster using Super Soldier	Duration increase	Do 20,000 headshot damage using Super Soldier	Duration increase

MASTERY UNLOCKS

You must complete all mastery challenges within the same tier set before moving on to the next set. Progress toward the next challenges will not be accrued before being unlocked.

TIER 1: Badge Foreground

TIER 2: Badge Foreground

TIER 3: Badge Foreground, Parnell Elite Skin

AWARDS

AWARD	DESCRIPTION	XP EARNED
STREET SWEEPER	Deal 2,000 damage to the Monster with the Combat Shotgun.	50
GOING NUCLEAR	Deal 2,000 damage to the Monster with the Multifire Rocket Launcher.	50
OVERPOWERED	Deal 3,500 damage while using Super Soldier.	50
SELF-DEFENSE	Absorb 800 damage with the Personal Shield.	50

LOADOUT

Parnell carries a couple weapons into battle: the Combat Shotgun and the Multifire Rocket Launcher. The former requires getting in nice and close to deal the damage, so his Personal Shield becomes really important. Flip on the Super Soldier ability to turn it up a notch. When out of range, the fully automatic launcher becomes the gun of choice to continue the barrage.

> **"EVACUATING A WHOLE COLONY IN FIVE DAYS... THIS IS NUTS."**
> – PARNELL

COMBAT SHOTGUN

Mastery Reward: Increased Damage

Damage per pellet: 14

Fire Rate: 170 Rounds per Minute

Ammo Capacity: 10 Rounds/80 Pellets

Parnell's shotgun deals some serious damage at a close range. Press the Primary button to equip the gun, and then squeeze the Fire button to fill your foe with some buckshot. You can refill ammo at any time by pressing the Reload button. The weapon is fully automatic, with 10 shells in each clip.

 As with Markov and Hyde, Parnell has a high damage, close-range weapon that requires him to get in close with the Monster. Be ready with your Personal Shield as you put the hurt on the Monster.

To continue your attack, make sure to switch to the longer-range Rocket Launcher when farther away. Parnell is limited to his two weapons, so there will be some down time, making Reload Speed a good Perk choice.

The Combat Shotgun is ideal when hunting the Monster since it takes care of most wildlife with ease. However, as you near a Monster's location, it is best to have the Rocket Launcher ready to get some early shots on the foe.

Unless you have a teammate who can bring the Kraken down, the Combat Shotgun is not very effective against the flying Monster. Switch to the Rocket Launcher to hit the distant foe, or jet pack to higher points to get in range.

MULTIFIRE ROCKET LAUNCHER

Mastery Reward: Increased Damage

Damager per Rocket: 90

Fire rate: 100 Rounds per Minute

Ammo Capacity: 5 Rockets

The Multifire Rocket Launcher gives Parnell a long-range option with decent damage output. The Secondary button equips the launcher, and then the Fire button shoots the explosives. This weapon is fully automatic, with five available rockets before you must reload. You can click the Reload button at any time to top it off.

As you get in range for the more powerful Combat Shotgun, or when the Monster retreats, use the Multifire Rocket Launcher to keep the attacks going from mid to long range.

These rockets fire in a straight line, so aim well. An alert foe can dodge many of your shots, but the continued barrage will reach your target as you move your reticle with the beast. Use the blast radius of the explosive to full effect by aiming at the beast's feet or a nearby wall.

This is the weapon of choice against the high-flying Kraken, as he is frequently out of the Combat Shotgun's range. Keep the rockets coming to weaken the beast.

SUPER SOLDIER

Mastery Reward: Increased Duration

Bonuses: 80% Increase in Fire Rate, 40% Increase in Reload Speed, 30% Increase in Sprint Speed, 300% Increase in Jump Height

Cooldown: 30 Seconds

Duration: 9 seconds

Utilizing the Super Soldier ability causes Parnell to move faster and gives his weapons a quicker fire rate, though at a small cost to his health. This significantly increases the damage that is done. Tap the Equipment button to use this skill. At first, it only lasts for three seconds, but max out Character Mastery, and it increases to nine seconds.

> ## "IF THAT'S TRUE, THEN WE'LL HAVE PLENTY OF JOB OFFERS AFTER THIS. AND PLENTY OF CHANCES TO LEARN MORE ABOUT THESE THINGS."
>
> — PARNELL

"ON THE OTHER HAND, EISENHOWER SAID, 'PLANS ARE USELESS, BUT PLANNING IS INDISPENSIBLE."

— PARNELL

When fighting the Monster, use this whenever available to maximize your damage output. Avoid using it when low on health, as it could knock you out. Team up with a good Medic who can keep you in the game longer.

This ability is best used in open areas where you have a clean shot at the Monster. Give yourself plenty of room to dodge incoming attacks as you quickly unload your ammo into the foe.

Like the Personal Shield, Super Soldier requires good timing to get the most out of it. It doesn't help to have the faster reload and movement if you can't get a shot on the Monster or if you don't have room to dodge incoming attacks.

FIGHTING THE MONSTER

Parnell only carries two weapons, so his roles in the group are not as extensive as the others. He is all about depleting the Monster's health, which he does very well. Use the Combat Shotgun as the team hunts their target to take down attacking wildlife.

As the team nears the Monster, have the Multifire Rocket Launcher ready. Start unloading the explosives at the foe as soon as it is spotted. Switch to the Combat Shotgun as you get into its range.

With Parnell's Super Soldier ability, he can deal out massive damage in little time. This makes him great against the heavily armored Goliath, which is slower to get away. Parnell is least effective against the Wraith, as she has an easier time escaping the barrage of attacks and avoiding his weapon fire.

Do not forget about your Personal Shield as you get in close with the Monster. Use the Super Soldier skill when you face the Monster out in the open, where you can get in a lot of shots and quickly dodge its attacks. Keep the ammo flying at the beast until it has fled out of sight.

TRAPPER

Group Role: Tracking the Monster and Pinning It Down

Class Ability: Mobile Arena

The Trapper has two major roles in Evolve: tracking the Monster down and trapping it inside the Mobile Arena. Both of these tasks are extremely important in the team's ultimate goal of taking down the enemy. Failing to find the Monster in a timely manner or missing the beast with the dome has a huge impact on your success.

Whether using Maggie's extremely effective pet Trapjaw, Griffin's Sound Spikes, or Abe's Tracking Dart Pistol, it is vital to reach the Monster as quickly as you can. Take full advantage of these skills, and call out anything you may find. There is more to it than simply spotting the Monster: anticipating or predicting where the target is headed is key in finding it during Stage 1.

Trappers may not have the firepower that the Assault class possesses, but they can still deal some damage. Each character is equipped with one weapon. Use it against hostile wildlife or the Monster when your other roles are complete.

Each Trapper also carries a device that can slow down the Monster. This item is more important than the damage that your weapon causes, so use it often. Abe's Stasis Grenades slow the enemy down for a period of time. A darting Wraith becomes an easier target when hit with this grenade.

Maggie's Harpoon Traps and Griffin's Harpoon Gun can immobilize the target for a short period. These tools work wonders on a flying Kraken, with the ability to bring it down to your level.

MOBILE ARENA

 Cooldown: 60 Seconds
Duration: 60 Seconds
Effective Radius: 50 Meters

Once the Monster is found, the Trapper's primary role is to trap it, which is accomplished with their class ability. Press the Ability button to equip the Mobile Arena, and then tap the Fire button to deploy. This energy dome is a half-sphere that captures any living creature within 60 meters. Hunters may still enter, but no one leaves.

Timing is extremely important with the Mobile Arena, as you must ensure that the Monster is within range before deploying. There is a long cooldown time between uses, so you won't get another chance for a while.

If the dome misses, you are informed as such, and the Trapper must take it down quickly to continue the pursuit. Hold the Ability button to bring it down, and immediately take off behind the Monster. It takes one minute for the dome to recharge.

Maggie and Abe are more maneuverable inside the arena because they have the ability to slow the Monster down. If you end up trapped alone with the adversary, stay on the move, and slow it down as much as possible.

The Trapper's dialogue will inform you when the arena is about to come down. This is a good time to hit the Monster with tracking devices. If Bucket is on the team, use his UAV to follow the enemy.

For the most part, the location you meet the Monster is not up to the Hunters, so it is tough to be particular about exactly where the arena is placed. Placement can be advantageous to the Monster as much as the Hunter. If you are not careful, you can easily trap the team in a tight space against the powerful Goliath. If you place the dome over a central pillar, a beast can hide from the group as it circles the structure.

When you first find the Monster, you must decide whether to deploy the Mobile Arena or wait. If the Monster engages the party in combat, it may be better to save the Mobile Arena until you have damaged the beast significantly. Then, you can trap it inside before it flees to prolong its pain.

MAGGIE

> ## "IT DOESN'T KNOW FEAR... BUT IT DOES KNOW PAIN."
> — MAGGIE

A quiet woman with a past shrouded in mystery, Maggie is a loner. For years, her only companion was Daisy, her faithful pet Trapjaw. Who needs friends when you have a 400-pound alien dogbeast at your side? When Daisy finds their prey, Maggie relies on her Machine Pistol and Harpoon Traps to bring it down.

SKINS

SKIN	HOW TO UNLOCK
DEFAULT	Unlocked from start.
MAGGIE ELITE SKIN	Earn 3 stars in all items in Character Mastery.

LOADOUT

	ITEM	DESCRIPTION
	MACHINE PISTOL	Efficient and deadly, just like Maggie.
	HARPOON TRAPS	Stationary harpoons that can immobilize the Monster.
	PET TRAPJAW	Daisy tracks the Monster and can also revive her human companions.
	MOBILE ARENA	Energy dome that traps the Monster and Hunters inside.

CHARACTER MASTERY

	TIER 1 REQUIREMENTS		TIER 2 REQUIREMENTS		TIER 3 REQUIREMENTS	
	REQUIREMENT	BUFF	REQUIREMENT	BUFF	REQUIREMENT	BUFF
MACHINE PISTOL	Do 8,000 damage	Damage increase	Do 21,000 damage to the Monster	Damage increase	Do 12,000 headshot damage to the Monster	Damage increase
HARPOON TRAPS	Harpoon the Monster 40 times	Range increase	Harpoon the Monster at least 8 times in 14 different matches	Range increase	Catch the Monster in 2 traps 50 times	Range increase
PET TRAPJAW	Follow Daisy for 2,600 meters	Health increase for Daisy	Revive 10 teammates with Daisy	Health increase for Daisy	Revive 2 teammates in a single match 30 times with Daisy	Health increase for Daisy

MASTERY UNLOCKS

You must complete all mastery challenges within the same tier set before moving on to the next set. Progress toward the next challenges will not be accrued before being unlocked.

TIER 1: Griffin

TIER 2: Badge Foreground

TIER 3: Badge Foreground, Maggie Elite Skin

AWARDS

AWARD	DESCRIPTION	XP EARNED
HAND CANNON	Deal 2,000 damage to the Monster with the Machine Pistol.	50
TRIPPED UP	Harpoon the Monster three times with the Harpoon Traps.	50
GOOD GIRL	Follow Daisy for 500 meters.	50
THUNDERDOME!	Trap the Monster in a Mobile Arena two times.	100

LOADOUT

Besides the very important Mobile Arena, Maggie comes equipped with a variety of toys. She deals decent damage with the Machine Pistol, while her Harpoon Traps stop the beast in its tracks. The Trapper's pet Trapjaw, Daisy, uses her amazing sniffing ability to lead the group straight to the Monster.

> "FACTOR WAS A ROUGH COLONY. VIOLENT. ONCE I HAD RUVA HERE, NO ONE WANTED TO MESS WITH ME."
>
> — MAGGIE

MACHINE PISTOL

Mastery Reward: Increased Damage

Damage per Bullet: 20

Fire Rate: 615 Rounds per Minute

Ammo Capacity: 60

The Machine Pistol is a powerful automatic weapon with poor accuracy. Press the Primary button to equip the gun, and then use the Fire button to discharge the bullets into your enemy. Use the Reload button at any time to top off the ammo.

The longer you hold the trigger down on the Machine Pistol, the wilder it gets. Instead, fire the weapon in bursts to keep the bullets close to your reticle.

Despite its shortcomings in accuracy, the gun packs a powerful punch. Aim for weak spots in the Monster's armor that Val or Lazarus has provided. Your first priority in combat should be to lay the Harpoon Traps, but once they are down, pull this guy out and make your enemy bleed.

HARPOON TRAPS

Mastery Reward: Increased Range

Trigger Radius: 18 Meters

Maximum Toss Distance: 10 Meters

Ammo Capacity: 1

Placed Harpoon Traps ensnare the Monster, holding it in place until the beast can swipe at it with a melee attack. Press the Secondary button to equip the device, and then squeeze the Fire button to place a trap on the ground in front of you. If the reticle is red, it cannot be placed at that location. Once it is blue, you can fire it into the surface. Note that it does take a few moments for it to set itself. You are limited to five at a time, which is indicated by the blue dashes along the bottom of your reticle.

Harpoon Traps are a great asset during all stages of *Evolve*. Place them along paths or at choke points to slow the Monster down. Hide them in the brush or next to walls so they go undetected until they are activated.

The Monster can destroy one before the trap is armed, so it's best to place them before engaging your opponent. The giant's smell ability can detect  Harpoon Traps, and attacks like Goliath's Fire Breath can easily take them out.

Against the high-flying Kraken, lay traps on the cliff edges above to bring him down to a manageable height. Since you are limited to five at a time, spread them around the battlefield wisely.

Lure the Monster into well-hidden Harpoon Traps, and have the team open fire on the stationary beast. Traps placed in the middle of the battlefield give the Hunters a spot they can retreat to. Call them out to your team so they know they have the option.

PET TRAPJAW

Mastery Reward: Increased Health for Daisy

Health: 1450

Smell Range: 100 Meters

Sprint Speed: 11 Meters per Second

Maggie's pet Trapjaw, Daisy, sniffs out the Monster and its tracks. The only thing you need to do to use her is to pay attention. Follow directly behind Daisy as she leads you to your target more quickly. Keep an eye on her icon, as the paw turns red when close and an exclamation point appears when she has found it. Daisy points at the Monster when it is nearby.

Stay close to your companion, or she will stop and wait. The less she stops, the quicker the team finds what they are looking for. You don't want to stray too far from her, but many times, you must leave her side to cut the Monster off. This is a good time to split up, as one pair stays with Daisy and the others attempt to anticipate the target's next move.

You may need to lead Daisy around if she loses the scent and stops tracking the Monster. It shouldn't take too long for her to get back on the scent, as she is great at her job.

Once you have found the Monster and deployed the Mobile Arena, plant the Harpoon Traps, and then pull out your Machine Pistol. During combat, Daisy's job isn't done: she will run around to downed Hunters and attempt to revive them.

Team up with Caira, and take full advantage of her Adrenaline Field. With her running alongside Daisy, the team can reach their target in no time.

Just like your other teammates, Daisy is worth protecting from the Monster. She is extremely efficient at picking up your allies, so have her back if she gets into trouble. Many times, though, she will be the Monster's final target. The game isn't over until all five of you have perished.

Daisy can detect a sneaking Monster, which she indicates by sniffing the ground. Rely on her to lead you to the stealthy beast.

> # "IT TOOK A LONG TIME FOR US TO REACH THE EVACUATION SHIP. LONGER TO FIGURE OUT HOW TO TURN IT ON."
>
> — MAGGIE

FIGHTING THE MONSTER

With Daisy by her side, Maggie has the easiest time tracking the Monster, though it still isn't a done deal. From touch down, rely on the Trapjaw to lead the group to their target. Daisy is well trained and extremely proficient at her job.

Keep an eye on Daisy's icon to know when the Monster has been found. Have someone break off from the group if it is necessary to cut the beast off.

Once the Monster is nearby, be ready with the Mobile Arena. Be sure you have it within range, and throw down the dome to entrap the beast. If it is Stage 1, it is very important that you do not miss. Later in the game, the Monster is more likely to engage you. At that time, it may be better to hold on to the arena and wait for the beast to lose some health before you deploy it.

With the Monster trapped inside the Mobile Arena, hide and defend yourself until the team arrives. If the Trapper is incapacitated or killed, the arena comes down. Once everyone is within the dome, it is time to get down to business.

Maggie's Harpoon Traps are more important to the team than doing damage with the Machine Pistol. Lay the five down in strategic locations, and deal out the damage.

The Wraith adds a couple of extra difficulties to Maggie's job. When you first find the Monster, she can release her Decoy in your direction and flee the other way. This can easily result in you trapping the fake Wraith inside the arena instead of the real one. On top of that, the Harpoon Traps will ensnare the Decoy.

Hank is a great teammate for Maggie. A Monster who has been grabbed by the Harpoon Traps is an easy target for his Orbital Barrage.

GRIFFIN

"BIG ENOUGH. BIGGER THAN ANYTHING ON THIS PLANET. NEVER HUNTED ANYTHING LIKE 'EM. CHALLENGE OF A LIFETIME, RIGHT THERE."

— GRIFFIN

They make horror movies about the things mounted on Griffin's wall. This veteran Trapper relies on deployable Sound Spikes to keep tabs on the Monster's movements. But when it's time to face off with his prey, he breaks out his Harpoon Gun to pin it down, like shooting a giant, angry fish in a space barrel.

SKINS

SKIN	HOW TO UNLOCK
DEFAULT	Unlocked with Griffin.
GRIFFIN ELITE SKIN	Earn 3 stars in all items in Character Mastery.

LOADOUT

	ITEM	DESCRIPTION
	GAUSS SMG	Best for dealing with the planet's lesser predators.
	HARPOON GUN	Fires an energy harpoon that immobilizes the Monster.
	SOUND SPIKES	Stalk the Monster with these remote sensors.
	MOBILE ARENA	Energy dome that traps the Monster and Hunters inside.

CHARACTER MASTERY

	TIER 1 REQUIREMENTS		TIER 2 REQUIREMENTS		TIER 3 REQUIREMENTS	
	REQUIREMENT	BUFF	REQUIREMENT	BUFF	REQUIREMENT	BUFF
GAUSS SMG	Do 10,000 damage	Damage increase	Do 14,000 damage to the Monster	Damage increase	Do 8,000 headshot damage to the Monster	Damage increase
HARPOON GUN	Hold Monster for one second 14 times	Range increase	Hold Monster for 115 seconds	Range increase	Harpoon the Monster in mid-air 80 times	Range increase
SOUND SPIKES	Plant 15 spikes at least 50 meters apart	Range increase	Reveal Monster 120 times	Range increase	Reveal a Stage 1 Monster 20 times	Range increase

MASTERY UNLOCKS

You must complete all mastery challenges within the same tier set before moving on to the next set. Progress toward the next challenges will not be accrued before being unlocked.

TIER 1: Abe

TIER 2: Badge Foreground

TIER 3: Badge Foreground, Griffin Elite Skin

AWARDS

AWARD	DESCRIPTION	XP EARNED
CLOSE QUARTERS	Deal 2,000 damage to the Monster with the Gauss SMG.	50
TUG O' WAR	Harpoon the Monster three times with the Harpoon Gun. It must hold the Monster.	50
UNCOVERED	Reveal the Monster two times with Sound Spikes.	50
THUNDERDOME!	Trap the Monster in a Mobile Arena two times.	100

LOADOUT

Griffin's biggest strength is with his Harpoon Gun, which has the ability to hold the Monster in place. His tracking device, the Sound Spikes, takes some getting used to, but once you figure out where to place them, they become invaluable. The Gauss SMG is best used to deal with the weaker creatures, but it can also contribute when taking on your main target.

"JUST DO YOUR JOB, COMMUNICATE WITH YOUR TEAMMATES, AND IF THINGS GO WRONG, IMPROVISE."

— GRIFFIN

GAUSS SMG

Mastery Reward: Increased Damage

Damage per Bullet: 21

Fire Rate: 450 Rounds per Minute

Ammo Capacity: 36

The Gauss SMG is best saved for Shear's weaker wildlife, but it can do some damage against all foes. Press the Primary button to equip the gun, and squeeze the Fire trigger. A clip holds 36 bullets, though you can top it off at any time with the Reload button.

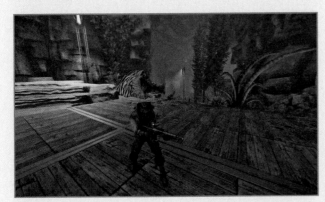

You can use the submachine gun to deal with the wildlife, but when in combat with the Monster, you should only use it as a last resort. After capturing the beast in the Mobile Arena and placing a Sound Spike, you should use the Harpoon Gun to slow it down. When this is not an option, then pull out the SMG.

HARPOON GUN

Mastery Reward: Increased Range

Damage: 150

Maximum Range: 41 Meters

Ammo Capacity: 1

The Harpoon Gun is a powerful weapon against the giant Monster. After equipping it with the Secondary button, aim at the foe, and hold the Fire button to shoot the harpoon and immobilize the Monster. The harpoon is released from the beast when it hits the device with a melee attack, or when you let go of the button.

The Harpoon Gun has a lengthy reload time, so use it efficiently. If you release the trigger just before the Monster breaks it, you can save valuable time and be ready sooner with your next harpoon.

This weapon is best used in the giant's back so that it must spin around first. Keep the Monster in between you and the rest of the team so you can bring it to a stop as it charges your allies. Note that the Harpoon Gun has a longer range than Harpoon Traps.

The Harpoon Gun should always be your weapon of choice when fighting the Monster. Switch to the Gauss SMG only when the Harpoon Gun is unavailable or when you are the last man standing.

SOUND SPIKES

Mastery Reward: Increased Range

Monster Detection Radius: 50 Meters

Maximum Allowed in World: 5

Sound Spikes are Griffin's means of tracking the Monster down. Once planted in the ground, it alerts you to the Monster's position when within range. Tap the Equipment button to ready the spike, and hold the Fire button to deploy it into the ground. Be sure to hold the trigger until the red bar fully fills up. Once the Monster is spotted near one of the spikes, an icon appears on your HUD.

You can only place five Sound Spikes at a time, as the blue dashes along the bottom of the reticle indicate. Place them wisely to get as much coverage as possible. Planting a sixth spike causes the first to be removed. The Monster and wildlife can destroy these devices, so try hiding them where they cannot be found.

Once spikes are placed, pull up your map to see their locations. Plant them at choke points, along paths, or simply at a location where you expect the Monster to go (such as feeding zones). Avoid overlapping them much to get as much coverage as possible. An icon also appears on the map when the Monster is detected.

Placement of the Sound Spikes depends somewhat on the shape of the map and where popular locations are found. On Dam, place them along the river to be alerted when the Monster crosses. If the map is narrow in the middle, fully cover that section with two or three spikes, and plant the remaining ones on each side.

Be alert, as a Monster can move near the Sound Spikes and not be detected. They do not work with a sneaking Monster. This isn't too bad, since the Monster is moving much slower,

but you could end up on the opposite side from the beast if you fully trust the sensors.

When the Mobile Arena is thrown and the Monster is trapped, immediately set down a Sound Spike so that your team can easily find the enemy and close in for the kill.

FIGHTING THE MONSTER

As you drop into a game of Hunt, look at the map and figure out where you want to place the Sound Spikes. Once you touch

down, split into groups of two. The other group can follow the Monster's tracks in hopes of finding the target that way, while your duo can move out to plant the spikes. The best bet is to flush the Stage 1 Monster directly to Griffin, who waits with his Mobile Arena.

Once the Monster has been spotted, close in. When you are within range, trap the beast within your Mobile Arena. Your first

priority inside the dome should be to plant a Sound Spike. This allows the others to immediately find the Monster and start their barrage of attacks.

Once in combat, try to keep the Monster between yourself and the other Hunters as you hold it in place with your Harpoon Gun. After the cable has been released, ready another one. A well-timed release as the Monster swings for it can gain you valuable time during the reload.

Once the sensor is placed and the Harpoon Gun is cooling down, pull out the Gauss SMG and deal out some damage. Quickly switch back to the harpoon when an opportunity for holding the beast arises. If you end up being the last one standing, you can use the submachine gun to deal a little pain, but it is usually a better option to run and hide.

ABE

> **"BOUNTY HUNTING IS THE KIND OF THING YOU DO WHEN YOU CAN'T DO ANYTHING ELSE. THIS IS WAY BETTER."**
> —ABE

Abe: the former intergalactic bounty hunter. A cowboy at heart, Abe hunts where the money is. His arsenal includes a Custom Shotgun, a pouch full of Stasis Grenades, and his homemade Tracking Darts. Oh, and his hat—he never forgets his hat.

SKINS

SKIN	HOW TO UNLOCK
DEFAULT	Unlocked with Abe.
ABE ELITE SKIN	Earn 3 stars in all items in Character Mastery.

LOADOUT

	ITEM	DESCRIPTION
	CUSTOM SHOTGUN	Effective at almost any range if you control your rate of fire.
	STASIS GRENADES	Slow the Monster down with these binding restrictors.
	TRACKING DART PISTOL	Track the Monster by tagging it or the wildlife it eats.
	MOBILE ARENA	Energy dome that traps the Monster and Hunters inside.

CHARACTER MASTERY

	TIER 1 REQUIREMENTS		TIER 2 REQUIREMENTS		TIER 3 REQUIREMENTS	
	REQUIREMENT	BUFF	REQUIREMENT	BUFF	REQUIREMENT	BUFF
CUSTOM SHOTGUN	Do 14,000 damage	Damage increase	Do 29,000 damage to the Monster	Damage increase	Do 12,000 headshot damage to the Monster	Damage increase
STASIS GRENADES	Slow the Monster 130 times	Radius increase	Slow the Monster for 800 seconds	Radius increase	Keep the Monster slowed for 3 seconds 160 times	Radius increase
TRACKING DART PISTOL	Dart the Monster 15 different times	Duration increase	Dart the Monster for 3,000 seconds	Duration increase	Dart the Monsters from 30 meters 60 times	Duration increase

MASTERY UNLOCKS

You must complete all mastery challenges within the same tier set before moving on to the next set. Progress toward the next challenges will not be accrued before being unlocked.

TIER 1: Badge Foreground

TIER 2: Badge Foreground

TIER 3: Badge Foreground, Abe Elite Skin

LOADOUT

Abe's tracking device is the Tracking Dart Pistol, which requires getting a bead on the Monster or marking its future food. When in combat, two weapons are a huge benefit to the team. Abe's Custom Shotgun deals out decent damage if used properly, and Stasis Grenades can greatly slow the beast down.

AWARDS

AWARD	DESCRIPTION	XP EARNED
BOOMSTICK	Deal 2,000 damage to the Monster with the Custom Shotgun.	50
SLOW AND STEADY	Slow the Monster three times with Abe's Stasis Grenade.	50
STICK AND BLINK	Mark the Monster with Abe's Tracking Dart twice.	50
THUNDERDOME!	Trap the Monster in a Mobile Arena two times.	100

CUSTOM SHOTGUN

Mastery Reward:

Increased Damage

Maximum Damage

per Shot: 88

Fire Rate:

300 Rounds per Minute

Ammo Capacity: 8

The Custom Shotgun is a decent weapon for the Trapper. It can be used at almost any range and deals a fair amount of damage, if used properly. Press the Primary button to equip the gun, and squeeze the Fire button to discharge the buckshot. You can reload the gun to its capacity of six shells at any time by pressing the Reload button.

The shotgun's accuracy becomes more inconsistent the quicker the weapon is fired. Slow down your fire rate to narrow the spread. At a slow enough pace, the accuracy is surprisingly good. Aim for weak spots that Val or Lazarus creates for extra damage.

Abe's Stasis Grenade is still his most important weapon in combat, but it is well worth your time to pull this one out and make the Monster bleed.

STASIS GRENADES

Mastery Reward: Increased Radius

Effect: 60% Slower Movement Speed

Max Duration: 15 Seconds

Effective Radius: 15 Meters

The Stasis Grenades dramatically slow the Monster's speed. This is extremely valuable in combat, as it allows teammates to stay out of the enemy's reach as they unload their weaponry. Tap the Secondary button to equip the grenades, and then press the Fire button to lob one toward your reticle. Hold the button down to display its trajectory for more accurate throws. You can place five of these grenades at one time. Blue dashes along the bottom of the reticle show how many have been used.

Stasis Grenades stick to any surface. For about 12 seconds, the grenade emits a field that slows the Monster down when within range. Spread these around the battlefield to slow the giant down. As the grenades die out, toss new ones around to maintain the effect.

These are extremely effective against the quick Wraith or Kraken, since they can be tough to hit when at full speed. Against any Monster, though, these grenades help the Hunters stay out of reach.

Out of combat, tossing these grenades into suspected paths of the Monster can help the team catch up to their objective more quickly. In Defend mode, use these to slow the Monster and its minions down as they attempt to reach the generators.

"LISTEN, SPOOKY: YOU DO NOT WANT TO MAKE A DEAL WITH THIS MAN. AND THAT'S COMING FROM *ME*."

—ABE

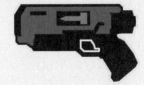
TRACKING DART PISTOL

Mastery Reward: Increased Duration

Tracking Duration: 45 Seconds

Fire Rate: 200 Rounds per Minute

Ammo Capacity: 6

Abe uses a Tracking Dart Pistol to find the Monster. Press the Equipment button to equip the gun, and pull the Fire button to shoot the dart. Six darts are held in a clip, which you can refill at any time with the Reload button.

You can track the Monster directly by hitting it with a dart. Alternately, by tagging wildlife and corpses, you create bait for the beast. When it devours one, the tracker continues to work from inside.

Hit as much wildlife with Tracking Darts as you can. The more tagged bodies out there, the more likely the Monster will ingest them. Dead tagged creatures may often be more tempting to the beast than live ones. Easy-kill Monsters are especially good targets for the Tracking Darts.

As the Mobile Arena is about to go down, tag the Monster with a Tracking Dart so that the team can quickly follow it. The longer the foe is tagged, the better chance there is to trap it again with another Mobile Arena.

FIGHTING THE MONSTER

As soon as the team touches down, pick up the Monster's tracks, and follow them. As you move through the map, hit any wildlife that you find with a Tracking Dart. Keep an eye out all around for acceptable targets.

When you find the Monster, make sure you are within range, and trap it within the Mobile Arena. Hit it with a Tracking Dart before or after deployment to help other Hunters spot the beast more quickly.

Spread Stasis Grenades around the battlefield. Placing them on the ground produces better coverage than sticking them on the walls. The Trapper is limited to five grenades at one time. As they disappear, toss new ones near the Monster to slow it down as much as possible.

When not tossing Stasis Grenades, pull out the Combat Shotgun and aim for the Monster's head or weak spots. It is good to deal out any damage that you can, but remember that slowing the Monster down for your teammates is often more effective than using the shotgun.

When facing the quick and stealthy Wraith, continue tossing the Stasis Grenades her way. One of the Wraith's strengths is her speed, so whenever that can be negated, the team has a better chance at success.

MEDIC

Group Role: Keep the Team Alive

Class Ability: Healing Burst

The Medic is quite often the most important Hunter on the team. It is up to that player to keep everyone alive as long as possible. Most Monsters come after her or him first, so staying out of sight is usually a good idea.

As the Medic, stick to the outsides of the battlefield or up high, where a nice vantage point gives you access to your teammates. For Lazarus, hiding is a little simpler with his Personal Cloak.

Each Medic has the Healing Burst, which can mend nearby Hunters, but Val and Caira also carry long-distance healing devices. This may sound like Lazarus is the inferior Medic, but his Lazarus Device is an amazing piece of technology that can bring the recently deceased back to life. This makes him a favorite among many of the other Hunters.

For the rest of the team, protecting the Medic is definitely in everyone's interest. Markov can lay down a field of mines, or Bucket can spread Sentry Guns around the battlefield. It is often necessary to gang up on the Monster in order to free your healer.

Beyond the healing and reviving, Medics each have their own unique loadouts that make them valuable in other roles, too. Caira can set enemies on fire with her Napalm Grenade, while her Acceleration Field speeds the group up as they run toward their objective.

Lazarus carries a sniper rifle that creates weak spots on the Monster, while a Personal Cloak allows him to stealthily move in to resurrect a teammate. Val carries a trio of guns, including her MedGun. One weakens the Monster, while the other slows it down.

HEALING BURST

Healing Amount: 350

Cooldown: 22 Seconds

Max radius: 15 Meters

Each Medic has the ability to release a burst of rejuvenating energy that heals any nearby characters, including the Medic. Tap the Ability button to release the cloud. There is a long recharge time between uses, so only use it when hurt.

The Medic is usually target number one, or at the least number two. When the Monster starts pounding on the Medic, use the Healing Burst, and immediately flee the area.

Be sure to communicate your intent to use the Healing Burst. Distant teammates may want to seek you out for the health boost.

With Val and Caira's healing abilities, it is very easy to forget about this skill. Any time you are not at full health, unload the Healing Burst to top off the Medic's HP.

"OF COURSE YOU DON'T NEED TO WORRY. YOU'VE GOT ME PATCHING YOU UP BEFORE YOU DIE."

— VAL

VAL

> "POINT IT AT THE MONSTER, PULL THE TRIGGER. UP TO YOU GUYS TO DO THE REST."
>
> — VAL

Sniper and Medic: two jobs that normally don't show up on the same résumé. Then again, Val doesn't apply for just any type of position. Her Armor-Piercing Sniper Rifle and Hunter-healing MedGun are the perfect qualifications for someone stalking prey the size of a small asteroid.

SKINS

SKIN	HOW TO UNLOCK
DEFAULT	Unlocked from start.
VAL ELITE SKIN	Earn 3 stars in all items in Character Mastery.

LOADOUT

ITEM		DESCRIPTION
	ARMOR-PIERCING SNIPER RIFLE	Punches holes in armor, creating weak points for teammates to target.
	MEDGUN	Fires a regenerative ray that continuously heals teammates.
	TRANQUILIZER GUN	Slows the Monster and tags it for an easier kill.
	HEALING BURST	Short burst of rejuvenating energy that heals Val and nearby allies.

CHARACTER MASTERY

	TIER 1 REQUIREMENTS		TIER 2 REQUIREMENTS		TIER 3 REQUIREMENTS	
	REQUIREMENT	BUFF	REQUIREMENT	BUFF	REQUIREMENT	BUFF
ARMOR-PIERCING RIFLE	Place 12 targets on the Monster	Damage increase	Enable teammates to deal 12,000 bonus damage to the Monster	Damage increase	Place 30 headshot targets on the Monster	Damage increase
MEDGUN	Heal 16,000 damage	Capacity increase	Revive 12 teammates with MedGun	Capacity increase	Heal 40 teammates before they're incapped	Capacity increase
TRANQUILIZER GUN	Tranquilize the Monster 14 times	Duration increase	Tranquilize the Monster for 400 seconds	Duration increase	Tranquilize the Monster from 100 meters away or more 60 times	Duration increase

MASTERY UNLOCKS

You must complete all mastery challenges within the same tier set before moving on to the next set. Progress toward the next challenges will not be accrued before being unlocked.

TIER 1: Lazarus

TIER 2: Badge Foreground

TIER 3: Badge Foreground, Val Elite Skin

AWARDS

AWARD	DESCRIPTION	XP EARNED
SURE SHOT	Mark the Monster four times with the Armor-Piercing Sniper Rifle.	100
QUICK FIX	Heal the Hunters for 3500 health with the MedGun.	50
SLEEPY TIME	Shoot the Monster three times with the Tranquilizer Gun.	50
MEDIC!	Heal two Hunters at once with the Healing Burst.	100

LOADOUT

Val is the ultimate Medic for any team looking to take down a giant Monster. She has great healing skills, along with the ability to weaken and slow down the target. Take full advantage of her entire loadout. Equip the Quick Switch Perk to cycle between them faster.

ARMOR-PIERCING SNIPER RIFLE

Mastery Reward: Increased Damage

Damage per Bullet: 140

Weak Spot Damage Multiplier: 2X

Ammo Capacity: 1 Round

Val's Armor-Piercing Sniper Rifle punches a hole in the Monster's armor, creating a weak spot for fellow Hunters to aim for. Tap the Primary button to equip the rifle, and squeeze the Fire button to fire the shot. The gun must be reloaded between every shot, so the fire rate is pretty slow.

The sniper rifle is extremely accurate, especially when using the scope. Hold down the Aim button to zoom in on your target. This allows you to place your targets wherever you please.

Hitting wildlife or the Monster with the Armor-Piercing Sniper Rifle places a circular target on the enemy. The other Hunters can hit this mark to deal twice the damage. These

weak points pair nicely with high-powered guns like the Rail Cannon.

When the Monster is first found and the Mobile Arena is deployed, hit it with as many shots from your sniper rifle as you can before switching over to MedGun duty.

MEDGUN

Mastery Reward: Increased Capacity

Heal Rate: 10% per Second

Maximum Range: 60 Meters

Max Fire Duration: 25 Seconds

The MedGun allows Val to perform her primary role from almost anywhere on the battlefield. Press the Secondary button to equip the device, face your injured target, and

squeeze the trigger to fire the regenerative ray. It continues healing the character until you release the button.

Val just needs to be facing toward a hurt teammate. Squeeze the trigger, and the gun auto aims at the character closest to your reticle. You do need to have a clear line of sight on the injured Hunter in order to heal.

Because of the MedGun's easy aim, Val can quickly spin around and start healing an ally. With multiple characters injured, give each one a short heal to keep them from being incapped.

You can use the MedGun to revive an incapacitated Hunter. As the Hunter bleeds out, fire the device his or her way. If the

Monster is pounding on the downed Hunter, the process essentially pauses. With the foe out of the way, the Hunter will be revived once the skull icon is filled completely.

TRANQUILIZER GUN

Mastery Reward: Increased Duration

Slow Effect Duration: 5 Seconds

Fire Rate: 70 Rounds per Minute

Ammo Capacity: 3 Rounds

A successful hit with the Tranquilizer Gun slows a Monster down and highlights it for a short time. Tap the Equipment button to switch to the gun, and then discharge the weapon with the Fire button. The gun holds three darts at a time. The Reload button tops it off at any time.

The fire rate is fairly slow and has a long reload time, so aim carefully. Hold down the Aim button to aim down the sights for a more accurate shot.

The Tranquilizer Gun is very effective against the Kraken and Wraith. Hitting the former with a tranq causes it to fall to the ground, while slowing the latter down takes away its valuable speed. As a bonus, it reveals their location as they hide behind obstacles for a short while.

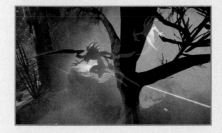

As the Mobile Arena is about to come down, hit the Monster with a tranquilizer dart. This makes it easier for the team to track the beast.

FIGHTING THE MONSTER

Val doesn't have much of a role during the hunt: just top off other Hunters' health when necessary, and place weak spots on the tougher wildlife. Once the Monster is found and the Mobile Arena is deployed, then she gets really busy.

Whenever you are closing in on the Monster, try to hit it with the Tranquilizer Gun to slow it down, making it easier for the Trapper to capture the beast.

Once the battle has begun, hit the Monster with several shots from the Armor-Piercing Sniper Rifle. Then, switch to the MedGun to keep your teammates' health topped off. Stay away from the action, positioning yourself on the outskirts of the arena or high above on a cliff.

Hit the Monster every once in a while with the Tranquilizer Gun to slow it down. This greatly helps the team, especially against Wraith and Kraken. With Hank on the team, hit the giant with a tranq dart before Hank releases his powerful Orbital Barrage, making it tougher for the Monster to flee the area.

Any time the other Hunters are healthy and the Monster is tranq'd, continue to fill it up with weak spots from your sniper rifle. The more holes in its armor, the faster it falls.

Remember, though, the biggest priority for the Medic is to keep everyone healthy. If you see a downed Hunter, use the MedGun to bring him or her back to life.

LAZARUS

> "THEY KNOW YOU ARE UNNATURAL, AND IT DISPLEASES THEM."
> — LAZARUS

What kind of Medic purposely lets his comrades die? One with a badass gun and the ability to restore life to the dead. Slipping past predators with a Silenced Sniper Rifle and Personal Cloak, Lazarus brings fallen allies back from death—even if they're now technically zombies.

SKINS

SKIN	HOW TO UNLOCK
DEFAULT	Unlocked with Lazarus
LAZARUS ELITE SKIN	Earn 3 stars in all items in Character Mastery.

LOADOUT

ITEM		DESCRIPTION
	SILENCED SNIPER RIFLE	Semi-automatic rifle that creates weak points in the Monster's armor.
	LAZARUS DEVICE	Slightly illegal device that instantly revives dead comrades.
	PERSONAL CLOAK	Temporary invisibility allows Lazarus to sneak past threats.
	HEALING BURST	Short burst of rejuvenating energy that heals Lazarus and nearby allies.

CHARACTER MASTERY

	TIER 1 REQUIREMENTS		TIER 2 REQUIREMENTS		TIER 3 REQUIREMENTS	
	REQUIREMENT	BUFF	REQUIREMENT	BUFF	REQUIREMENT	BUFF
SILENCED SNIPER RIFLE	Place 200 targets on the Monster	Damage increase	Teammates must do 270 damage by hitting Lazarus's targets on the Monster	Damage increase	Place 150 headshot targets on the Monster	Damage increase
LAZARUS DEVICE	Use the Lazarus Device 4 times	Recharge rate increase	Use the Lazarus Device 28 times on teammates	Recharge rate increase	Use the Lazarus Device on 3 teammates in a single match 25 times	Recharge rate increase
PERSONAL CLOAK	Cloak revive 7 creatures with the Lazarus Device	Duration increase	Cloak revive 22 teammates with the Lazarus Device	Duration increase	Cloak revive 3 teammates in a single match 25 times with the Lazarus Device	Duration increase

MASTERY UNLOCKS

You must complete all mastery challenges within the same tier set before moving on to the next set. Progress toward the next challenges will not be accrued before being unlocked.

TIER 1: Caira

TIER 2: Badge Foreground

TIER 3: Badge Foreground, Lazarus Elite Skin

AWARDS

AWARD	DESCRIPTION	XP EARNED
SILENT AND DEADLY	Mark the Monster four times with the Silenced Sniper Rifle.	50
REVIVIFIED	Revivify two Hunters with the Lazarus Device.	100
FRIENDLY GHOST	Revive or revivify multiple Hunters while using Personal Cloak.	50
MEDIC!	Heal two Hunters at once with the Healing Burst.	100

LOADOUT

Lazarus is the only Medic who doesn't possess a second healing ability. Instead, his Lazarus Device brings a character back from the dead, an extremely valuable skill—provided the team can keep him alive. Lazarus also carries a sniper rifle similar to Val's, but his has a faster fire rate.

SILENCED SNIPER RIFLE

Mastery Reward: Increased Damage

Damage per Bullet: 30

Weak Spot Damage Multiplier: 1.5X

Ammo Capacity: 10 Rounds

Lazarus' Silenced Sniper Rifle is a semi-automatic rifle that creates weak spots in the Monster's armor. Press the Primary button to equip the gun, and squeeze the trigger to fire. The Aim button allows you to zoom in through the built-in scope, granting more accurate shots. You can press the Reload button any time before the 10-bullet clip runs out to fill it back up.

Hitting wildlife or the Monster with Lazarus' sniper rifle places diamond-shaped targets on the enemy. The Hunters can then hit these marks for extra damage. This pairs nicely with high-powered guns like the Rail Cannon.

This may sound similar to Val's sniper rifle, but Lazarus' weapon is semi-automatic and produces no tracers. It shoots as fast as you can tap the Fire button. This allows you to spread out many weak spots in the Monster's armor, while spending less time doing so. However, the damage bonus is less than what Val's gun produces.

When the Monster is first found and the Mobile Arena is deployed, hit the beast with as many shots from your sniper rifle as possible. Line the foe up in your sights, and rapidly tap the Fire button to lay down as many weak spots as you can. Spread them out so that inaccurate weapons have a better shot of getting the damage boost.

LAZARUS DEVICE

Mastery Reward:

Increased Recharge Rate

Cooldown: 12 Seconds

Trigger Time: 1 Second

The Lazarus Device is what makes Lazarus who he is. With it, he can bring dead Hunters back to life. Tap the Secondary button to equip the device. Approach a downed or dead character, and hold the Fire button until the red charging meter fills up. Reviving a Hunter with this device does not add a strike to his or her health.

When a Hunter dies, an icon appears above with a semi-circle meter over the top. This slowly counts down until that Hunter can no longer be revived. Get to the victim before the body disappears. Remember that you can use the device on an incapacitated character.

When Lazarus is on the team, it is important to avoid picking up downed Hunters, unless of course it is the Medic who has been incapacitated. Avoiding strikes against the Hunters helps greatly down the road.

Be patient with your revives. There is plenty of time to get to the Hunter once he or she has been incapacitated. Wait for the Monster to lose interest, use the Personal Cloak, and sneak over to the Hunter corpse unnoticed.

Note that a Hunter's health will be low after being revived. Immediately use a Healing Burst if available.

When Lazarus is teamed up with Maggie, Daisy tends to avoid reviving the Hunters unless necessary. This helps when trying to avoid strikes.

PERSONAL CLOAK

Mastery Reward: Increased Duration

Cooldown: 35 Seconds

Max Duration: 12 Seconds

"THE REVIVER IS FULLY CHARGED! YOU MAY DIE AS OFTEN AS YOU WISH!"
— LAZARUS

The Support class has the Cloaking Field ability, but Lazarus has his own personal one. Tap the Equipment button to go invisible temporarily. This allows Lazarus to sneak past enemies or walk over to a helpless Hunter.

Call out to your team when deploying the Personal Cloak. That way, your Support Hunter doesn't double up with his Cloaking Field. When a fight turns bad, Lazarus needs as much invisibility time as he can get.

Whenever possible, save the Personal Cloak for revives. Frequently, the Monster will keep an eye on downed Hunters, especially when Lazarus is on the team, so stealth is vital for getting to them. Go invisible, sneak over to the incapacitated character, perform the resurrection, and quickly get out.

Watch out, as Goliath's Fire Breath can reveal a cloaked Hunter's location. Try to stay out of reach of his attacks. Water puts out the flame, if there happens to be any nearby.

FIGHTING THE MONSTER

During the hunt, Lazarus' main focus is keeping the team healthy and tagging the tougher wildlife with weak spots. The sniper rifle does a little damage, so it is possible to take down weaker creatures, but you may want to channel your time and effort toward your core strengths.

Lazarus really earns his money when it comes to the big Monster battles. First thing after the enemy is captured in the Mobile Arena is to load it up with weak spots from the sniper rifle.

At this point, Lazarus should flee to the outside edges of the battlefield or up high on the cliffs. Higher vantage points give you a better view of your entire team. When someone requires medical attention, drop down, use a

Healing Burst, and quickly flee again. Wherever you watch the action from, try to keep teammates in between you and the Monster.

Teammates should plant traps on these high points, but immediately get out to avoid attracting any unneeded attention. Mines, Sentry Guns, and Harpoon Traps make great deterrents.

When a Hunter goes down, use the Personal Cloak, and drop down to his or her side. Bring

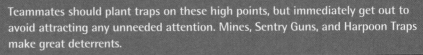

the character back to life, and again, flee to your safe spot. There is a cooldown time between uses of the Lazarus Device, so you must time the revives well when multiple Hunters get in trouble.

Watch out if Lazarus is downed, as the Monster will often camp his body. This Medic is an important target for the enemy, which goes out of its way to ensure

that Lazarus is out of the game as much as possible. Try distracting the beast to move it away from the body.

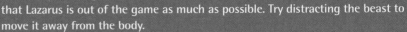

Lazarus is tough to get the hang of, but he is a very powerful Hunter when played well. Remember to stay out of sight as much as possible when in combat, and silently swoop in for revives when characters are incapped.

"WHAT POSSIBLE REASON WOULD I HAVE TO BEND THE LAWS OF LIFE AND DEATH IN THIS MANNER?"

— LAZARUS

CAIRA

"HUNTING ALIEN MONSTERS. THIS IS NOT HOW I THOUGHT MY CAREER WOULD GO. NOT COMPLAINING! JUST... WOW."

— CAIRA

One can only imagine the confusion at the weapons lab when Caira put in her order for a Grenade Launcher that shoots both Napalm and Healing rounds. As a qualified combat Medic, she thoroughly enjoys both saving lives and setting stuff on fire. Her Acceleration Field is also the perfect pick-me-up for an all-night hunt.

SKINS

SKIN	HOW TO UNLOCK
DEFAULT	Unlocked with Caira
CAIRA ELITE SKIN	Earn 3 stars in all items in Character Mastery.

LOADOUT

ITEM		DESCRIPTION
	NAPALM GRENADE LAUNCHER	Launch these incendiary grenades to ignite your foes.
	HEALING GRENADE LAUNCHER	The best type of friendly fire! Shoot at your teammates to heal them.
	ACCELERATION FIELD	Give those in proximity to you a speed boost to catch up to your prey, or make them more effective in combat.
	HEALING BURST	Short burst of rejuvenating energy that heals Caira and nearby allies.

CHARACTER MASTERY

	TIER 1 REQUIREMENTS		TIER 2 REQUIREMENTS		TIER 3 REQUIREMENTS	
	REQUIREMENT	BUFF	REQUIREMENT	BUFF	REQUIREMENT	BUFF
NAPALM GRENADE LAUNCHER	Do 3,300 damage	Range increase	Do 4,000 damage to the Monster	Range increase	Get 170 direct hits on the Monster	Range increase
HEALING GRENADE LAUNCHER	Heal 32,000 damage	Range increase on area of effect burst	Revive 15 teammates	Range increase on area of effect burst	Heal multiple teammates 900 times	Range increase on area of effect burst
ACCELERATION FIELD	Cover 2,200 meters using Acceleration Field	Duration increase	Give teammates a boost 74 times	Duration increase	Cover 50 meters with teammates in a single match 100 times	Duration increase

MASTERY UNLOCKS

You must complete all mastery challenges within the same tier set before moving on to the next set. Progress toward the next challenges will not be accrued before being unlocked.

TIER 1: Badge Foreground

TIER 2: Badge Foreground

TIER 3: Badge Foreground, Caira Elite Skin

LOADOUT

Caira has an interesting loadout for a Medic. Her grenade launcher can fire both Napalm and Healing Grenades—set the enemy on fire and heal fellow Hunters with the same weapon. Her third skill, Acceleration Field, is unique to the game. Release the speed boost to help your team catch up with the Monster.

AWARDS

AWARD	DESCRIPTION	XP EARNED
SCORCHED	Deal 2,000 damage to the Monster with the Napalm Grenade Launcher.	50
HEALTHSPLOSION	Heal a teammate for 1,000 HP with the Healing Grenade Launcher.	50
SPEEDY	Over 500 meters with Acceleration Field.	50
MEDIC!	Heal two Hunters at once with the Healing Burst.	100

NAPALM GRENADE LAUNCHER

Mastery Reward: Increased Range

Damage: 35 Plus Residual Burn Damage

Explosion Radius: 5 Meters

Ammo Capacity: 4 Grenades

The Napalm Grenade Launcher launches incendiary grenades at your foes, setting them ablaze. Tap the Primary button to select the weapon, and squeeze the Fire trigger to toss the grenade. Hold the button down to display an arc for precise aiming. The enemy continues to burn after impact, keeping the hurt on for a number of seconds. You can reload the launcher at any time with the Reload button.

Once the Monster has been captured within the Mobile Arena, hit it with a Napalm Grenade, and then switch to healing if necessary. Keep the fire going throughout the battle to maximize damage.

Napalm Grenades work well against Wraith, as long as you can make contact with it. After it sends out its Decoy, the Monster is cloaked for a short time. Hitting it with the grenade sets it on fire, revealing its location.

HEALING GRENADE LAUNCHER

Mastery Reward:

Increased Range on Area of Effect Burst

Healing Amount: 125

Explosion Radius: 10 Meters

Ammo Capacity: 4 Grenades

The Healing Grenade Launcher creates radial blasts of healing energy wherever it impacts. Press the Secondary button, followed by the Fire trigger to throw the grenade toward the reticle. Hold the button down to bring up an aiming arc that allows for more precise tosses. You can reload the launcher at any time with the Reload button.

Look for allies who are currently engaged with the Monster, and launch Healing Grenades at them to keep them in the fight longer. The area of effect burst allows Caira to heal multiple targets at once. Line up your throws so that they land between two or three Hunters to maximize the healing.

You can use the Healing Grenades to pick up an incapped Hunter from afar. As a character bleeds out, toss the healing projectiles their way until he or she stands again.

Unlike Val's MedGun, Caira can use the Healing Grenade Launcher on herself. Fire the projectiles at Caira's feet for some self-healing.

ACCELERATION FIELD

Mastery Reward: Increased Duration

Bonuses: 40% Increase in Sprint Speed, 50% Increase in Jump Height

Cooldown: 45 Seconds

Max Duration: 13.5 Seconds

Once the Acceleration Field has been used, Caira and anyone surrounding her are sped up to incredible speeds. Tap the Equipment button to release the speed boost. Lines appearing to come at the group indicate that a character is under the speed effect. Caira also informs the team about the start and end of the ability. Other Hunters must stay near Caira to keep the speed up.

This boost in speed works very well when the group needs to get to an objective quickly, such as the Monster, an egg, or a survivor. From the back of the pack, release the field to bunch everyone up and avoid leaving Hunters behind.

Caira's Acceleration Field is also useful in combat. Activating the speed boost as the group battles the Monster can help the Hunters move more quickly and dodge its attacks.

Combine Caira with Maggie for a rush tactic in Hunt mode. As soon as the team touches down and Daisy picks up the Monster's scent, move up beside the Trapjaw and use the Acceleration Field to get the speed boost. Use it again

when it becomes available. This gives the group a much better chance in reaching the Monster at Stage 1.

FIGHTING THE MONSTER

Unlike the other Medics, Caira plays a big part in the hunt for the Monster. If Maggie is the Trapper, group up with Daisy at the start. If not, get the group to follow the Monster tracks. Release the Acceleration Field, and speed off toward your target.

The Napalm Grenade Launcher works well against the wildlife that hinder your progress. Do not waste too much time on them, unless there is a worthwhile Buff you can obtain from an elite wildlife.

Once the Monster is found and it has been trapped inside the Mobile Arena, hit the enemy with a Napalm Grenade, and then switch your focus to healing if needed. Caira's Healing Grenade has an area of effect

burst that can heal multiple Hunters at once. Launch them at any Hunters engaged with the enemy.

Find a high perch or stick to the outside of the arena to stay out of harm's way. An elevated vantage point allows Caira to launch grenades down on enemies and allies alike.

Every now and then, hit the Monster with Napalm Grenades to maximize the fire

damage. Help out your teammates whenever possible by releasing the Acceleration Field in the middle of the battlefield. The speed boost allows them to avoid incoming attacks more easily. Take the opportunity to use a Healing Burst while out there if the team has taken damage.

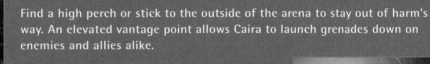

Remember to heal yourself when Caira is hurt. Use the Healing Burst, or fire a Healing Grenade at her feet. Just as the Mobile Arena is about to go down and the Monster is looking to flee, hit the Acceleration Field to hurry directly behind the target.

The Acceleration boost works well in Nest and Rescue modes, when it is vital that you reach the next objective quickly.

SUPPORT

Group Role: Assist Teammates while Also Dealing out Damage

Class Ability: Cloaking Field

Just as their title suggests, this eclectic selection of Hunters supports the team, though they also have the ability to deal out some serious damage. Each character comes equipped with a high-damage weapon and the class ability, Cloaking Field. Otherwise, they are quite diverse in their skills, with each character having his own way to assist the team.

Hank's Orbital Barrage can be a game changer when dropped on a slow or stationary Monster. Combine that with his Shield Projector, which is guaranteed to save many Hunters from getting a beatdown, and he becomes a huge asset for any Hunter squad.

Bucket's everyday job may be to pilot the ship, but this machine packs quite a punch on the battlefield. Besides his extremely satisfying Guided Missile Launcher, this Hunter has the ability to deploy five Sentry Guns, which can make any Monster think twice. On top of that, he can use his head as a UAV that can survey the area and tag the Monster once spotted.

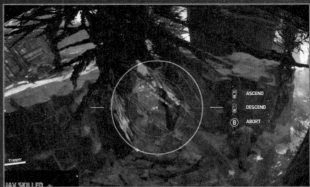

The third and final Hunter is Cabot, the creator of this crew. This Hunter is best at spoiling a good game for the Monster. Get a lucky toss with his tagging dust, and things can quickly change to the Hunters' favor. Pull out the powerful Rail Cannon, and shoot your target through any surface. Once fully engaged with the beast, his Damage Amplifier makes everyone's shots hurt even more.

This leaves a tough decision for any player: which Support character should be taken into the fight?

CLOAKING FIELD

Active Radius: 10 Meters

Cooldown: 30 Seconds

Duration: 20 Seconds

Cloaking Field is extremely valuable on the battlefield, with its ability to help a struggling team escape. Tap the Ability button, and any nearby Hunters temporarily become invisible. This allows your teammates to sneak past threats, flee from trouble, or stealthily revive another Hunter.

As the squad tracks the Monster, many aggressive wildlife get in your way—some small, some big. Timely use of the Cloaking Field helps the team move past them so that the Hunters can remain focused on the task at hand. This is especially helpful when passing bigger creatures that can easily remove a Hunter from the pack, such as the Tyrant.

In battle, help out the higher-value targets like the Medic by allowing them to do their job from the safety of the Cloaking Field. Teammates who get in trouble can use the invisibility to flee from trouble. Call out to your squad when the ability is available.

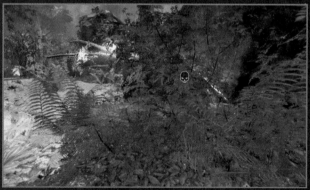

The invisibility is extremely helpful for incapped Hunters. Once cloaked, there is a good chance the Monster will leave them alone. This cloaking also allows Support to move in and pick the character up. With Lazarus on the team, the cloak gets less use since he has his own Personal Cloak.

Remember that firing a weapon reveals your location, even when cloaked. This includes Cabot's Damage Amplifier, so there is no hiding this assistance from the Monster.

HANK

"OH YEAH. NOTHIN' LIKE A COOKOUT TO WASH AWAY THE TASTE OF A STANDARD SYNTHPASTE RATION. ANY REQUESTS?"

— HANK

Hank believes in the simple things, like the value of a hard day's work or the joy of indiscriminately firing a Laser Cutter at bloodthirsty predators. Which is why he cherishes the quiet moment after calling down an Orbital Barrage on whatever creature is currently pissing him off. The ensuing bombardment of fiery death really puts things into perspective.

SKINS

SKIN	HOW TO UNLOCK
DEFAULT	Unlocked from start.
HANK ELITE SKIN	Earn 3 stars in all items in Character Mastery.

LOADOUT

ITEM	DESCRIPTION
LASER CUTTER	Cannon that rapidly fires a volley of laser bolts.
SHIELD PROTECTOR	Single-target shield that protects fellow Hunters.
ORBITAL BARRAGE	Summons a massive bombardment from an orbital mining satellite.
CLOAKING FIELD	Grants temporary invisibility to Hank and nearby allies.

CHARACTER MASTERY

	TIER 1 REQUIREMENTS		TIER 2 REQUIREMENTS		TIER 3 REQUIREMENTS	
	REQUIREMENT	BUFF	REQUIREMENT	BUFF	REQUIREMENT	BUFF
LASER CUTTER	Do 6,000 damage	Damage increase	Do 20,000 damage to the Monster	Damage increase	Do 5,000 headshot damage to the Monster	Damage increase
SHIELD PROJECTOR	Shield teammates from damage 20 times	Capacity increase	Shield 35,000 damage	Capacity increase	Prevent 30 teammates from becoming incapped	Capacity increase
ORBITAL BARRAGE	Do 6,600 damage	Damage increase	Do 24,000 damage to the Monster	Damage increase	Damage the Monster 30 times from a distance greater than 50 meters	Damage increase

MASTERY UNLOCKS

You must complete all mastery challenges within the same tier set before moving on to the next set. Progress toward the next challenges will not be accrued before being unlocked.

TIER 1: Bucket

TIER 2: Badge Foreground

TIER 3: Badge Foreground, Hank Elite Skin

AWARDS

AWARD	DESCRIPTION	XP EARNED
LASER SHOW	Deal 2,000 damage to the Monster with the Laser Cutter.	50
PROTECTOR	Shield the Hunters for 2,000 damage with the Shield Projector.	50
DUCK AND COVER	Deal 2,000 damage to the Monster with Orbital Barrage.	50
NOW YOU SEE ME	Cloak two Hunters at once with the Cloaking Field.	100

LOADOUT

Hank is equipped to both deal out the pain and save his comrades in battle. The Laser Cutter does its job when he isn't needed elsewhere, but his Orbital Barrage can really tear a Monster up—provided it doesn't flee that location. At the least, the explosives can drive the enemy away from the area. But Hank's Shield Projector provides the most benefit to the team. It allows the Medic to continue healing while the Monster focuses its attention their way, or it keeps the Assault's attacks up when his Personal Shield is no longer available.

"GEAR CHECK, FOLKS. CAN'T TAKE ANY RISKS ON THIS ONE. SHIELDS FULL OF JUICE?"

— HANK

LASER CUTTER

Mastery Reward: Increased Damage

Damage: 160 per Second

Recharge Time from Empty: 3 Seconds

Max Fire Duration: 5 seconds

Hank's Laser Cutter rapidly fires a volley of lasers. Press the Primary button to select the weapon. The Fire trigger releases the projectiles at your target. Holding the Aim button gives you a slightly zoomed-in view, but this gun works just as well fired from the hip.

The Laser Cutter has incredible accuracy. Go for headshots or aim at weak spots to maximize damage to the Monster. Ensure that your teammates do not need protection, and then pull this weapon out to help bring the beast down.

You should equip this weapon as the team hunts the Monster so Hank can deal with pesky creatures along the way.

SHIELD PROJECTOR

Mastery Reward: Increased Capacity

Max Damage Absorbed: 800

Recharge Time from Empty: 11 Seconds

Max Range: 60 Meters

The Shield Projector protects a Hunter from all damage dealt to them for a short period and is used in the same manner as Val's Medgun. Press the Secondary button to equip the device, face the friendly character, and hold the Fire button. Releasing the button stops the protection and allows the device to recharge its battery.

As long as Hank has an ally close to the aiming reticle, the Shield Projector will lock on to the Hunter. Use the Shield Projector on allies who are currently engaged with the Monster. The Shield Projector's battery depletes only if the player that it is shielding is being damaged. Otherwise, you can hold the beam on the targeted player forever without draining the battery.

The Shield Projector is vital during combat to keep Assault Hunters alive longer. Since many Monsters tend to focus on the Medic, they may need the protection more. Learn the enemy's attack animations, and squeeze the trigger just as it strikes your comrades. Efficient use of the device goes a long way in keeping the team around longer.

The Shield Projector has incredible range. Besides giving a teammate temporary invisibility, Hank's duties can all be performed from a high perch. Move the Monster around with the Orbital Barrage, protect teammates who engage the foe, and hit the beast with the Laser Cutter whenever possible.

Teaming up with Val is a great way to mess with the Monster. Shield her as she heals you when you both are under fire. Be sure to communicate use of the Shield Projector so that your Assault Hunter doesn't waste his Personal Shield.

ORBITAL BARRAGE

Mastery Reward: Increased Damage

Max Damage per Missile: 360

Max Damage Radius per Missile: 8

Number of Missiles in Barrage: 17

Hank's Orbital Barrage can deal some serious damage to the Monster, but its best use may be in moving the foe away from an objective. Tap the Equipment button to bring up a reticle. Place the reticle where you want the explosives to land. A red circle with three bombs crossed out indicates that they cannot be dropped there. Once ready, hold the Fire button down until the red bar is filled to unleash the devastation.

> **"THIS IS LASER-DEATH, BABY! GOOD ENOUGH FOR A SHIP'S HULL, IT'S GOOD ENOUGH FOR YOU."**
>
> — HANK

The Orbital Barrage is a very powerful attack with a direct blow, but hitting a moving target with it is impossible. It is best used on a Monster that is in the process of evolving, being held down by harpoons, or possibly slowed down.

The explosives start out dropping where the attack was aimed, but they move farther out as it continues. A fleeing Monster may still get hit as it attempts to dodge them.

Watch out for an incoming Orbital Barrage, as it knocks any Hunters caught in the blast far away. Quickly dodge out of the area to avoid losing your position. Always communicate when using this attack so that your allies can exit the area in time.

The Orbital Barrage's best use may be as a defensive measure. Drop them near an objective or incapped Hunter to force the Monster away. The best hope is that the beast will panic and make a mistake.

Since the explosives rain from the skies above, this ability is ineffective under cover. The "unable to use" graphic is shown whenever you attempt to do so.

FIGHTING THE MONSTER

As the team hunts the Monster, you can use Hank's Laser Cutter to fend off pesky wildlife. Group the team when approaching

dangerous creatures like the Tyrant, and use the Cloaking Field to move past without losing time. The Shield Projector comes in handy if a Hunter is swiped.

Once the Monster is found and the Mobile Arena is deployed, pull out the Laser Cutter and do some damage to the foe. Avoid attracting too much attention; your team needs your protection.

If the group lucked out and the Monster is evolving, quickly hit it with the Orbital Barrage. Otherwise, you should save this

ability for when the beast is harpooned or needs moving.

Hank can do most of his work from a high position, so seek out a safe spot with a good view of the action. Project the shield on

Hunters who are currently engaged with the Monster. If possible, get in some pot shots with your laser, but your primary job should be to protect the team. Use the shield efficiently to keep its battery charged.

If the squad gets into trouble, drop down and use the Cloaking Field so that they can escape with ease. You can also assist by sending in the Orbital Barrage, but be sure to announce the move since Hunters caught in the blasts will be sent flying away.

Hank requires a lot of pre-empting. You must anticipate whom the Monster is going to attack next and predict where enemies are heading. Actually, though, much of *Evolve* requires a little prediction and luck.

In Defend mode, drop the Orbital Barrage on minions that attack the generator. In Rescue, use the Shield Generator to assist survivors to the evacuation point.

BUCKET

"AH YES. THIS 'WINGING IT' THING THAT YOU HUMANS ARE SO FOND OF. OF COURSE..."
— BUCKET

Normally charged with flying the ship, Bucket uses a modified repair drone chassis when the time comes to support his human comrades on the ground. His Guided Missile Launcher, deployable Sentry Guns, and detachable UAV make him more than a match for anything organic.

SKINS

SKIN	HOW TO UNLOCK
DEFAULT	Unlocked with Bucket.
BUCKET ELITE SKIN	Earn 3 stars in all items in Character Mastery.

LOADOUT

ITEM	DESCRIPTION
GUIDED MISSILE LAUNCHER	Who needs a right hand when you've got guided missiles?
SENTRY GUNS	Multiple floating weapon platforms deploy from Bucket's "chest."
UAV	Bucket's detachable head recons the area and tags the Monster if he spots it.
CLOAKING FIELD	Grants temporary invisibility to Bucket and nearby Hunters.

CHARACTER MASTERY

	TIER 1 REQUIREMENTS		TIER 2 REQUIREMENTS		TIER 3 REQUIREMENTS	
	REQUIREMENT	BUFF	REQUIREMENT	BUFF	REQUIREMENT	BUFF
GUIDED MISSILE LAUNCHER	Do 9,000 damage	Damage increase	Do 25,000 damage to the Monster	Damage increase	Get 390 direct hits to the Monster	Damage increase
SENTRY GUNS	Do 15,000 damage	Range increase	Do 20,000 damage to the Monster	Range increase	Have 3 Sentry Guns firing at once 30 times	Range increase
UAV	Travel 3,000 meters in Hunt or Rescue	Tracker duration increase	Find the Monster 30 times in Hunt or Rescue	Tracker duration increase	Find 25 Stage 1 Monsters in Hunt or Rescue	Tracker duration increase

MASTERY UNLOCKS

You must complete all mastery challenges within the same tier set before moving on to the next set. Progress toward the next challenges will not be accrued before being unlocked.

TIER 1: Cabot

TIER 2: Badge Foreground

TIER 3: Badge Foreground, Bucket Elite Skin

AWARDS

AWARD	DESCRIPTION	XP EARNED
STEADY HAND	Deal 2,000 damage to the Monster with the Guided Missile Launcher.	50
SET AND FORGET	Deal 2,000 damage to the Monster with the Sentry Guns.	50
HIDE AND SEEK	Reveal the Monster two times with the UAV.	100
NOW YOU SEE ME	Cloak two Hunters at once with the Cloaking Field.	100

LOADOUT

Bucket was built to both track down a target and deal out some heavy damage. The UAV allows Bucket to go out on his own to find and tag the Monster. Well-placed Sentry Guns and a Guided Missile Launcher make him extremely beneficial in combat.

GUIDED MISSILE LAUNCHER

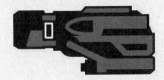

Mastery Reward: Increased Damage

Damage per Rocket: 68

Fire rate: 60 Rounds per Minute

Ammo Capacity: 4

The Guided Missile Launcher fires high-powered rockets that you can control in flight. Tap the Primary button to switch to the weapon. Pull the Fire trigger to let the projectile go. At this point, the rocket moves toward the reticle. As long as it does not run into an obstacle, it will make impact there. Four rockets are available at a time, which you can refill at any time by pressing the Reload button.

The next rocket takes a few moments to load up, so space is needed to get multiple projectiles in the air. However, it is possible to guide as many as four missiles into a target. An extremely skilled user could fire all four into the air, and then pull down the aiming reticle to rain fire from above. This requires a lot of luck to actually make contact, but you can use it to flush a Monster out.

The guided missiles detonate as they near their target, so it is not necessary to be too accurate. Launch them into the air, and get the reticle close to have an impact.

Bucket's first priority in combat should be to place his Sentry Guns, but once they are ready, switch to the Guided Missile Launcher.

SENTRY GUNS

Mastery Reward: Increased Range

Damage rate: 85 Damage per Second

Max Fire Range: 22.5 Meters

Max Toss Distance: 6 Meters

Bucket can deploy Sentry Guns that automatically fire at nearby hostiles. Tap the Secondary button to equip them. As you run around, a blue hologram appears where the gun will be placed. If it is red, one cannot be used there. You can place five turrets at a time, as the blue dashes along the bottom of the reticle indicate.

Place them around the battlefield or near objectives for great effect. Monsters may think twice before entering an area that is well guarded. An enemy's long-range abilities can destroy these turrets, so do not expect them to last too long against a good Monster. If the guns are grouped too close together, they can be destroyed with a single attack. Be sure that all five are deployed with plenty of space between them before you start thinking about firing missiles at the foe.

The Sentry Guns can protect incapacitated Hunters. Place them near the downed character to keep a Monster at bay. This allows a cloaked Bucket to move in and get him or her back into the fight.

These turrets are great against the eggs in Nest mode. Break away from the group, and plant some Sentry Guns around an egg. Select one that is far from the Monster so the guns can do their job. Make sure that they are placed close enough to the objective, or they will not fire.

Moving and looking around are performed as normal. The Fire button ascends, the Aim button descends, and B aborts the operation. A red bar on the bottom of your HUD indicates the battery remaining in the UAV. Once empty, a Battery Depleted message appears, and it crashes to the ground as you are returned to Bucket's body. There is a long cooldown timer for the UAV, so obviously, it is best to get the Monster marked.

UAV

Mastery Reward: Increased Tracker Duration

Duration of UAV Tag:

30 Seconds

Max Speed: 12 Meters per Second

Max Flight Duration: 54 Seconds

Bucket's head can be removed and used as a UAV to seek out the Monster. Tap the Equipment button to grab ahold of the device, and then hold the Fire trigger until a red bar fills up to launch the UAV. This switches your view to the device.

> **"THAT IS RATHER THE POINT, ACTUALLY. I BELIEVE THE NATIVE WILDLIFE FOUND MY PREVIOUS FLUIDS DELICIOUS. WHY ELSE WOULD THEY CONTINUE TO ATTEMPT TO EAT ME?"**
>
> — BUCKET

Once the Monster is spotted, keep it within the inner reticle. A circular meter around the outside fills up as it attempts to mark the beast. Once complete, abort the UAV, as a red icon now shows the team where they can find the Monster.

While searching for the Monster with the UAV, follow any Monster tracks you can find, listen for sounds from the Monster, and keep an eye out for the usual clues like flying birds. The UAV is best used when the team has a fairly good idea where the enemy is.

Avoid straying too far with the UAV because your body is left behind, possibly unprotected. Leave Sentry Guns around Bucket for some added protection. The team should go toward the UAV to get a quicker start on the Monster. It takes Bucket a minute to catch up with the group.

As the Mobile Arena expires, send the UAV after the Monster. This way, the squad can track it for a while longer. Be careful, as the Monster can shoot the UAV out of the air.

FIGHTING THE MONSTER

During the hunt for the Monster, Bucket can be a huge help to the Trapper with his UAV. There is a lot of territory to cover, but if you have a good idea of the direction where the beast has gone, launch the device and track it down. If the team has kept tabs on Bucket's head, they should be in a good position once the target has been tagged.

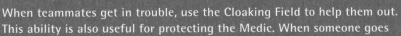

In combat, Bucket's support is more offensive than defensive with his guided missiles and Sentry Guns. The first priority should be to lay down the five turrets. Once they are in position, light the Monster up with the rockets.

When teammates get in trouble, use the Cloaking Field to help them out. This ability is also useful for protecting the Medic. When someone goes down, throw out Sentry Guns to protect the character who decides to pick the downed Hunter up.

A good tactic with any trap is to flush the Monster into it. Place Sentry Guns at a cave opening or choke point, and have the team move the enemy toward them.

Before the Mobile Arena goes down, launch the UAV, and follow the Monster if it flees. This allows the team to keep track of the enemy for longer.

CABOT

"EVERYONE GEAR UP. LET'S FIND THIS THING AND EARN OUR KEEP."
— CABOT

If we judge a man by the friends he keeps, then Cabot has some explaining to do. As the wrangler of this motley crew, Cabot helps teammates by using his Dust Tagging to track the Monster and his Rail Cannon to put it down. But there's nothing more helpful than his trusty Damage Amp, which makes his squad pack an even bigger punch.

SKINS

SKIN	HOW TO UNLOCK
DEFAULT	Unlocked with Cabot.
CABOT ELITE SKIN	Earn 3 stars in all items in Character Mastery.

LOADOUT

	ITEM	DESCRIPTION
	RAIL CANNON	Prey can't hide when you can fire through objects with your trusty Railgun.
	DAMAGE AMPLIFIER	Target your enemy to boost the damage done by your teammates' weapons.
	DUST TAGGING	Drop tagging dust in an area to mark all life forms.
	CLOAKING FIELD	Grants temporary invisibility to Cabot and nearby Hunters.

CHARACTER MASTERY

	TIER 1 REQUIREMENTS		TIER 2 REQUIREMENTS		TIER 3 REQUIREMENTS	
	REQUIREMENT	BUFF	REQUIREMENT	BUFF	REQUIREMENT	BUFF
RAIL CANNON	Do 12,000 damage	Damage increase	Do 34,000 damage to the Monster	Damage increase	Do 26,000 headshot damage to the Monster	Damage increase
DAMAGE AMPLIFIER	Amplify 9,000 damage	Energy pool increase	Amplify 24,000 damage to the Monster	Energy pool increase	Amplify 54 damage in a single use 250 times	Energy pool increase
DUST TAGGING	Reveal 70 creatures	Radius increase	Reveal the Monster 60 times	Radius increase	Reveal the Stage 1 Monster 25 times	Radius increase

MASTERY UNLOCKS

You must complete all mastery challenges within the same tier set before moving on to the next set. Progress toward the next challenges will not be accrued before being unlocked.

TIER 1: Badge Foreground

TIER 2: Badge Foreground

TIER 3: Badge Foreground, Cabot Elite Skin

LOADOUT

Cabot is in charge of this odd bunch of Hunters and is equipped with one of the more interesting loadouts in the game. His Dust Tagging ability allows him to mark the Monster and all wildlife within the dust's radius. Pair that with a Rail Cannon that can shoot through walls, and many a Monster will be surprised. Finally, you can use a Damage Amplifier in combat to boost everyone's damage output.

AWARDS

AWARD	DESCRIPTION	XP EARNED
HYPERSONIC	Deal 2000 damage to the Monster with the Rail Cannon.	50
AMPED UP	Provide 1000 Damage Amplification.	50
TAG AND BAG	Reveal the Monster two times with Dust Tagging.	100
NOW YOU SEE ME	Cloak two Hunters at once with the Cloaking Field.	100

RAIL CANNON

Mastery Reward: Increased Damage

Max damage: 210 Damage on a Direct Hit

Max Obstacle Penetration: 40 Meters

Ammo Capacity: 1 Round

The Rail Cannon is a powerful single-shot weapon that can fire through walls. Press the Primary button to equip the rifle, and squeeze the Fire trigger to discharge the instantaneous blast. The gun is automatically reloaded after every shot, giving it a poor fire rate.

This weapon pairs very well with Cabot's Dust Tagging ability. Being able to see a highlight of marked wildlife or the Monster allows Cabot to injure an enemy that believes they are safe behind an object. Note that it is at a reduction of damage because the shot is weakened as it travels through an obstacle.

In combat, when near the Monster, it is best to use the Damage Amplifier to support the rest of the team. But it is worth switching over to the Rail Cannon to get in the occasional shot, especially as the other ability recharges.

DAMAGE AMPLIFIER

Mastery Reward: Increased Energy Pool

Max Amount of Bonus Damage: 1000

Recharge Time from Empty: 17 Seconds

Max Range: 35 Meters

The rest of the team can get a nice boost in damage output when Cabot uses the Damage Amplifier. Tap the Secondary button to switch to the device. Aim at the enemy, and squeeze the Fire trigger. A ray between the gun and target indicates that it is working. Anyone who fires on the foe

gets a damage bonus. Hold the button down to maintain the effect. Once released, there is no bonus.

Coordinate this ability with your Assault Hunter since he will be engaged most with the Monster. Call it out when available, and release the trigger when nobody attacks. Learn to use it efficiently to maximize the effect. Switch to the Rail Cannon when the Damage Amplifier does not make sense.

Using the Damage Amplifier is typically more important during a fight than doing damage yourself with the Rail Cannon. Remember that

using this device reveals your location when cloaked.

DUST TAGGING

Mastery Reward: Increased Radius

Outline Duration: 20 Seconds

Cooldown: 70 Seconds

Effective Radius: 60 Meters

Dust Tagging allows Cabot to do his own Monster tracking. Tap the Equipment button to equip the radioactive dust. Using the ability is similar to Hank's Orbital Barrage. A green graphic of a bomb indicates that the dust can be dropped at that location. The reticle must be placed on the ground. To drop it on a higher location, aim at the edge of the structure or cliff. Hold the Fire trigger down until the red bar fills up.

Just like Orbital Barrage, you cannot use this ability under cover. A red graphic of a bomb crossed out signifies when it cannot be used. Dust Tagging does not knock teammates away, but you don't want to waste the stuff by dropping it next to anyone.

The Dust Tagging outlines any creatures within the dust cloud, allowing you to see where they go through any objects. Ideally, this is used to find a hiding Monster, but it is also good to see what wildlife lies ahead. If a feeding zone is found, there is a chance the big guy is going to pass through at some point.

If you are at a loss, toss some dust into a probable location in hopes of getting a lucky find. At the very least, you can figure out where the Monster is not. Remember that there is also a Trapper on the team who is doing their own tracking.

> ## "AND YOU ALL KNOW WHAT HAPPENS IF WE MESS THIS UP..."
>
> — CABOT

FIGHTING THE MONSTER

As soon as Cabot touches down from the dropship, spot the Monster tracks, and toss some dust beyond them to try to immediately spot the beast. Use Dust Tagging early and often to narrow down the Monster's location. It can also have the effect of keeping the enemy moving. Troublesome creatures also come in view, in case the team wants to alter their route.

As the squad nears the Monster's position, use Dust Tagging to pinpoint its location. Once found, use the Rail Cannon to get in some shots through obstacles.

Once the team is engaged with the foe, switch over to the Damage Amplifier to assist the team in taking it down. This is primarily useful as your Assault Hunter attacks the Monster, but boosting anyone's damage is beneficial.

When no one targets the Monster or as the amplifier regenerates, pull out the Rail Cannon to get in some pot shots. Do not forget about the Cloaking Field: use it to assist teammates in trouble or incapped Hunters.

When the Mobile Arena goes down, hit the Monster with some dust. Then, pull out the Rail Cannon to get in some final shots as it flees the area.

MONSTERS

The Monster's role is pretty clear: kill everything and survive. If the battle runs longer, the Monster only grows in strength as time goes on, gaining a sizeable advantage in the final stage of evolution. How the Monster chooses to play sets the pace of the entire match.

There are three distinctly different Monsters: the Goliath, the Kraken, and the Wraith. Each class is suited to a different style of combat, giving some of them an edge in certain game modes. Although one Monster may be better than another in a certain mode or map, the main component to being a good Monster is player skill.

Unlike the Hunters, the Monster is left to fight alone, forcing it to learn quickly without the help of a team. The following three sections break down effective use of abilities, as well as strengths and weaknesses against each class of Hunter.

CHOOSING THE BEST MONSTER

Choosing the best Monster for a specific game mode can make or break an inexperienced Monster player. Below are suggested Monster choices for each mode.

MODE	MONSTER	SUGGESTION
HUNT	Kraken	The Kraken's ability to get high in the sky allows it to easily spot creatures and Hunters out of the smell range, helping to evolve quickly and stay away from a Hunter ambush.
NEST	Goliath	When an egg is hatched in nest, it spawns a level 1 Goliath. Use this to cause confusion and rush the Hunters early with the help of the minion.
RESCUE	Wraith	The Wraith can abduct a downed survivor to move it to a position that will benefit the Wraith. This tactic can be used to set a trap for the Hunters, or to move the survivors close together to double your attack's effectiveness.
DEFEND	Goliath	The Goliath can one-shot the basic turrets that surround the objective with a fully upgraded rock throw. It also has the highest health value in the game, allowing you to be a little more aggressive in the fight and keep the pressure on the Hunters.

Although these Monster choices can make it easier by playing to their strengths in each of these modes, an experienced Monster player can successfully compete in any game mode. A good Monster is a confident Monster, so choose whichever beast you feel can achieve victory.

MONSTER AWARDS

Awards are single match achievements that award stackable achievement bonuses.

NAME	DESCRIPTION	EXPERIENCE AWARDED
DNR	Incapacitate two Hunters.	50
Bulletproof	Evolve without losing any health.	100
It's Evolution	Evolve to Stage 3.	150

GOLIATH

The Goliath is a high-armor, melee-oriented powerhouse.

BIO

Goliath woke up on the wrong side of angry this morning. Little is known about this Monster because scientists studying the beast wind up getting torn in half. Proving just how unfair natural selection can be, Goliath cannot only punch through the hull of a starship, but he can also breathe fire.

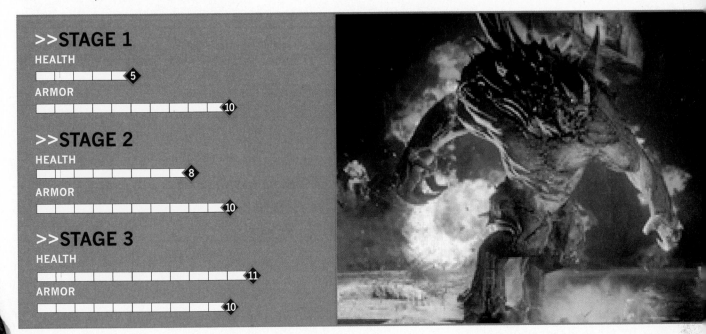

>>STAGE 1
HEALTH — 5
ARMOR — 10

>>STAGE 2
HEALTH — 8
ARMOR — 10

>>STAGE 3
HEALTH — 11
ARMOR — 10

SKINS

Skins grant no ability bonus, but the alternate color schemes may help the Monster blend into the environment.

SKIN	HOW TO UNLOCK
DEFAULT	Unlocked from start.
ELITE SKIN	Complete all Character Mastery challenges for Goliath.

CHARACTER MASTERY

	LEVEL 1		LEVEL 2		LEVEL 3	
	REQUIREMENT	BUFF	REQUIREMENT	BUFF	REQUIREMENT	BUFF
ROCK THROW	Do 12,000 damage	Damage bonus %	Damage multiple targets 35 times	Damage bonus %	Hit mid-air Hunters 150 times	Damage bonus %
LEAP SMASH	Do 12,000 damage	Range bonus %	Damage multiple targets 50 times	Range bonus %	Hit Hunters from 20 meters 50 times	Range bonus %
FIRE BREATH	Do 12,000 damage	Range bonus %	Damage multiple targets 175 times	Range bonus %	Do 80,000 damage to mid-air Hunters	Range bonus %
CHARGE	Do 8,000 damage	Duration bonus %	Damage multiple targets 50 times	Duration bonus %	Damage multiple Hunters 100 times	Duration bonus %

MASTERY UNLOCKS

You must complete all mastery challenges within the same level set before moving on to the next set. Progress toward the next challenges will not be accrued before being unlocked.

TIER 1: New Badge, Kraken Becomes Unlocked

TIER 2: New Badge

TIER 3: New Badge and Goliath Elite Skin

AWARDS

AWARD	DESCRIPTION	XP EARNED
AIR STRIKE	Deal 2000 damage to the Hunters with Leap Smash	50
BARBARIC	Deal 2000 damage to the Hunters with Rock Throw	50
CHARGER	Deal 2000 damage to the Hunters with Charge	50
FIRE STARTER	Deal 2000 damage to the Hunters with Flame Breath	50

FEEDING

The Goliath can go longer periods between eating due to its high armor. Unlike the other Monsters, it's best to just gorge yourself on groups of animals before moving on. Even pausing during battles to tear through the flesh of a few creatures isn't a bad idea, especially if the Hunters can't find you. Using attacks like Charge and Leap Smash can help Goliath quickly close in and eliminate creatures before they have to spread out and escape. This drastically increases the amount of time the Monster has to feed.

ABILITIES

ICON	ABILITY NAME	★	★ ★	★ ★ ★
	ROCK THROW	Damage 100% Radius 100%	Damage 130% Radius 130%	Damage 169% Radius 169%
	LEAP SMASH	Damage 100% Radius 100%	Damage 130% Radius 130%	Damage 169% Radius 169%
	FIRE BREATH	Damage 100% Range 100%	Damage 130% Range 130%	Damage 169% Range 169%
	CHARGE	Damage 100% Radius 100%	Damage 130% Radius 130%	Damage 169% Radius 169%

CHARGE

Activating Charge causes Goliath to rush forward at a high rate of speed, dealing damage and knockback. You can use Charge to separate Hunters or push them into a better position during a fight. Since the Hunters get sent tumbling, it makes them easier to target for a follow-up Leap Smash or Rock Throw. When hunting, use Charge to quickly close the distance and dispatch a small group of creatures. Although Charge is mainly an offensive ability, you can also use it to quickly escape from the Hunters or dodge a Mobile Arena that's about to go down.

FIRE BREATH

Fire Breath spits a jet of liquid flame that deals damage to Hunters for a short period of time. Although some may argue that this ability lacks offensive power, you can effectively use it to counter some of the Hunters' deployable weapons, like Markov's Arc Mines or Maggie's Harpoon Traps. If the Hunters are being cloaked, use this ability to set them on fire, revealing their location for the time that they are on fire. Hunters near water cause this ability to be much less effective. In that scenario, try using a Charge to push them away from the water before activating Fire Breath.

LEAP SMASH

Goliath's strong legs enable him to leap into the air, unleashing a devastating jump attack that deals splash damage where it lands. If you catch a group of Hunters sticking a little too close together, activate Leap Smash to initiate contact from any direction. If you have no special movement Leaps, you can use Leap Smash for a quick getaway in a bind. Be sure to clear any traps before leap smashing into an area, as Goliath is still vulnerable to attacks while in the air and landing.

ROCK THROW

Hunters may think they are safe when flying through the air against Goliath; they couldn't be more wrong. Ripping a huge boulder from the earth, Goliath launches it into the air, doing splash damage to the target location. Although it takes some skill to throw the boulder accurately, there are small things you can do to increase the chances of a direct hit. For example, using Charge to send enemies tumbling, then following up with a Rock Throw to the location they are tumbling to prevents them from being able to dodge the attack.

SPECIAL MOVEMENT ABILITY: LEAP

Goliath's Leap is his best tool for evading Hunters. When used off of taller objects, Goliath can cover great distances in a single bound. For most effective use, aim slightly above the horizon line (center point). If aimed too high or too low, Goliath will not travel as much distance, effectively wasting a stamina bar.

To evade the Hunters, take a long Leap into some water. Landing in water leaves no tracks for the Hunters to detect the direction you have jumped in. Simply sneak out of the water, and the Hunters will have no idea in which direction this gigantic Monster went.

FIGHTING AS GOLIATH

Goliath is a close-quarters, heavily armored powerhouse. His main focus in combat is to knock the Hunters around as much as possible, as this prevents them from attacking and forming a solid plan of offense against him. Use your abilities mixed with leaping to pop in and out of combat, topping off your armor in between engagements. Goliath has more armor than Kraken or Wraith, making him the most resilient Stage 1 Monster in the game. Don't be afraid to attack the Hunters with full armor at Stage 1 to get a few strikes in before evolving. If you are looking to rush the Hunters as Goliath, get your armor up quickly, then find an elite animal and initiate contact with the Hunters nearby. Getting wildlife involved in battle is the key to having an early game victory.

ASSAULT

When fighting the Assault character, keep him off balance by charging and leap smashing into him. If you have to be in close, you don't want him to be able to attack. Alternative methods could include using the Rock Throw ability to keep the Assault guy at bay.

If the Assault Hunter activates his Personal Shield, leave him alone and focus on another Hunter. Attacking an Assault Hunter with a Personal Shield is just wasting potential DPS against other targets.

Watch out for Markov's Arc Mines: even a Stage 3 Goliath can have his armor taken down quickly by walking through a mine field. Counter the mines by either throwing rocks at them or using Fire Breath. Using Fire Breath doesn't instantly detonate the mines, so make sure they explode before entering the battle.

MEDIC

The Medic is the priority target for Goliath. Val and Caira's ability to heal their teammates at range while staying out of Goliath's close-range attacks makes them big pests. If the Medic is keeping his or her distance from the team, use a quick series of Leaps or a Leap Smash to get to them. Then, use a quick Pounce to force their teammates to come closer to rescue the Medic.

When playing against Lazarus, be sure to choose Fire Breath early in the game, as this helps combat his Personal Cloak. Using abilities on incapacitated Hunters and then eating their bodies is another easy way for Goliath to combat Lazarus.

SUPPORT

The Support class can create some dangerous environments for Goliath to fight in, with Hank's Orbital Barrage or Bucket's Sentry Turrets. Combat these easily with a quick Leap

or burst of Fire Breath. Team cloaking is not effective against a Goliath's Fire Breath attack; just make sure to keep the fights away from water so the Hunters cannot put out the flames.

If you encounter a Hunter playing as Hank, take them out at the beginning of the fight. If Hank uses his Shield Projector efficiently, he can drastically decrease Goliath's ability to take down Hunters, including pounced targets.

TRAPPER

Trappers try to slow you down at all costs. Sneak past Maggie's Harpoon Traps to prevent them from activating, and then start your attack or use Fire Breath to eliminate all of the traps quickly. If caught

by a harpoon, quickly turn and attack the cable before trying to leap away. When caught in the area of a Stasis Grenade, use your abilities or perform a Leap to escape the stasis field.

Leaving the Trapper for the final kill may help Goliath in a team fight by keeping the group of Hunters inside the Mobile Arena. If you can work the Hunters into a corner, or trap them in a cave with the help of the arena, the Trapper will be forced to deactivate the Mobile Arena.

FIGHTING AGAINST GOLIATH

When fighting Goliath, focus on surrounding him and attacking from all directions. Stay away from caves and areas that enable Goliath to get to high ground. If possible, take the fight to the water, as this takes away Goliath's ability to catch the Hunters on fire.

Keep your distance from elite animals in a team fight. Since Goliath stays close to the ground when running, it may aggro a few of the Monsters during travel.

ASSAULT

Make yourself a target! If playing with Hank, take turns activating your shield and having him shield you with the Shield Projector. A smart Goliath will leap away from you when you activate your shield; get in close, and make him pay. When playing as Markov, place mines on higher ground or in bushes to make them harder for Goliath to spot. Although Hyde's Toxic Grenade is good for flushing the Monster out, if Goliath chooses to run away from the Hunters, the cloud will stay and slow you and your fellow Hunters down.

The only possible way Goliath can counter any of Parnell's attacks is to knock him off his feet and send him tumbling. This makes Parnell an effective weapon at getting the Monster's attention while maintaining constant damage. Use Super Soldier mixed with the Multifire Rocket Launcher when the Monster is at a distance. Once he is in close, pop your Personal Shield, and switch to the shotgun to maximize your damage.

MEDIC

Although you may not try to make your presence known on the battlefield, the Monster will try to incapacitate you as soon as you are spotted. Stick to high ground and keep at a distance while you heal other Hunters. Using Val or Caira allows you to revive other Hunters from afar, which is a crucial tactic to keep you out of the Goliath's range of attack. Stay in the other Hunters' line of sight to prevent Goliath from pouncing you. In team battles, Caira's Acceleration Field enables the Hunters to dodge Goliath's attacks with ease.

Tranquilizing Goliath helps prevent his onslaught of melee attacks and decreases his ability to close the distance between his enemies. Using the Armor-piercing Sniper Rifle, Val can place weak points in the Monster's armor, helping to destroy the armor quickly. All of this, paired with Val's pinpoint ability to heal other Hunters at a distance, makes her the most effective Medic against the Goliath.

SUPPORT

The Support class can turn the tides in battle against the Goliath. Utilizing Bucket's Sentry Guns can help increase the DPS during a fight, although Goliath's Fire Breath can easily take them out.

Using Hank's Shield Projector on Goliath's current target instantly negates its attack. This makes him a valuable asset when taking on this Monster. However, doing so also makes Hank a target, so consider cloaking if Goliath turns to charge him. Using the Orbital Strike on a pounced Hunter deals a high amount of damage while breaking the Hunter free and buying them some valuable space to get away.

TRAPPER

This is the only Monster that you don't want to trap in a small space with you, especially at the beginning of a fight. Due to Goliath's high armor, trapping it in the Mobile Arena early lets the Monster deal a lot of damage without much permanent effect. To defeat this, become a master of the "late dome." Wait until you force Goliath to run from the fight, and in that moment, drop the Mobile Arena and take the fight to him.

Taking down Goliath's health is important early on, especially if your team of Hunters isn't able to take him out early game. This makes hunting the Monster down quickly very important, and there is no better team than Maggie and Daisy the Trapjaw. Daisy can narrow in on the Goliath with little help from the Hunters. The loyal Trapjaw also revives incapacitated Hunters, enabling your Medic to stay out of combat for longer periods of time. Try to keep Maggie's Harpoon Traps a good distance apart to prevent Goliath from taking out multiple traps with a single melee attack or a burst of Fire Breath. Before the Mobile Arena is dropped, focus on slowing down Goliath and dealing damage when possible. Once the arena drops, the angry Monster comes at you with full force, so try to conceal yourself somewhere and stay alive. When Goliath's attention is diverted, resume placing Harpoon Traps.

KRAKEN

The Kraken is a high-flying terror, charged with electricity.

BIO

If the dictionary ever decided it needed a new word to describe a mix between waking nightmare and ungodly horror, it would undoubtedly include an image of Kraken. This tentacled monstrosity unleashes electric death on Hunters who get too close, and even those who think they are safely out of range.

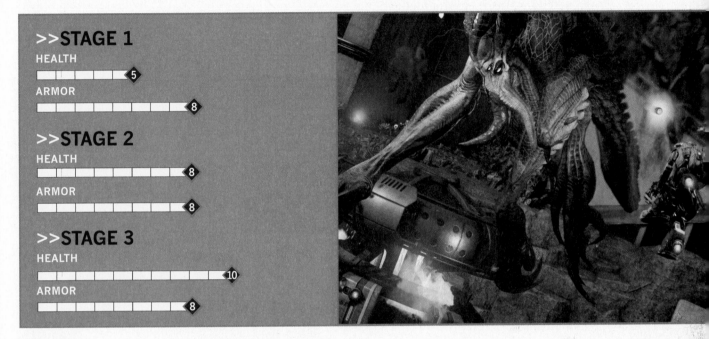

>>STAGE 1
HEALTH 5
ARMOR 8

>>STAGE 2
HEALTH 8
ARMOR 8

>>STAGE 3
HEALTH 10
ARMOR 8

SKINS

Skins grant no ability bonus, but the alternate color schemes may help the Monster blend into the environment.

SKIN	HOW TO UNLOCK
DEFAULT	Unlocked from start.
ELITE SKIN	Complete all Character Mastery challenges for the Kraken.

CHARACTER MASTERY

	LEVEL 1		LEVEL 2		LEVEL 3	
	REQUIREMENT	BUFF	REQUIREMENT	BUFF	REQUIREMENT	BUFF
LIGHTNING STRIKE	Do 20,000 damage	Damage bonus %	Damage multiple targets 50 times	Damage bonus %	Do damage to multiple Hunters 80 times	Damage bonus %
BANSHEE MINES	Do 27,000 damage	Damage bonus %	Do 80,000 damage to Hunters	Damage bonus %	Do damage to multiple Hunters 60 times	Damage bonus %
AFTERSHOCK	Do 15,000 damage	Damage bonus %	Damage multiple targets 40 times	Damage bonus %	Damage multiple Hunters 60 times	Damage bonus %
VORTEX	Do 30,000 damage	Blast speed increase %	Do damage to multiple Hunters 80 times	Blast speed increase %	Knock back 360 mid-air Hunters	Blast speed increase %

MASTERY UNLOCKS

You must complete all mastery challenges within the same level set before moving on to the next set. Progress toward the next challenges will not be accrued before being unlocked.

TIER 1: New Badge, Wraith Becomes Unlocked

TIER 2: New Badge

TIER 3: New Badge and Kraken Elite Skin

AWARDS

AWARD	DESCRIPTION	EXPERIENCE
GROUNDER	Deal 2000 damage to the Hunters with Lightning Strike.	50
SCREECHING HALT	Hit three Hunters with Banshee Mines.	50
DAISY CHAINED	Deal 1000 damage to the Hunters with Aftershock.	50
ELEMENTALIST	Knock down three Hunters with Vortex.	50

FEEDING

Although the Kraken spends much of his time flying high above the battlefield, he must descend to eat. Use Kraken's ability to fly and smell to find groups of creatures to consume. Use ranged attacks or abilities to take down small packs of animals from the sky, then descend to gorge on the carcasses without worrying about them getting spooked and running away.

ABILITIES

ICON	ABILITY	★	★ ★	★ ★ ★
	LIGHTNING STRIKE	Damage 100% Radius 100%	Damage 130% Radius 130%	Damage 169% Radius 169%
	BANSHEE MINES	Damage 100% Radius 100%	Damage 130% Radius 130%	Damage 169% Radius 169%
	AFTERSHOCK	Damage 100% Range 100%	Damage 130% Range 130%	Damage 169% Range 169%
	VORTEX	Damage 100% Radius 100%	Damage 130% Radius 130%	Damage 169% Radius 169%

AFTERSHOCK

Aftershock is the Kraken's answer to close-quarters combat. Although this ability may take a few moments to charge, once it finishes, it unleashes a powerful multitarget attack to all enemies within the blast radius. When timed correctly, you can use Aftershock to shake the Hunters off of you when you are pulled to the ground.

Attacking Hunters is not Aftershock's only use. When hunting a pack of creatures, activating Aftershock is an effective way to take them all down at once. It's also an easy way to eliminate a pack of Trapjaws or other smaller aggressive predators when in Stage 1.

BANSHEE MINES

Banshee Mines require only a third of the cooldown meter to fire, allowing you to fire up to three banshee rounds in a quick burst, if needed. You can leave Banshee Mines as traps for Hunters or wildlife. When

an enemy draws near to one of the mines, it changes shape and color, then begins to track toward the target. Since the Hunters can shoot these mines, it is helpful to leave them around blind corners, or generally hide them when not in active combat. Mines can also be launched a good distance, granting Kraken the ability to take out creatures before coming in contact with them. Using this tactic helps give you more time to eat, helping you evolve early.

If selected at Stage 1, the Monster can leave a few Banshee Mines at the Hunters' drop-in point. Doing so damages and slows down the Hunters, giving the Kraken more time to escape.

LIGHTNING STRIKE

The Lightning Strike is a devastating ranged blast that comes down in the form of a pillar. Like Aftershock, the Lightning Strike has a short charge time, making it possible for Hunters to dodge it.

Effectiveness with the Lightning Strike is dramatically increased when called in after using some of the Kraken's other abilities. These other abilities may force the Hunters to use up their Jet Packs, leaving them incredibly vulnerable to the Lightning Strike. When a Hunter is incapacitated, you can use the Lightning Strike to help finish them off.

When chosen alongside the Banshee Mines at Stage 1, the Kraken can use the previously mentioned tactic of dropping mines at the Hunters' drop-in point. Called in from a distance amidst the confusion could result in getting a very early strike against one of the Hunters.

VORTEX

Vortex is a moving wall of elemental energy that deals damage and knocks back enemies from afar. When called down from the sky on a lone Hunter, the Vortex can single them out and push them a good distance from Kraken. This leaves the Hunter an easy target for a quick Pounce. Hunting down groups of creatures is very easy when using Vortex; just aim for the center of the group. Unlike the Hunters, creatures are not affected by the knockback, so you do not have to go far to claim your bounty.

Stuck in a bad place during a fight? Targeting multiple Hunters with Vortex helps push them into an area that may better suit you in combat.

SPECIAL MOVEMENT ABILITY: AIRBURST

Airburst enables the Kraken to fly up into the air to gain an advantage when fighting creatures and Hunters. Once in the air, you can activate Airburst again to quickly move in the direction you are currently aiming. Use this ability to cover vast amounts of ground quickly. When high enough in the sky, the Kraken does not leave tracks. However, when lower, the Kraken leaves a different-shaped footprint. Hunters then know to look upward. To descend from the air, press and hold the Sneak button.

FIGHTING AS THE KRAKEN

The Kraken is a high-flying Monster dealing death from above. Staying in the air and on high ground is the key to being a successful Kraken. Although the Kraken has a decent amount of armor, it is recommended to maintain distance from the Hunters.

When in the air, the Kraken's melee attack changes to a ranged attack. Use this to your advantage, as the Kraken is currently the only Monster to offer a ranged basic attack. The ranged attack deals a small amount of AOE damage, so don't be afraid to spam the attack even if you don't have a direct shot.

ASSAULT

The Kraken is the worst enemy of the Assault class. Since most Assault characters are only effective at close range, the Kraken can gain altitude and distance, and then continue to attack and call down abilities with relative ease. When up against Markov's Arc Mines, use the basic ranged attack from the air to destroy them. If you're getting pulled out of the sky into close range, use a quick Vortex just before landing to push the Assault Hunters away and keep your ranged advantage.

MEDIC

From the sky, it is usually easy to spot the Medics (with the exception of Lazarus). To help prevent Lazarus from reviving his dead teammates, throw some Banshee Mines at the dead Hunters. If a Hunter is only incapacitated, the Banshee Mines will track to that Hunter. Try to avoid hits from Lazarus or Val's rifles: once they land a few hits, the rest of the Hunters' attacks become much more effective, even at longer ranges.

Val's Tranquilizer Gun will slowly bring the Kraken out of the sky. Either focus on eliminating her early in the fight, or deal damage to other Hunters to force her to focus on healing teammates.

If a Medic is doing a good job at evading your attacks, get in close, and send them away with a Vortex attack. Once they are separated, you can either continue attacking them and pushing them farther, or turn back and continue your attack on the team of Hunters.

SUPPORT

Support Hunters all have weapons that can deal damage at decent ranges, making them one of the Kraken's greatest threats. Get some strikes in early, and keep them separated from the other Hunters to prevent them from effectively using the Cloaking Field. When struggling to find the Support class, just watch for other Hunters going in and out of cloak to pinpoint their location. Don't become stagnant when calling in abilities; keep moving to become a harder target for Support Hunters to hit.

When facing Cabot, focus on taking him down as soon as possible. It is impossible to hide from the Rail Cannon, even behind other objects.

TRAPPER

The Trapper is the priority target for the Kraken. The dome takes away one of the main advantages of the Monster, forcing the Kraken to move toward the center of the dome to gain its height advantage. You should immediately focus on eliminating the Trapper by cycling through the Kraken's abilities and using your ranged melee attack. Watch out for Harpoon Traps, Stasis Grenades, and Griffin's Harpoon Gun. When the Harpoon Gun hits you, immediately focus on breaking the chain so you don't get pulled out of the sky.

FIGHTING AGAINST THE KRAKEN

The Kraken gains its advantage from flying high and calling down ranged attacks and abilities. As a team, the main focus should be to bring the Kraken to the ground by any means necessary. Be sure to conserve your Jet Pack so that you have fuel to dodge this Monster's abilities. When setting up a team fight or ambush, try to trap the Kraken inside a cave. Keep a small spread when fighting the Kraken to prevent the Monster from striking multiple Hunters with its attacks.

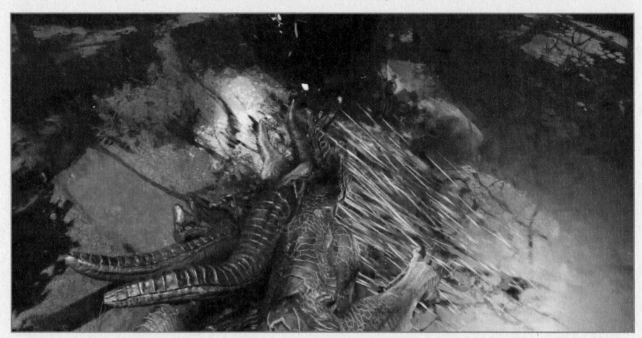

ASSAULT

All Assault classes have a medium-range weapon; be prepared to use it! The Kraken tries to stay high in the sky, so pester it with as many bullets as possible when it is not in range of your close-quarters weapons. If you run out of Jet Pack during a team battle, use your Personal Shield to absorb attacks. It is a good idea to take some damage first, however. For example, letting the Kraken hit you with the ability the first time and then using your shield to block it the second time will have the Kraken wasting much more of its time trying to eliminate you.

At first, Markov's Arc Mines may seem ineffective against the Kraken. However, if you combine them with Maggie's Harpoon Traps, you may be able to pull the Monster into them. This is not always effective, though, due to the Kraken's ability to combat any type of deployable object at range.

The best choice when combatting the Kraken is Parnell. Using his Super Soldier ability, combined with his long-range Rocket Launcher, inflicts massive amounts of damage on the Kraken.

MEDIC

As the Medic, focus on keeping your distance from the other Hunters in a team battle. This tactic (for the most part) keeps the Monster from targeting you. Use Val or Caira's ability to revive incapacitated Hunters at a range to prevent being a stationary target for the Kraken.

Val is best equipped for taking down the Kraken. Using the Tranquilizer Gun slowly pulls the Kraken directly out of the sky, and unlike the Harpoon Traps, the Monster cannot do anything to wear off the slowing effect of the dart early. Once you have the Monster slowed, use your Armor-Piercing Sniper Rifle to put a few critical points onto the Monster. Critical points increase all of the Hunters' abilities to deal damage at range. Use the Medgun and Healing Bursts to revive Hunters. Keep them moving, and prevent them from getting hit by the Kraken's abilities.

SUPPORT

All Support Hunters have decent weapons to combat the Kraken even when the Monster is high in the sky. When the Mobile Arena is in full effect, activate your Cloaking Field, and stay close to the Trapper to prevent the Kraken from taking down the arena.

Cabot's Rail Cannon is the best weapon for fighting the Kraken. Its high damage at range and ability to shoot through objects definitely gives him an edge over the other Support-class Hunters. Once the Monster is trapped in the Mobile Arena, drop a Dust Tag to keep track of him, and then spam the Rail Cannon. After you've brought the Monster down to the ground, switch to the Damage Amplifier to maximize the damage your team does for the few moments the Monster is on the ground.

TRAPPER

The Mobile Arena is the best tool to turn the tides against the Kraken during a fight. This makes the Trapper a key tool to gain a victory against this Monster. An advanced Hunter will drop the Mobile Arena on a fleeing Kraken. Doing this forces the Kraken closer to the ground. Try to work the fight into the corners by using Griffin's Harpoon Gun or Maggie's Harpoon Traps. Since the Kraken can fly, it may be hard to track using only footsteps. Definitely keep an eye out for broken trees and other environmental clues.

When playing against the Kraken, the Trapper must spend most of their time keeping the Kraken slowed and pinned to the ground. Keep this in mind, and let the rest of the Hunters focus on dealing the damage!

Bringing the Kraken down to fight on the ground and keeping the Monster there is the most important job for the Trapper. Griffin can easily accomplish this task, as he can use his Harpoon Gun to pull the Kraken directly out of the sky. To get an even better edge when using the Harpoon Gun, aim for the backside of the Monster. Then, just as the Monster is about to break the harpoon link, let go and reposition while you begin to reload. This technique gives the Monster less time in between being harpooned. When placing Sound Spikes, keep in mind that most Kraken players will avoid caves, so try to place them in open ground around the map.

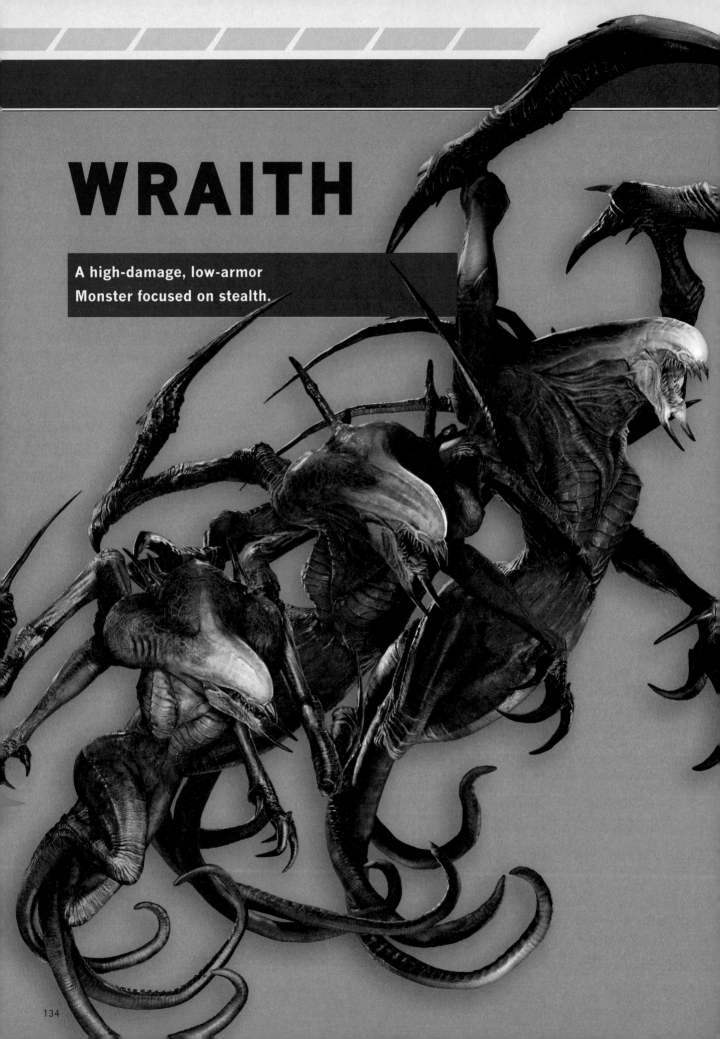

WRAITH

A high-damage, low-armor
Monster focused on stealth.

BIO

The most frightening enemy is the one you cannot see. And once you spot her, chances are you are shooting at her Decoy. Armed with two piercing blades, Wraith is not a monster you want to be alone with. But don't let your teammates give you a false sense of security, because in the blink of an eye, she can abduct you into the darkness.

>>STAGE 1

HEALTH 4

ARMOR 5

>>STAGE 2

HEALTH 6

ARMOR 5

>>STAGE 3

HEALTH 8

ARMOR 5

SKINS

Skins grant no ability bonus, but the alternate color schemes may help the Monster blend into the environment.

SKIN	HOW TO UNLOCK
DEFAULT	Unlocked from start.
ELITE SKIN	Complete all Character Mastery challenges for the Wraith.

CHARACTER MASTERY

	TIER 1 REQUIREMENTS		TIER 2 REQUIREMENTS		TIER 1 REQUIREMENTS	
	REQUIREMENT	BUFF	REQUIREMENT	BUFF	REQUIREMENT	BUFF
WARP BLAST	Do 30,000 damage	Damage bonus %	Damage multiple targets 90 times	Damage bonus %	Damage multiple Hunters 15 times	Damage bonus %
ABDUCTION	Abduct 35 targets	Increased range %	Abduct 45 mid-air Hunters	Increased range %	Abduct Hunters from team 225 times	Increased range %
DECOY	Do 12,500 damage with Decoy	Damage bonus %	Do 32,000 damage to Hunters with Decoy	Damage bonus %	Stealth pounce 30 times while invisible	Damage bonus %
SUPERNOVA	Do 34,500 damage while Supernova is active	Increased duration (x) seconds	Do 125,000 damage to Hunters while Supernova is active	Increased duration (x) seconds	Damage using abilities 70 times while Supernova is active	Increased duration (x) seconds

MASTERY UNLOCKS

You must complete all mastery challenges within the same level set before moving on to the next set. Progress toward the next challenges will not be accrued before being unlocked.

TIER 1: New Badge

TIER 2: New Badge

TIER 3: New Badge and Wraith Elite Skin

AWARDS

AWARD	DESCRIPTION	XP EARNED
KAMIKAZE	Deal 1000 damage to Hunters with Warp Blast.	50
SNEAK ATTACK	Abduct two Hunters.	50
BODY DOUBLE	Decoy delivers 500 damage to Hunters.	50
VOID	Deal 1000 damage to Hunters while in Supernova.	50

FEEDING

Wraith is a hit-and-run predator. Take down one or two creatures, and consume them quickly before moving on. Since Wraith has low armor, this negates the value of eating a large amount of creatures. When trying to evolve quickly, use the little bit of armor gained from smaller prey to attack a larger creature. If done correctly, you'll regain your armor from the Monster at the end of the fight, and maybe even a Buff if you took down an Elite (Albino) creature. Make sure to consume creatures carrying Buffs all the way before moving on so that the Hunters cannot pick up the Buff.

ABILITIES

ICON	ABILITY	★	★ ★	★ ★ ★
	WARP BLAST	Damage 100% Range 100%	Damage 130% Range 130%	Damage 169% Range 169%
	ABDUCTION	Damage 100% Range 100%	Damage 130% Range 130%	Damage 169% Range 169%
	DECOY	Duration 100% Damage 100%	Duration 130% Damage 175%	Duration 169% Damage 250%
	SUPERNOVA	Damage 100% Radius 100%	Damage 130% Radius 130%	Damage 169% Radius 169%

ABDUCTION

Abduction is a high-speed attack that latches onto a Hunter and immediately pulls them away from the group to a new location. When activated, Wraith warps toward the target and immediately pulls them back to the point where the ability was activated. You can combine the attack with Pounce to easily take down the now-isolated Hunter. You can also use Abduction to snipe enemies out of the air, which is very effective against escaping foes or for singling out the Medic. Be warned: any mines or other deployables in the path of the Abduction damage the Wraith. Even if Wraith fails to land the attack, she still moves at a high rate of speed between the targeted point and the point in which Abduction was activated. Combined with a few Warp moves, this can really throw off the Hunters and provide you time to reposition safely. Even if you miss the Abduction, you still damage a small area near the point of contact.

Abduction can also be used on incapacitated Hunters to quickly move them to a different point. Moving downed Hunters will help keep the other Hunters from being able to revive them safely.

DECOY

Decoy summons a copy of Wraith that can activate deployables and deal damage to the Hunters. While the Decoy is summoned, Wraith remains completely cloaked. This gives you a chance to ready for a Pounce on an unsuspecting Hunter, or provides you some valuable time to escape and regenerate some armor. Wraith can eat while cloaked, helping to keep her armor up while trapped in a dome. You can use this ability to clear mines away from choke points or objectives without doing damage to Wraith. You can also use Decoy to take down turrets in Defend mode. If the Hunters are hot on your tail and haven't spotted you yet, consider sending your Decoy toward them. You can also use Decoy to flank the Hunters. For example, send your Decoy around a small rock or boulder at the Hunters, and then while cloaked, move around to the rear and pounce on an unsuspecting Hunter.

SUPERNOVA

Supernova activates a small arena that grants Wraith a damage and armor bonus. Although this ability is effective against a single target, it really shines when you can corner multiple enemies. If you can gather your foes close enough, Wraith's melee can damage them all at once. When an enemy escapes the arena, use Abduction to quickly pull them back in and resume your attack. If activated before using Decoy, the Decoy will carry the effects of the Wraith, including the visual effects.

WARP BLAST

Warp Blast warps Wraith toward a target and then fires off a blast, doing high damage in a small area. Activating this ability to initiate a team fight with the Hunters is a good idea. It quickly brings your opponents into close-quarters range while separating the Hunters from each other. When hunting for food, you can use Warp Blast to quickly catch and take out a group of creatures. Much like Abduction, you are vulnerable to mines and other deployable abilities with warping to a target before the explosion. Colliding with a character or object stops Wraith and activates the blast. Keep in mind that the blast still takes time to activate once you reach the target, so try to use it against unsuspecting targets or cornered Hunters. You can use Warp Blast to take down turrets in Defend mode, but Wraith must immediately disengage the turret to prevent her from taking permanent damage.

SPECIAL MOVEMENT ABILITY: WARP

Wraith's ability to punch holes through time and space enables her to warp from point to point quickly. Using Warp from point to point still leaves claw prints if you are close enough to the ground, so like Goliath, use Warp from high ground to maximize its effect.

Warping while in combat is an effective way of confusing the Hunters while dodging a fair amount of damage. Try warping out of a Hunter's line of sight before activating Decoy to really put some distance between yourself and the enemy.

FIGHTING AS WRAITH

Wraith is all about speed, stealth, and damage. While she is the most fragile of all the Monsters, she deals the highest damage and keeps a lower profile. Use stealth to your advantage by sneaking around and pouncing unsuspecting Hunters who stray from their team.

Due to Wraith's lower armor, the player must focus on fighting in "bursts," breaking out of combat to regenerate armor before fighting again. Whenever full armor is achieved, it is a good idea to go engage the Hunters to get a few early strikes on them. Doing so puts you at a great advantage after evolving.

ASSAULT

Assault Hunters are a priority target for Wraith due to their high damage capabilities. The best possible way to combat the Assault class is isolating them from other Hunters and pouncing. A quick way to get an easy Pounce is using Abduction, then quickly activating Sneak and pouncing. Isolating the Assault class isn't always possible; in these cases, use your Decoy to deal some damage to the Assault character without taking any yourself. Watch out for Markov's Arc Mines: the only way you can clear them is by sacrificing your Decoy. When in a team fight with the Hunters, the goal is either to isolate and eliminate the Assault class, or to keep distance so you can avoid the high amounts of damage they can inflict at close range.

MEDIC

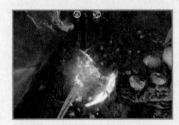

Since most of the Medic's weapons require pinpoint accuracy, movement is again key in evading and countering the Hunter's attack. Try to keep them busy by damaging the other Hunters, then pounce when they are vulnerable. The Medic is generally fairly harmless against Wraith, but if you come across Val, focus on incapacitating her immediately to prevent getting tagged and slowed by the Tranquilizer Gun. If the Tranquilizer Gun hits you, activate Decoy. This unmarks Wraith while cloaked, giving you a chance to put some distance in between you and the Hunters. When the cloak runs out, Wraith remains marked and slowed until the effects of the Tranquilizer Gun wear off. If you are playing against Lazarus, it is a good idea to attack an incapacitated enemy until they are killed, then quickly use Decoy and consume the Hunter while cloaked. Lazarus cannot bring a Hunter that you have eaten back to life.

SUPPORT

Try to keep the Support Hunter separate from the group of Hunters to eliminate the effectiveness of the team cloak ability. Using Abduction is a great way of accomplishing this. If the team is fully cloaked, look for signs of movement from the Hunters, and use a Warp Blast in that direction to separate them. Moving around during a fight greatly reduces the effectiveness of any Support Hunter. Watch out for Hank's Orbital Barrage; if the Wraith gets caught in the area of effect, the barrage will eat through all of its armor very quickly. The most effective way to combat Bucket's turrets is to simply avoid them, but if this is not possible, counter them with a well-placed Warp Blast.

TRAPPER

The Trapper should be the first target for Wraith. Getting trapped inside of the dome is a death sentence for a low-armor, high-movement speed Monster like Wraith. Harpoon Traps placed by a Hunter not only slow Wraith down, but they can also stop a Warp Blast from reaching the Hunter. One way to avoid getting hit by Harpoon Traps is to activate Sneak, and work your way through them. However, sneaking isn't always possible in combat. If you are caught in the Mobile Arena, activate Supernova, followed by your Decoy. Doing so gives your Decoy a damage boost while giving you a chance to single out and pounce an unsuspecting Trapper.

FIGHTING AGAINST WRAITH

When up against Wraith, the Hunters must focus on sticking together and trying to hunt down Wraith as soon as possible. The Trapper is the most important member of the team when fighting Wraith, so do your best as a team to keep them alive.

ASSAULT

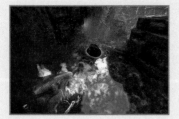

Stay in close, and force Wraith to fight you over your teammates. Markov is a strong choice when fighting Wraith thanks to his ability to surround himself and his teammates with mines. During team battles, mines force Wraith to take loads of damage if she chooses to engage your team. When playing as Hyde, use your Flamethrower the instant you see Wraith activate Decoy to catch the invisible Wraith on fire, keeping her in the line of sight.

MEDIC

The Medic should always focus on keeping their team of Hunters alive. However, against Wraith, the Medic can play a little more of an advanced damage-dealing role. The best Medic for combatting the Wraith is Val, thanks to her Armor-Piercing Sniper Rifle and Tranquilizer Gun. Against Val, Wraith slows down considerably and crumbles underneath the damage put out by your teammates.

Caira's Adrenaline Field can come in handy while trying to hunt down Wraith early on. You can use the Napalm Grenade option on her launcher to damage and mark a cloaked Wraith.

SUPPORT

Wraith can cloak, and so can you! Use the team cloak ability to keep your team hidden from Wraith and turn the tides in a team fight. If Wraith can't see you, she can't target you for Abduction or a Pounce. Be aware that even during a cloak, your Jet Pack can be seen.

Because Wraith must attack at close range, Bucket is a great decision for the fight. Using Bucket's Sentry Guns can do a lot of damage to a Wraith trapped in the area during a fight. Although Wraith may be hard to spot from the ground, the perspective granted from the UAV makes spotting Wraith much easier. You can also use it to scout around corners to look for a possible ambush.

TRAPPER

Taking away Wraith's speed is crucial to defeating her. This makes the Trapper the most important piece to the puzzle during the battle. When Wraith is slowed and trapped in a dome, she becomes an easy target for the rest of the Hunters. Wraith can dodge Maggie's Harpoon Traps by sneaking, but she cannot dodge Stasis Grenades, even when cloaked. This makes Abe the definitive choice for slowing down Wraith. Stasis Grenades do not stay placed indefinitely; from the moment they are thrown, they start to decay (check out Abe's section for more information). As soon as you drop the dome to trap Wraith, try to find a safe spot to support your team, and stay out of direct combat. Once the dome is in full effect, work with the Support class to keep yourself cloaked.

PERKS

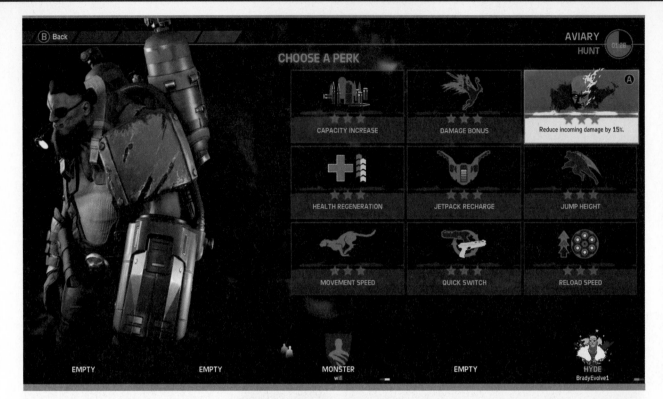

After selecting a Hunter or Monster and choosing the Monster abilities, a Perk is selected amongst the nine choices for each side. Your choice of Perk often comes down to your play style, but specific characters and game modes match up well with certain ones.

Perks are unlocked as a player advances through level progression. Each level opens up another Perk. The max level in *Evolve* is 40. Hunters begin the game with Tier 3 Jump Height, and Monsters get Tier 3 Climb Speed. Damage Bonus, Damage Resistance, and Movement Speed are shared between the Hunters and Monsters. The rest are unique to each side.

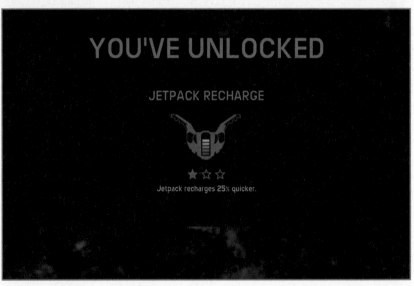

There are nine total Perks for each side. Taking away the two original Perks and counting the shared ones only once gives you 13 that require unlocking. Each one has three tiers; therefore, they must be unlocked three times. This means that 39 Perks get unlocked, which results in the max level of 40.

HUNTER PERKS

CAPACITY INCREASE

TIER	LEVELS UNLOCKED	DESCRIPTION
1	10	Increase battery or clip size by 25%.
2	23	Increase battery or clip size by 38%.
3	36	Increase battery or clip size by 50%.

Capacity Increase allows the Hunter to use any equipment that requires ammo or a battery longer. If your weapons are not lasting long enough for your taste, pick this Perk up.

DAMAGE BONUS

TIER	LEVELS UNLOCKED	DESCRIPTION
1	5	Increase damage output by 7%.
2	18	Increase damage output by 11%.
3	31	Increase damage output by 15%.

Damage Bonus increases all damage done by the Hunter. This is always a good choice for Assault or even Support classes, making their high-damage attacks even stronger.

DAMAGE RESISTANCE

TIER	LEVELS UNLOCKED	DESCRIPTION
1	8	Reduce incoming damage by 7%.
2	21	Reduce incoming damage by 11%.
3	34	Reduce incoming damage by 15%.

Damage Resistance decreases the damage done by the Monster or wildlife. This can be good for Medic or Trapper Hunters, who are often the primary target of the Monster's attacks. However, there is usually a better choice for a Perk.

HEALTH REGENERATION

TIER	LEVELS UNLOCKED	DESCRIPTION
1	13	Heal 15 points per second.
2	26	Heal 23 points per second.
3	39	Heal 30 points per second.

Health Regeneration is a nice choice for any Hunter, especially those who are high-value targets. There are better choices out there, but you cannot go wrong with a constant heal.

JET PACK RECHARGE

TIER	LEVELS UNLOCKED	DESCRIPTION
1	4	Jet Pack recharges 37% quicker.
2	17	Jet Pack recharges 55% quicker.
3	30	Jet Pack recharges 75% quicker.

The Jet Pack's fuel refills quicker with this Perk, allowing the player to use it more often—especially useful in battle when the Monster throws every ability their way. This is a good choice for those beginners who are having trouble getting used to their Hunter's Jet Pack.

JUMP HEIGHT

TIER	LEVELS UNLOCKED	DESCRIPTION
1	N/A	N/A
2	N/A	N/A
3	1	Increase jump height by 200%.

A maxed-out Jump Height Perk is the initial Buff given to the Hunters, so the first few games will be played with this Perk. The Hunter's jump height is doubled, allowing them to clear bigger obstacles—including a charging Goliath. Time your jump as he heads your way, add a little fuel, and leave the Goliath wondering where you went.

MOVEMENT SPEED

TIER	LEVELS UNLOCKED	DESCRIPTION
1	11	Increase top speed by 10%.
2	24	Increase top speed by 15%.
3	37	Increase top speed by 20%.

Increase your speed by up to 20% with this Perk, which is beneficial to any Hunter who has trouble catching up with the Monster. This is also helpful in combat, allowing you to dodge attacks more easily.

QUICK SWITCH

TIER	LEVELS UNLOCKED	DESCRIPTION
1	2	Cycle between items 50% faster.
2	15	Cycle between items 75% faster.
3	28	Cycle between items 100% faster.

Many of the Hunters have multiple items that are useful during combat. Because of this, there is a lot of down time as the player switches between them. With Quick Switch, that time is reduced greatly. This is a great choice for several of the characters, such as Caira. The quicker you can cycle between the two grenade launchers, the more effective she is.

RELOAD SPEED

TIER	LEVELS UNLOCKED	DESCRIPTION
1	7	Items recharge or reload 15% more quickly.
2	20	Items recharge or reload 23% more quickly.
3	33	Items recharge or reload 30% more quickly.

Reload Speed reduces the cooldown time between uses of a Hunter's equipment. This allows the player to use weapons and skills more often, making it a useful Perk for all characters.

MONSTER PERKS

ARMOR REGENERATION

TIER	LEVELS UNLOCKED	DESCRIPTION
1	14	Armor regenerates 25% faster.
2	27	Armor regenerates 38% faster.
3	40	Armor regenerates 50% faster.

Armor Regeneration is the last Perk that unlocks, and it is a good one: the Monster gets armor back at much quicker rate. It is extremely useful for any Monster, since it requires the Hunters to work that much harder during combat. After your armor runs out in a battle, flee the area. Quickly top it off again, and return to the surprised humans.

CLIMB SPEED

TIER	LEVELS UNLOCKED	DESCRIPTION
1	N/A	N/A
2	N/A	N/A
3	1	Increase climb speed by 30%.

A maxed-out Climb Speed Perk is the initial Buff given to the Monsters, so the first few games will be played with this Perk. Monsters can scale walls and cliffs that much faster, allowing them to flee quicker.

COOLDOWN REDUCTION

TIER	LEVELS UNLOCKED	DESCRIPTION
1	9	Abilities recharge 15% faster.
2	22	Abilities recharge 23% faster.
3	35	Abilities recharge 30% faster.

Very similar to the Hunters' Reload Speed Perk, Cooldown Reduction reduces the time between ability uses. This is one of the most valuable Perks for Monsters, especially early on, when the player may only have one or two Perks.

DAMAGE BONUS

TIER	LEVELS UNLOCKED	DESCRIPTION
1	5	Increase damage output by 7%.
2	18	Increase damage output by 11%.
3	31	Increase damage output by 15%.

Damage Bonus increases all damage dealt by the Monster. This is a great choice for Goliath or Kraken, which already do quite a bit with their big attacks.

DAMAGE RESISTANCE

TIER	LEVELS UNLOCKED	DESCRIPTION
1	8	Reduce incoming damage by 7%.
2	21	Reduce incoming damage by 11%.
3	34	Reduce incoming damage by 15%.

Damage Resistance decreases the damage done by the Hunters against the Monster. This is an obvious choice for any Monster. This Perk aggravates many Hunters while they wonder why their attacks are not having the usual effect.

FEEDING SPEED

TIER	LEVELS UNLOCKED	DESCRIPTION
1	3	Increase feeding rate by 37%.
2	16	Increase feeding rate by 55%.
3	29	Increase feeding rate by 75%.

Feeding Speed increases the rate at which the Monster eats dead wildlife. This allows it to reach Stage 2 and 3 that much quicker, but it is not limited to the early game; there are often times where the Monster benefits by feeding during combat. With the boost in feeding speed, it is more likely to get something eaten before being attacked again.

MOVEMENT SPEED

TIER	LEVELS UNLOCKED	DESCRIPTION
1	11	Increase top speed by 10%.
2	24	Increase top speed by 15%.
3	37	Increase top speed by 20%.

Increase your speed by up to 20% with this Perk, which is beneficial to any Monster as it attempts to flee the Hunters. A boost in speed is great at all stages of the game: feeding, fleeing, and fighting.

SMELL RANGE

TIER	LEVELS UNLOCKED	DESCRIPTION
1	6	Smell range increased by 37%.
2	19	Smell range increased by 55%.
3	32	Smell range increased by 75%.

The Monster's smell ability is extremely important when desperately searching for food and avoiding surprise appearances of the Hunters. Pick up the Smell Range Perk to spot both that much sooner.

STAMINA INCREASE

TIER	LEVELS UNLOCKED	DESCRIPTION
1	12	Traversal stamina recharges 25% faster.
2	25	Traversal stamina recharges 38% faster.
3	38	Traversal stamina recharges 50% faster.

Stamina Increase is the equivalent to the Hunters' Jetpack Recharge. Faster recharging stamina allows the Monster to leap, airburst, and warp more often.

ELITE WILDLIFE BUFFS

Elite wildlife, found around the planet of Shear, are indicated by a white plus icon above the creature. Once you've killed the creature, you can grab a Buff from its corpse. This is like having two Perks. Now, an icon is displayed in the upper-right corner for the five minutes that the Buff lasts. Looking at the map also displays the current Buff. The following wildlife give the listed Buffs to Hunters and Monsters.

ARMADON

	BUFF	DESCRIPTION
HUNTER	Damage Resistance	35% damage resistance, does not affect shields.
MONSTER	Damage Resistance	35% damage resistance, does not affect armor.

BLITZLEOPARD

	BUFF	DESCRIPTION
HUNTER	Jump Bonus	Jump four times higher.
MONSTER	Climb Speed Bonus	Climb 50% faster.

BASKING CEPHALADON

	BUFF	DESCRIPTION
HUNTER	Wildlife Defense	All wildlife runs away from the Hunter.
MONSTER	Feeding Bonus	100% feeding speed.

CANYON STRIDER

	BUFF	DESCRIPTION
HUNTER	Movement Speed	35% faster movement speed.
MONSTER	Movement Speed	35% faster movement speed.

CROWBILL SLOTH

	BUFF	DESCRIPTION
HUNTER	Damage Bonus	35% increases in damage output.
MONSTER	Damage Bonus	35% increases in damage output.

REAVER

	BUFF	DESCRIPTION
HUNTER	Jetpack Flight Bonus	Use 35% less fuel when flying.
MONSTER	No Bird Indicator	There is no indicator for the Hunters when birds are scared.

MAMMOTH BIRD

	BUFF	DESCRIPTION
HUNTER	Reload Speed	50% faster reload, quick weapon switch.
MONSTER	Cooldown Reduction	Abilities cool down 50% quicker.

SPOTTER

	BUFF	DESCRIPTION
HUNTER	Animal Sense	Hunters can see outlines of creatures within a 50-meter radius.
MONSTER	Smell Range Increases	200% increase in smell range, 75m -> 100m.

MARSH STRIDER

	BUFF	DESCRIPTION
HUNTER	Movement Speed	35% faster movement speed.
MONSTER	Movement Speed	35% faster movement speed.

STEAMADON

	BUFF	DESCRIPTION
HUNTER	Stun Bonus	Slows the Monster for one second when shot.
MONSTER	Stun Bonus	Slows the Hunters for one second when shot.

MEGAMOUTH

	BUFF	DESCRIPTION
HUNTER	Ability Bonus	Cooldown is reduced for special ability.
MONSTER	Stealth Pounce Bonus	Stealth attack damage is dealt quicker.

TYRANT

	BUFF	DESCRIPTION
HUNTER	Health Regeneration	Regenerates health over time.
MONSTER	Health Regeneration	Regenerates health over time.

NOMAD

	BUFF	DESCRIPTION
HUNTER	Jetpack Recharge	Jet Pack fuel recharges faster.
MONSTER	Special Ability Bonus	Monster special ability cooldown reduction.

VENOMHOUND

	BUFF	DESCRIPTION
HUNTER	Poison Target	Bullets poison the Monster.
MONSTER	Poison Target	Poison damage added to melee attacks.

OBSIDIAN GRUB

	BUFF	DESCRIPTION
HUNTER	Stability Bonus	Hunters still take damage, but they don't get knocked down.
MONSTER	Armor Regeneration	Armor regenerates over time.

WILDLIFE

An assortment of wildlife inhabits all area of the planet Shear. The Monster needs these creatures to gain armor and evolve. The key as a Monster is to figure out the most efficient wildlife in the current biome, meaning that it is easy to kill the animal and that the Monster will gain a lot of energy. Meanwhile, these pests harass Hunters as they search for the Monster or complete objectives. The wildlife are found in specific biomes, and most species can show up as an elite, which means a Buff for either side. This chapter lists all of the wildlife in the game, along with where they are found and available Buffs.

ARMADON

Biomes: Forest

Elite Buff for Hunters: Damage Resistance

Elite Buff for Monsters: Damage Resistance

A three-stomached grazing ruminant that feeds primarily on grasses (both the leaves of grass and the grubs that live in the soil), the Armadon is technically an omnivore, capable of eating and digesting almost anything.

Though solitary and normally docile, Armadons are highly territorial. Colonists often mistake their distinctive call for a mating cry, but it is actually the territorial bellow of one male sensing the subsonic vibrations of another distant male infringing on his territory.

Much like the Steamadon, Armadons are well armored, but much bigger with a load of HP. This means a long fight for both Hunters and Monsters. The reward is worth it for the Monster, but Hunters should avoid the Armadons' area unless a Buff is available.

BASKING CEPHALADON

Biomes: Acid, Ice

Elite Buff for Hunters: Wildlife Defense

Elite Buff for Monsters: Feeding Bonus

A close relative of the Mammoth Bird, the Basking Cephaladon is a "living fossil." One of the first of Shear's aquatic cephalopods to emerge from the seas and make its home on land, the Cephaladon is the last living remnant of Shear's Demozoic period.

Basking Cephaladons are typically found near water in the ice biomes. The alligator-looking creatures become aggressive if their space is disturbed. A good amount of health takes a decent amount of time for either side to fight through. An albino provides a nice Buff for Hunters who keep wildlife away from the group.

BLITZ LEOPARD

Biomes: Forest, Acid, Ice, Desert

Elite Buff for Hunters: Jump Bonus

Elite Buff for Monsters: Climb Speed Bonus

Blitzleopards are powerful ambush predators descended from seal-like aquatic pack hunters. Like their distant cousins the Mammoth Birds, Blitzleopards deploy bioluminescence, but this is purely for mating purposes. In fact, although the Blitzleopard's distinctive tail glow looks identical to the glow from a Mammoth Bird's tentacles (at least to humans), they are different. Only humans and Blitzleopards can see the tail glow; Shear's other creatures are blind in that spectrum.

Blitzleopards are often found in a small pack and can do their share of damage to a group of Hunters. Hit these guys early, as they can leap on to a Hunter from a long distance. A Monster has a much easier time dealing with them, as long as it can catch up with them.

CANYON EEL

Biomes: Desert

Elite Buff for Hunters: None

Elite Buff for Monsters: None

Canyon Eels are elasmobranches native to Shear's freshwater rivers. They are sightless scavengers, carnivores, and swarm hunters. They hunt based on sensing vibration in the water.

An extremely rare wildlife species, Canyon Eels are only found in water when the Man-eating Eels map effect is enabled. Enter the water, and these little creatures can eat through a character's health.

CANYON STRIDER

Biomes: Acid, Desert

Elite Buff for Hunters: Movement Speed

Elite Buff for Monsters: Movement Speed

The Canyon Strider is a fast, agile pack animal that grazes across several of Shear's biomes. Its primary defenses are its speed and sense of smell. Striders can detect the distinct aroma of Megamouths and easily avoid them.

These small creatures are extremely easy to kill. Even a shot from Val's sniper rifle can take one down from a distance. One simple swipe from a Monster knocks it down, but it may take some effort to catch up. If the Monster can sneak up on a pack, they are very efficient when feeding.

CROWBILL SLOTH

Biomes: Forest, Acid, Ice, Desert

Elite Buff for Hunters: Damage Bonus

Elite Buff for Monsters: Damage Bonus

A large, typically docile herbivore, the quick-to-anger Crowbill gets its name from its distinctive beak, used to dig grubs out of soil and the bark of trees.

The Crowbill Sloth, first seen in the tutorial, charges Hunters quickly whenever disturbed. It's not the toughest creature to take down, but it does have a good amount of health. As the Hunters, avoid them if at all possible, unless it possesses the extremely valuable Damage Bonus Buff. Monsters should take their time killing this guy, as it rewards with plenty of energy.

DUNE BEETLE

Biomes: Acid, Desert

Elite Buff for Hunters: None

Elite Buff for Monsters: None

The Dune Beetle is a huge arthropod, one of the deadliest predators on Shear. Its claws are specially adapted to pierce the ignimbrite husks of creatures living near magma deposits.

They are extremely aggressive against Hunters, as they charge and use their claws. There no Buffs available from Dune Beetles, so steer clear of them when playing as a Hunter. Beetles have a decent amount of HP, making them a tougher kill for both Hunters and Monsters.

GLACIOPOD

Biomes: Ice

Elite Buff for Hunters: None

Elite Buff for Monsters: None

The small, sturdy Glaciopod happily whiles away the hours scraping lichen off glaciers. Its incredibly nutrient-rich scat gets its distinctive color and caloric value from the fungal spores contained within. The algae it eats depends on the Glaciopod to digest the fungus and disperse its spores for it.

These little guys do not harm either side, but they are a huge benefit to the Monster. As they slowly move around, they occasionally drop white algae behind them. The Monster can eat these to build armor and evolve. Whenever a Hunter encounters one, the player should kill it to keep the Monster from getting more energy from it.

MAMMOTH BIRD

Biomes: Forest, Acid, Ice, Desert

Elite Buff for Hunters: Reload Speed

Elite Buff for Monsters: Cooldown Reduction

Descended from aquatic cephalopods, Mammoth Birds are not avians. Their closest land-dwelling relatives are the Blitzleopards.

Their legs are specially adapted tentacles, leaving their other tentacles free as prehensile grasping, hunting, and eating tools. Two of its tentacles evolved into sophisticated bioluminescent lures that store a potent electric charge.

Mammoth Birds use the lure/charge combination to ferret out Spotters in their dens. The tentacles worm their way into the Spotters' den, the Spotters investigate the light, and the electric charge stuns the Spotters.

Mammoth Birds are quick but easy kills for a Monster once they have been caught. Hunters should steer clear of them, unless a Buff is available. They typically flee from the group, but their defensive electric charge can damage a character fairly quickly.

MARSH STRIDER

Biomes: Forest

Elite Buff for Hunters: Movement Speed

Elite Buff for Monsters: Movement Speed

Marsh Striders are easily preyed-upon omnivores that exist primarily on a diet of grubs, bark, and moss. Apart from a high breeding rate, their only defense when attacked is to fall to the ground and mimic the behavior of a sick animal. This confuses many of Shear's ambush predators, which instinctively avoid attacking an apparently ill creature.

When found by a Monster, these creatures should be dealt with quickly if safe from the Hunters. Take them out before they notice your presence, and feast on the energy. Marsh Striders are very efficient kills. Hunters can easily ignore these guys as they flee from the team, unless, of course, the Movement Speed Buff is available. If one is downed but not killed, do it a favor and put it out of its misery as it crawls along the ground.

MEGAMOUTH

Biomes: Acid, Desert

Elite Buff for Hunters: Ability Bonus

Elite Buff for Monsters: Stealth Pounce Bonus

One of the most distinctive of Shear's vast collection of unique wildlife, the Megamouth is an aptly named ambush predator that uses camouflage to hide from prospective prey.

The well-armored, boulder-looking enemy sits and waits for the Hunters to move nearby. Then, it pounces and snatches one of the Hunters. It is up to another Hunter to free the victim by damaging the creature. Be sure to move the group well wide of these guys, unless it is an albino. In that case, kill it from afar to nab a Buff. This is likewise a relatively tough kill for a Monster and may not be worth the trouble, unless there is not much choice.

NOMAD

Biomes: Acid, Desert

Elite Buff for Hunters: Jet Pack Recharge

Elite Buff for Monsters: Special Ability Bonus

It is a popular misconception among Shear's colonists that the Nomad's long legs and great height are adaptations to allow it to feed on the leaves of tall trees. In fact, the Nomad's height is part of a mating display. Taller male Nomads attract more mates, so over many generations, the Nomad has grown to the size we encounter now.

These long-legged creatures are slow to react to the Hunters and easy to slip past. However, they charge when Hunters get close. While not the easiest kill on Shear, the animal goes down after a short while.

OBSIDIAN GRUB

Biomes: Ice

Elite Buff for Hunters: Capacity Increase

Elite Buff for Monsters: Armor Regeneration

Like its close cousin the Lava Strider, the Obsidian Grub evolved several pairs of eyes. It has seven but keeps only two open at a time to minimize exposure to the extreme heat of its native lava flow environment.

The grub scours the newly created igneous plains in volcanically active regions looking for any of the many small insects specially adapted to Shear's pyroclastic environments.

Obsidian Grubs are tiny, armored, and very docile. As Hunters, just let them be, unless one possesses a delicious Buff. Its armor does prove to be a bit of an obstacle for the humans. Monsters have a relatively easy time swiping through the armor to get to the energy.

PHANTOM

Biomes: Forest

Elite Buff for Hunters: None

Elite Buff for Monsters: None

Phantoms are large, nearly man-sized flying mammalian scavengers. Highly social, they patrol in packs known as blights and use advanced chirps as signals to coordinate their hunting and alert each other to threats.

Though placental mammals that give live birth and are covered with fine hairs, Phantoms sport hard, bird-like beaks composed entirely of keratin. They use these beaks to rip and tear at the flesh of their prey. The beak's smooth, hairless texture prevents the bacteria on the carrion they eat from growing on or near their mouths.

The Phantom's map effect brings these flying pests out to the forest maps. Shoot or knock these guys out of the air. They attack Hunters but are easy prey for Monsters.

REAVER

Biomes: Forest, Acid, Ice, Desert

Elite Buff for Hunters: Jet Pack Flight Bonus

Elite Buff for Monsters: No Bird Indicator

Reavers are social pack animals and scavenging hunters. They are one of a number of amniotic tetrapod species on Shear collectively known as synapsids. Like mammals, they are warm-blooded, but unlike mammals, they do not give live birth to their young and lay eggs instead.

Reavers can be found in packs or occasionally on their own. They are very aggressive and are best avoided by Hunters, unless a Buff is available. They are easy kills for a Monster and worth spending the small amount of time to get the energy.

SPOTTER

Biomes: Forest, Ice

Elite Buff for Hunters: Animal Sense

Elite Buff for Monsters: Smell Range Increase

Spotters are highly social reptilian omnivores that make the wide, temperate flatlands of Shear home. Living in tightly knit extended family units (colonies), they are communicative and cooperative. They nest in self-built mounds created from their own regurgitated food. These mounds act as compost piles, allowing them to easily regulate their heat.

The tiny creature is an easy kill, if you can catch one. The only trouble one produces for the Hunters is trying to pick one off for their Animal Sense Buff. Their small size and quick feet make them tough targets. If a Monster can sneak up behind one, a quick swipe ends the Spotter's life.

STEAMADON

Biomes: Ice

Elite Buff for Hunters: Stun Bonus

Elite Buff for Monsters: Stun Bonus

A close relative of the Armadon, the Steamadon's third stomach is isolated from the other two. Most food goes into the first two stomachs, but the special algae the Steamadon uses to regulate its heat goes into the third stomach, where it is fermented into a compost. The compost reaches temperatures of over 100 degrees Celsius.

This normally allows the Steamadon to keep its body toasty warm, even in the freezing arctic biomes of Shear. When threatened, the Steamadon releases some of the superheated nitrous oxide from its third stomach into a special bladder it keeps filled with water.

Steamadons are very similar to their cousin the Armadon, but much smaller. They are well-armored and emit steam which obscures vision, giving a nearby Monster time to get away.

TRAPJAW

Biomes: Forest, Acid, Ice, Desert

Elite Buff for Hunters: None

Elite Buff for Monsters: None

The Trapjaw is a successful and highly varied pack hunter found in all four climates on Shear. Like its distant cousin the Harpy, the Trapjaw is a scavenger, preferring to prey on sick and elderly animals and often stealing kills from larger predators.

Trapjaw have poor eyesight but excellent hearing, allowing them to dig their heads into a carrion corpse and root around for bones or nutrient-rich organs while still being able to hear approaching predators.

These cousins of Maggie's pet, Daisy, travel around in packs and are extremely aggressive to Hunters. Use widespread weapons or Markov's Lightning Gun to eliminate them quickly. The team must steer very wide to avoid them. A Monster that can sneak up on a group of Trapjaws can rack up some quick energy.

TYRANT

Biomes: Forest, Ice

Elite Buff for Hunters: Health Regeneration

Elite Buff for Monsters: Health Regeneration

One of Shear's iconic dominant apex predators, Tyrants can be found lurking in any freshwater lake on Shear. Equally adapted to desert and arctic conditions, these aggressive ambush hunters lunge at their prey, snapping their beak-like jaws around their victim and pulling them back into the water. Prey that are not killed by the crushing force of their jaws are quickly drowned.

Tyrants hang out in the water and are fairly slow, but they are still one of the biggest threats for Hunters outside of the Monster and its minions. Jet pack past these guys whenever possible, and if the beast grabs a teammate, free him or her with some weapon fire. A Monster will get on a Tyrant's bad side if provoked, and the creature is a handful to take down.

VENOMHOUND

Biomes: Forest, Acid

Elite Buff for Hunters: Poison Target

Elite Buff for Monsters: Poison Target

Solitary ambush predators, Venomhounds lurk in Shear's heavy undergrowth, striking out at any herbivores unlucky enough to wander by. Their high-molecular mass neurotoxin is chemically similar to terrestrial latrotoxin. The poison is not fatal to a full-grown human, but colonists with weakened immune systems may die if bitten.

These greenish creatures jump out of nowhere and grab ahold of a helpless Hunter. If one succeeds at grabbing a Hunter, he or she is poisoned, slowly draining health for a short while. This won't kill a healthy Hunter, but it can cause trouble if the character is already badly injured, or if the creature gets ahold of a weak colonist.

GAME MODES

Hunters must revive and evacuate 5 survivors before the Monster kills 5 of them.

There are four basic game modes in *Evolve*: Hunt, Nest, Rescue, and Defend. These offer a variety of gameplay options for the Monsters and Hunters. Simply hunt each other in Hunt mode, or fight over objectives.

A fifth mode called Evacuation pits the Hunters against the Monster in five days of matches—

four rounds occurring in Hunt, Nest, or Rescue modes, and a fifth taking place in Defend mode. The game balance is shifted between the two sides depending on how each fares.

First, this chapter provides you with in-depth coverage of the two tutorials. Then, you'll learn about the game modes themselves. Detailed descriptions on how each work and strategies for both sides give you everything you need to enter the wild with confidence.

EVACUATION

Hunter Objective: Save the Shear Colonists by Protecting the Evacuation Ship

Monster Objective: Destroy the Colonists and the Evacuation Ship

Evacuation mode pits the four Hunters against the Monster in five rounds, or days, of gameplay. The first round is always Hunt mode on any of the main 12 maps. For the next three rounds, the players vote on two options, which can be Hunt, Rescue, or Nest mode. These take place on an adjacent map to the previous day. It is possible to get the same map in both options. Refer to the map above to see how the maps connect.

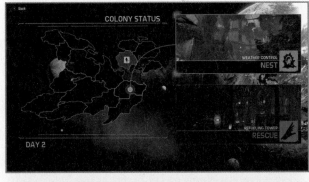

The players continue making their way across the map until the fifth and final round, which is a game of Defend. This one takes place on one of the four special maps. By getting a majority of the votes, it is possible to force the game toward a favorite Defend map. No matter where the Evacuation game begins, any of the four Defend maps is accessible.

After each day, based on how well each side performed, the Colony Status is given—displaying the number of people that the Hunters saved and the number that the Monster killed. The winning side typically ends up with the bigger number, as the colonies are tallied after each round.

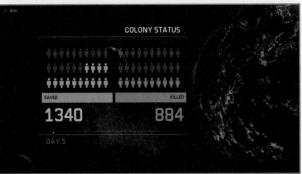

The next screen shows the Auto Balance, as the loser of the previous round gets a nudge in their favor. The advantage may bounce back and forth between even teams, or a dominant squad may always have the balance against them. It is possible to lose the first four days and go into the Defend stage with full favor, but your team will always have a disadvantage with the map effects.

Based on which side won the previous round and where it took place, a map effect is added to the next day. If the Monster won, it favors the beast, and vice versa. Each map has a selection

of possible effects. Refer to the Map chapter for a full rundown of each location, along with the map effects that can take place at each. Final round map effects are always Armored Sentry Guns for Hunters and Extra Armor for the Monster.

 HUNT

Hunter Objective: Take down the Monster, or Last until the Timer Reaches Zero

Monster Objective: Kill All Hunters at Once, or Destroy Power Relay

A Stage 1 Monster has been spotted, and four Hunters have been called in to take care of it. The Hunters must track down the beast as quickly as they can while the Monster flees through the environment. The Monster gets a 30-second head start on the Hunters.

While the Monster feasts on the local wildlife, the Trapper uses his or her unique ability to track down the big foe. Along with cues from the environment, the four-person group works hard and fast to reach the Monster before it becomes even more powerful.

As the Monster devours the wildlife, it is powering up as it evolves to Stage 2 and then to its ultimate form, Stage 3. At this point, the fiend gains the upper hand, with the choice of either eliminating the Hunters or destroying the now-vulnerable Power Relay. As the Monster, step up to the Power Relay, and hold the Melee button to rip it apart. This is extremely time-consuming, and more than likely, the Hunters will interrupt.

Once the Monster hits Stage 3, it must make a play at the Power Relay or the Hunters. After awhile, a timer counts down from three minutes. The Monster must destroy the Power Relay before it reaches zero, or the Hunters win the round. The timer is paused when there is a lull in the fight.

HUNTER STRATEGY

Finding the Monster as quickly as possible is the key to victory for the Hunters, though it is not impossible to take it down at Stage 3. Use all of the environment cues, as well as your Trapper, to track it down. Monster tracks, broken branches, animal corpses, and scattered birds are all useful in finding the objective.

Becoming familiar with the maps is key to cutting the adversary off. Once you find the Monster, communication and teamwork are necessary to defeat the giant. Each Hunter must play their specific role; one mistake can be the difference in the game.

Monsters are only able to regenerate armor, so any health loss stays with it for the entire game. Eat away at its HP any chance you get. Every shot may be the difference the next time you meet.

MONSTER STRATEGY

As soon as the match starts, flee the area as the Hunters drop nearby. Quickly feed on any wildlife you encounter. At Stage 1, the Monster is an easier kill for the pursuers. Reach Stage 2, and the two sides tend to even out. Fully evolving to Stage 3 greatly increases your chances for survival.

At Stage 3, make a choice whether to go after the Power Relay or take your improved power against the Hunters. The three Monsters have their own unique abilities, and learning the ins and outs of each goes a long way when facing a well-organized Hunter team.

As Hunters are taken down and revived, a strike is given that reduces their maximum health by 25%. Bleed out or get a third strike, and the player must wait for the next dropship. Use these strikes and missing Hunters to your advantage.

NEST

Hunter Objective: Destroy All Six Eggs or Minions, or Kill the Monster

Monster Objective: Eliminate the Hunters before the Eggs or Minions are Destroyed

Six eggs are scattered around the map, as noted on the map and on your heads-up display. The Hunters must destroy the eggs within 10 minutes, or the Monster wins. Simply attack the outer shell until it flakes off, and then destroy the egg. A bar above designates the health of the egg. Ensure that it is completely demolished before moving on. The Monster can use an egg no matter how damaged it is.

In the meantime, the Monster can hatch a minion from an egg by standing nearby and holding the Eat/Climb button. This eliminates one of the eggs, which benefits the Hunters, but the minion heads straight for the Hunters. Only one minion can be hatched at a time. Once the Hunters kill it, another can be grabbed from an egg. If all six eggs or the minions hatched from them are destroyed, the Monster loses.

HUNTER STRATEGY

The team must make a choice when the game starts. Do you make a run for the Monster and take it out before it reaches Stage 2, or do you concentrate on destroying the eggs? The Monster typically goes after the closest egg and hatches it. This gives away its location, but more than likely, a minion joins the beast.

If the team decides to take out the eggs, head to the closest one. Numbers underneath the egg's health bar indicate the distance from that objective; the smaller the number, the closer it is. Once the shell of an egg is broken, you can place weak spots on the surface for added bonus. With Bucket, place Sentry Guns near an egg, and let them take one out while the team works on another.

Another tactic is to have the Trapper capture the Monster in the Mobile Arena away from any eggs, while the rest of the team destroys the eggs. The unlucky Hunter inside the dome must run and hide to avoid causing the arena to fall.

MONSTER STRATEGY

Use the Smell ability to find nearby wildlife and feed on their corpses. Evolve once the opportunity arises, head for the closest egg, and hatch a minion. The minion heads straight for the Hunters, so follow him there. Continue to feed on any creature you find along the way to build up armor. Assist your helper, and take the Hunter squad down.

RESCUE

Hunter Objective: Locate, Revive, and Escort Five Survivors to a Rescue Shuttle

Monster Objective: Kill Five Survivors before They can be Rescued

A Monster roams the area as survivors have fled into the wilderness. It is up to the four Hunters to locate, revive, and escort the survivors to a rescue shuttle.

When the Hunters land, two survivors are revealed to both sides. The Hunters must move out and revive them before the Monster can kill them. Once the two have been revived or killed, a dropship appears in 30 seconds. Now, the Hunters must escort the colonists to the extraction point, protecting them from the Monster.

At this point, two more survivors appear. Repeat the same process as with the first group. Next, five survivors are revealed. Again, after all five are revived or killed, a dropship shows up to take the colonists away. The Hunters must escort any remaining survivors to the shuttle. In a close match, this is just enough to make it come down to the final survivor.

When the survivors are first revealed, they bleed out just as teammates do when the Monster downs them. Once the red drains from the skull icon, he or she dies. A number underneath the icon represents the distance to the survivor: the smaller the number, the closer the person.

The current objective is shown in the top-left corner, along with icons for the survivors. Each round is shown on a separate line. The icon turns white once the colonist is picked up, and an X is marked through anyone who is killed.

HUNTER STRATEGY

 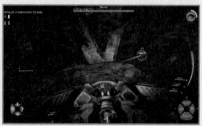

Move to the survivors quickly, using the distance to decide priority. Maggie and Lazarus are good choices for this mode. Maggie's pet Trapjaw assists in reviving the survivors, and Lazarus can bring them back after bleeding out. Caira can also be very useful with her Adrenaline Field.

Survivors can be a pain when you're attempting to lead them to the extraction point. If Hunters stand around, the colonists also stand around. Have the group move to the shuttle to encourage them along. During this stage, Hank is extremely valuable, as he can shield any survivors who get in trouble.

Set traps around the extraction point to keep the Monster at bay. Markov's Arc Mines and Bucket's Sentry Guns work well here. Hank's Orbital Barrage at the point of extraction helps keep the enemy away, too.

MONSTER STRATEGY

The Monster must make a tough decision at the start of a game of Rescue. Quickly move over to the first survivors and risk confronting the Hunters at Stage 1, or let them have the first two while you feed up to Stage 2. For most people, the latter is the best choice. Facing the Hunters too early can be extremely tough for any Monster.

Once you've achieved Stage 2, immediately head for the next survivors, and start attacking as soon as they are within range. To make the kills easier, try to isolate the survivors as they head for the extraction point.

DEFEND

Hunter Objective: Defend Generators and Ship until It Takes Off, or Kill the Alpha Monster

Monster Objective: Destroy the Generators and Ship before the Timers Run Out

A transport ship refuels as a Stage 3 Alpha Monster and two minions enter the area. The Hunters must defend the generator from the bad guys for six minutes. If the Hunters can keep the generator going as the timer runs out, they win. Otherwise, if it is taken out, access is given to a second generator.

Three minutes are added to the timer as the enemies move toward the next objective. Again, if the timer hits zero with the generator surviving, the Hunters win. If the Monsters destroy both objectives, doors are opened to the power source. Another three minutes are added as everyone moves toward the final objective.

The same objectives hold for the third and final target. If the power source survives through the rest of the timer, the Hunters win. If it is destroyed, the Monster wins.

The dropship returns dead Hunters to the game every 30 seconds instead of the normal two minutes. A message appears on screen for a character who bleeds out as the dropship shows up. Pressing the given button immediately sends the Hunter to the shuttle. Even if the entire team is wiped out, they all return on the next ship.

Once the minions are defeated, a timer counts down until another duo is hatched. These guys appear at the start for the first generator and then at the last destroyed objective.

Turrets around each objective assist the Hunters against the minions and Monster.

HUNTER STRATEGY

For a short time at the start of the match, the Monsters are in the distance, making their way to the first generator. There are three lanes for them to enter. Set up traps along each one to slow them down. As they get closer, protect the generators with the traps. Markov's Arc Mines eat away at the minions as they move toward the next objective.

Since the dropship shows up more frequently in Defend mode, it is less important to revive teammates. It is often better to let them bleed out and continue fending off the minions and Monsters. Call out to teammates if you want a revive or not. Due to the increased dropship frequency, Lazarus is not a good choice for Defend.

Kraken may be the best choice for the Monster, which means that Val is great as the Medic. Her Tranquilizer Gun knocks the giant out of the air and slows it down.

As the Trapper, meet up with the incoming Alpha Monster at least 60 meters away from the generator, and put up the Mobile Arena. The generator must still be defended from any untrapped minions, so have others stay behind.

MONSTER STRATEGY

The Monster starts out at Stage 3. Load up on your favorite abilities, and use this power to your advantage. Kraken is a great choice for Defend. He is quick, better armored than Wraith, and his long-range attacks work well on the turrets.

Wait for the minions before going after the generators. Let them attack the objectives while Kraken harasses the Hunters. Once you've taken care of the minions, pull out, and wait for the next helpers. Get in some shots at the generators whenever the opportunity arises, but it is better to have the minions there.

DEFEND MAPS

Defend mode takes place on four special maps instead of the usual 12. These include Colonial Water & Power, King's Fort, New Calico, and Salveron Industries. Get more information about each in the Maps chapter.

MAPS

DISTILLERY FUSION PLANT MEDLAB ORBITAL DRILL **REFUELING TOWER** RENDERING PLANT

A Rank-Rajat self-repairing 'Refuel, Repair, and Resupply' depot sits alone in the forest, tended by its worker-crew of 18 engineers and servicemen.
Periodically, vehicles visit for repair and to load up on supplies for their colony.

There are four biomes on planet Shear: acid, desert, forest, and ice. All of these feature a unique selection of wildlife, as listed below. The biomes each have three normal maps, which are playable on Hunt, Nest, and Rescue modes. Each habitat also has a fourth Defend-only map.

ACID BIOME

Creature Inhabitants: Basking Cephaladon, Blitzleopard, Canyon Strider, Crowbill Sloth, Dune Beetle, Mammoth Bird, Megamouth, Nomad, Reaver, Trapjaw, Venomhound

Avoid the water and geysers in the acid biome, which can slowly drain the health of Hunters and Monsters.

BARRACKS

Potential Map Effect with Hunter Win: Space Laser, Colonists, Forcefield, Fair Weather

Potential Map Effect with Monster Win: Falling Satellite, Canyon Striders, Man-Eating Eels, Storms

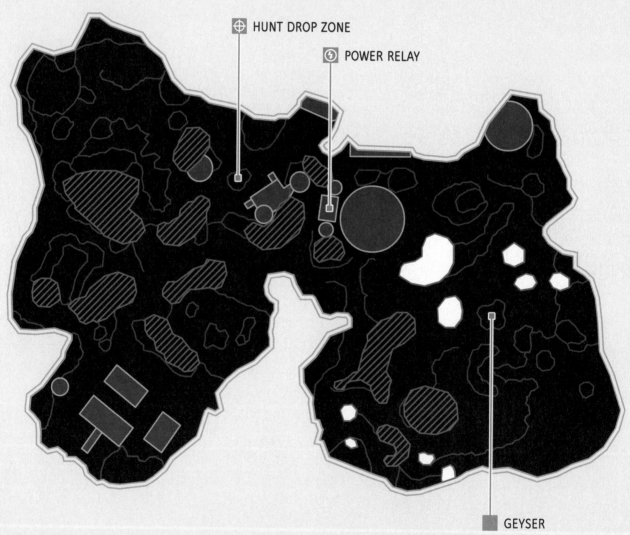

⊕ HUNT DROP ZONE

⊙ POWER RELAY

■ GEYSER

EbonStar Tactical Solutions offers a range of outposts and armed contingents to choose from when contracting them to protect your settlement, like the ES29 "Three of a Kind" outpost fitted with quasar-class anti-artillery multicannons! Even a Sol Guard frigate must take notice and consider retreat when these babies start firing.

Tall geysers spew steam high into the air around the east side of the map. Climbing to the top damages Hunters and Monsters. The landing pad is a great fight location for the Hunters with its openness. Much of the west half of the map offers tighter spaces. The Power Relay sits in an enclosed area just west of the circular platform. Three entrances should be protected once the Monster reaches Stage 3.

ORBITAL DRILL

Potential Map Effect with Hunter Win: EbonStar Ally, Colonists, Fair Weather

Potential Map Effect with Monster Win: EbonStar Corpses, Canyon Striders, Storms

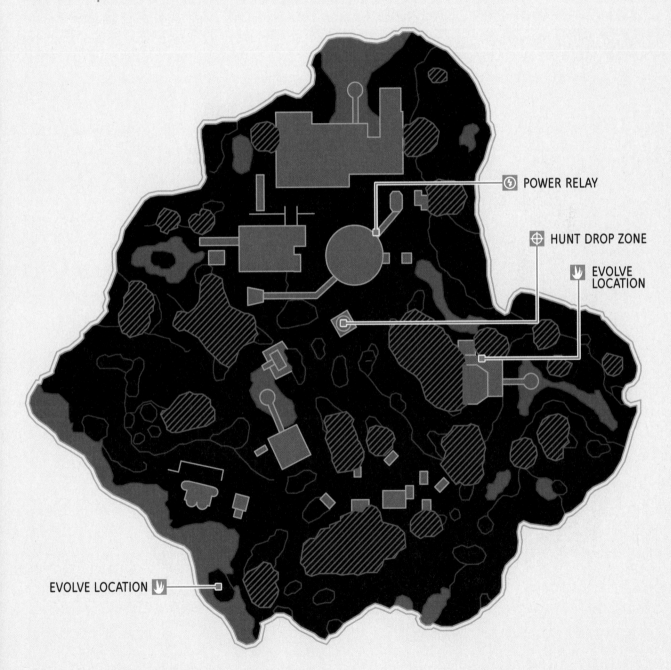

NORDITA employs lots of tricks to tease heavy elements out of Shear's crust. One is the Orbital Asthenospheric Fermionic Condenser, a deep-bore orbital energy drill that can punch a hole in the planet's crust. The OAFC is controlled via satellite from this remote location.

The group of NORDITA buildings on the north side of Orbital Drill is the focus of a map that presents many nooks and crannies for the Monster to hide in. There are a few good, private spots around the area that are great to evolve in. The Power Relay sits inside the small circular building toward the center of the map. Entrances on the north and south sides are the only ways in. This makes it fairly easy to defend, but be careful that the team doesn't group for an easier shot.

RENDERING PLANT

Potential Map Effect with Hunter Win: EbonStar Ally, Space Laser, Forcefield, Teleport Gates, Cargo Ship, Fair Weather

Potential Map Effect with Monster Win: EbonStar Corpses, Falling Satellite, Man-Eating Eels, Teleport Rifts, Second Monster, Storms

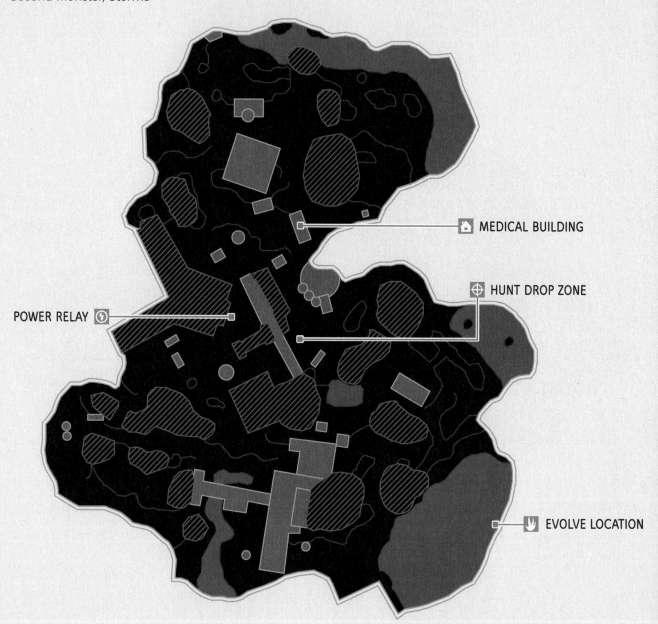

This settlement renders Marsh Striders down into the fatty oils, lipids, and other organic chemicals the colony uses as raw materials for a million everyday uses. It's much cheaper and more efficient to mine the necessary hydrocarbons from the local wildlife rather than synthesize it all.

Rendering Plant is littered with buildings and rock ledges. Roads leading through the mostly man-made environment are vulnerable to attacks from above. Dangerous bodies of water surround the east and south, with rocks jutting out that allow the Monster to evolve in relative safety. The Power Relay is located on the side of one of the plant's buildings. It has no cover at all, though surrounding structures give some protection.

COLONIAL WATER & POWER

Potential Map Effect with Hunter Win: Armored Turrets

Potential Map Effect with Monster Win: Armored Minions

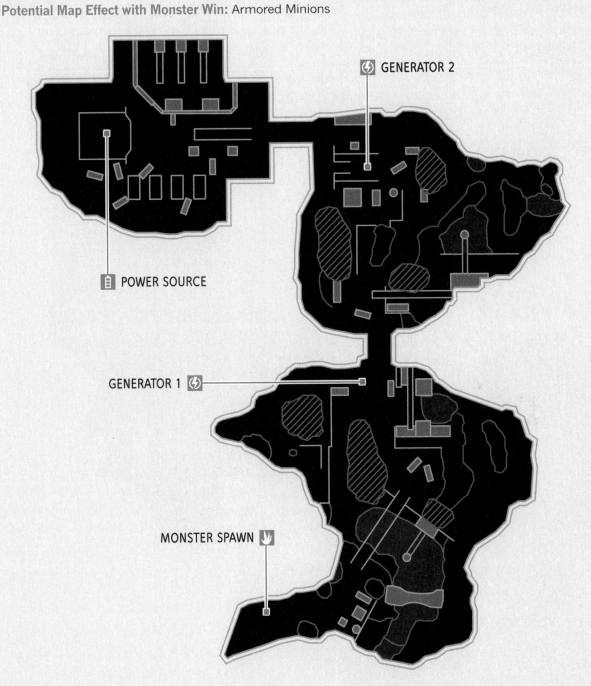

GENERATOR 2

POWER SOURCE

GENERATOR 1

MONSTER SPAWN

One of the largest man-made structures on Shear, CW&P routes all power generated at the fusion plant and hydroelectric plant, as well as all fresh water. Built over a hydrologically active geothermal site, the plant is self-powered and self-sustaining. It has to be, as all life in the colony depends on its water and energy.

Colonial Water & Power is only available in Defend mode. Monsters spawn at the very bottom, in a narrow strip to the left. The final objective lies all the way in the northwest corner. While the minions may take the long way to the first generator, it is a relatively close hike for the Monster. You can find a natural environment along the east edge of the map, but most of the action takes place at the facility. An upper floor surrounds the power source, which allows the Hunters to protect it from above.

DESERT BIOME

Creature Inhabitants: Blitzleopard, Canyon Eel, Canyon Strider, Crowbill Sloth, Dune Beetle, Mammoth Bird, Megamouth, Nomad, Reaver, Trapjaw

ARMORY

Potential Map Effect with Hunter Win: Teleport Gates, Forcefield, Fair Weather

Potential Map Effect with Monster Win: Teleport Rifts, Man- Eating Eels, Storms

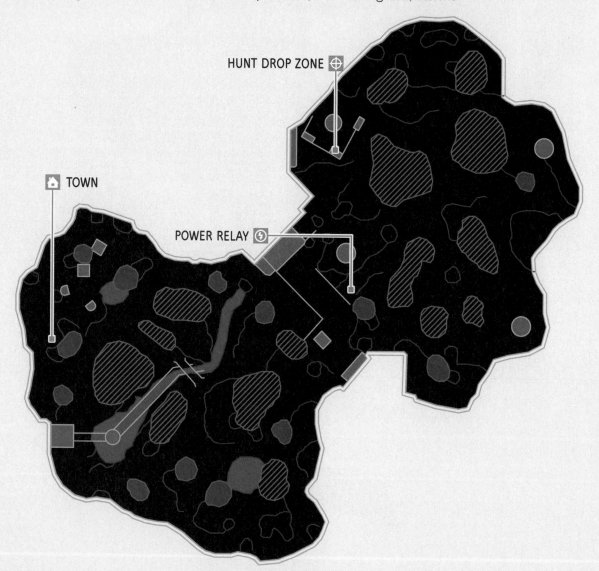

Designed to repel attacks from the most aggressive Corp Pirates, EbonStar's armory is fitted with an EMP cannon. When attacked, the cannon fires its EMP rockets, shutting down the electronic systems of any would-be invader.

EbonStar's armory is located in the desert biome, with many high cliffs and tall structures looking down on open areas. A narrowing in the middle of the map allows it to be split into two distinct zones, letting the Hunters narrow their search area. A small town on the far west side offers up some corpses for the Monster at the start of the match. The Power Relay is located on the central tower, which results in a wide-open fight. This can favor the Hunters.

THE DAM

Potential Map Effect with Hunter Win: Teleport Gates, Attack Drones, Colonists, EbonStar Ally, Fair Weather
Potential Map Effect with Monster Win: Teleport Rifts, EMP, Canyon Striders, EbonStar Corpses, Storms

The Celestial self-surveying, self-deploying hydroelectric power station is designed to be dropped into orbit on any world, survey the planet from orbit, identify potential locations suitable for hydroelectric power, intelligently choose the best location, and then drop out of orbit and deploy itself, all without human supervision.

Once deployed, the plant produces enough power to sustain three Type-M NORDITA colonies, two Darwin-class ERI research facilities, or one "Straight Flush" EbonStar facility.

Magnetically sealed overflow doors regulate the twin reservoirs created by the facility. The doors are designed to be failsafe, opening and releasing dangerous excess water should the power completely fail.

The match starts directly on top of the dam. Water runs through the middle, allowing the Monster to easily hide its tracks as it roams between the north and south. A pair of Pumping Stations and a high platform in the southeast give the Monster some nice options where it can get away and evolve. The Power Relay is located on top of the dam, with really only one way in. The high setting means that the Hunters can see the enemy coming from afar.

WRAITH TRAP

Potential Map Effect with Hunter Win: Cargo Ship, Sentry Guns, Colonists, Forcefield, Attack Drones, Fair Weather

Potential Map Effect with Monster Win: Second Monster, Radioactive Clouds, Canyon Striders, Man-Eating Eels, EMP, Storms

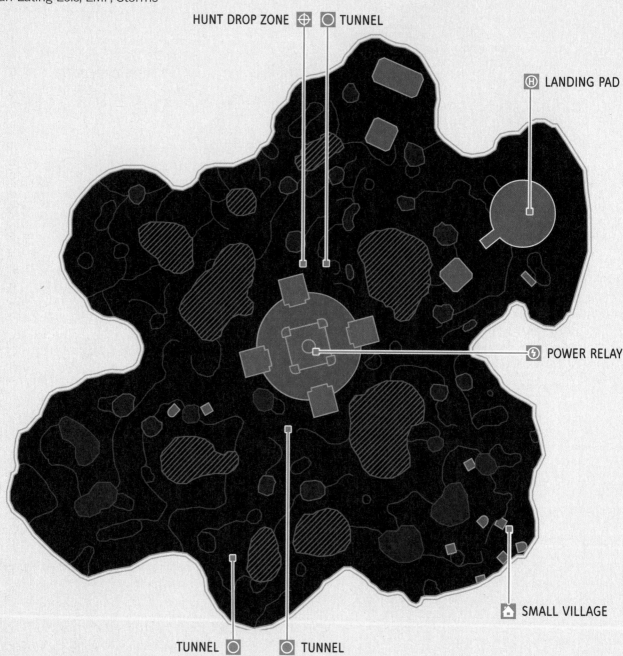

Desperate, EbonStar constructs a hideous, terrifying experiment at a secret desert base.

Wraith Trap is centered around a concrete bunker that houses a captured Wraith. This is also where the Power Relay sits. Many clashes will take place near this bunker. It is very open, with tunnels leading out the north and south. A landing pad in the far northeast side offers up another wide-open environment. Much of the south side is the typical desert, rocky environment, with a few decent locations for the Monster to get some privacy.

SALVERON INDUSTRIES

Potential Map Effect with Hunter Win: Armored Turrets

Potential Map Effect with Monster Win: Armored Minions

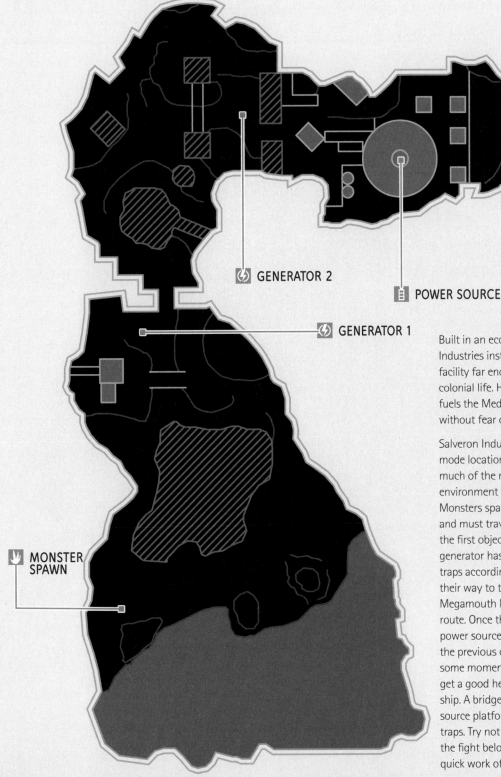

GENERATOR 2

POWER SOURCE

GENERATOR 1

MONSTER
SPAWN

Built in an ecological dead zone, Salveron Industries installed a Generyst processing facility far enough away from the rest of colonial life. Here, the alien fungus that fuels the Medgun can be bred in isolation without fear of contaminating the locals.

Salveron Industries is the desert Defend mode location. A big facility makes up much of the map, with a little natural environment thrown in at the start. The Monsters spawn in the southwest corner and must travel north and then east once the first objective is destroyed. The first generator has only two ways in, so lay traps accordingly. As the players make their way to the second generator, an elite Megamouth lies in wait along the lower route. Once the Monster has access to the power source, it is a short journey from the previous objective. Push through with some momentum, and the bad guys can get a good head start on destroying the ship. A bridge that leads to the power source platform is a great location for traps. Try not to get too distracted: take the fight below, or the minions may make quick work of their final target.

FOREST BIOME

Creature Inhabitants: Armadon, Blitzleopard, Crowbill Sloth, Mammoth Bird, Marsh Strider, Phantom, Reaver, Spotter, Trapjaw, Tyrant, Venomhound

FUSION PLANT

Potential Map Effect with Hunter Win: Cargo Ship, Teleport Gates, Clear Skies

Potential Map Effect with Monster Win: Second Monster, Teleport Rifts, Carnivorous Plants

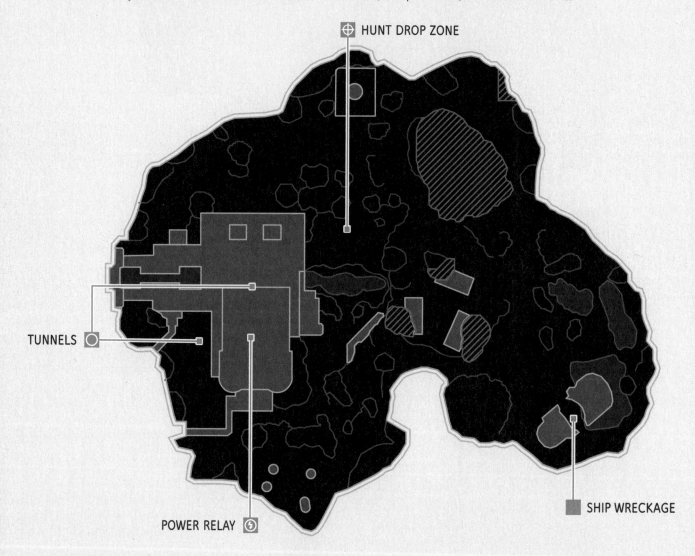

⊕ HUNT DROP ZONE

TUNNELS

POWER RELAY ⚡

SHIP WRECKAGE

A Celestial Fission-Electric Type IV power plant provides electrical power to several nearby settlements. Dropped over a naturally occurring thorium deposit, the plant mines and processes the ore it needs to power the steam turbines. Its crew of 22 is needed only to maintain the plant and operate the control systems.

Fusion Plant is a relatively small map, with the big, complex NORDITA facility taking up much of the west side. Many levels of the structure allow a Monster or Hunter to hide if things get hairy in combat. Storage tanks litter the area just to the south, while ship wreckage is the only unnatural thing in the far east. A small fenced-in area to the far north makes a decent location for the Hunters to fight their foe. The Power Relay sits inside the plant on the bottom floor. Multiple entrances along the three levels can be defended with well-placed traps. Once the fight is taken inside, it can get very dangerous.

REFUELING TOWER

Potential Map Effect with Hunter Win: Colonists, Sentry Guns, Teleport Gates, Birds, Clear Skies

Potential Map Effect with Monster Win: Canyon Striders, Radioactive Clouds, Teleport Rifts, Phantoms, Carnivorous Plants

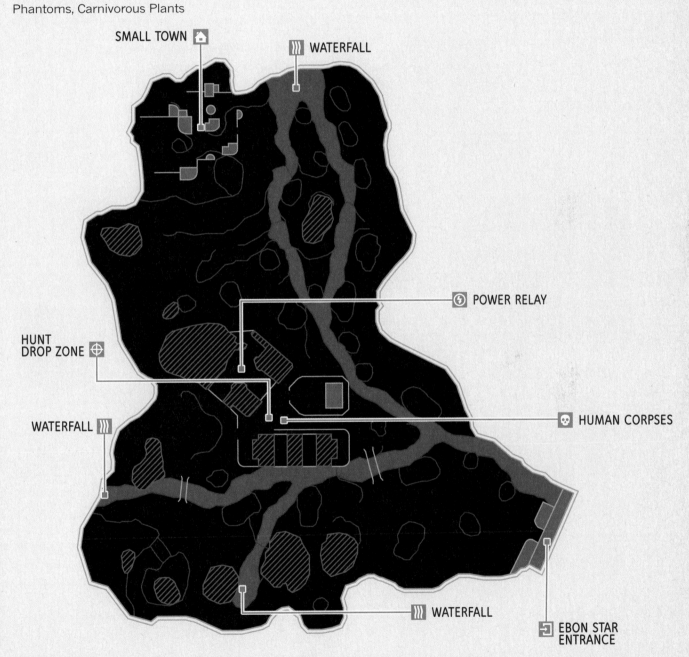

A Rank-Rajat self-repairing "Refuel, Repair, & Resupply" depot sits alone in the forest, tended by its worker crew of 18 engineers and servicemen.

Periodically, vehicles visit for repair and to load up on supplies for their colony.

The big tower that sits in the middle of this map may be the main focus, but the winding river that runs throughout the east and south makes the environment what it is. The Monster can easily hide its tracks as it traverses between the zones. Human corpses lying around the start give the Monster a head start on feeding. The Power Relay sits inside the tower, with three ways in. Defend them all as the Monster attempts to fight its way in.

WEATHER CONTROL

Potential Map Effect with Hunter Win: Cargo Ship, Sentry Guns, Birds, Medbays, Fair Weather

Potential Map Effect with Monster Win: Second Monster, Radioactive Clouds, Phantoms, Mutated Plants, Storms

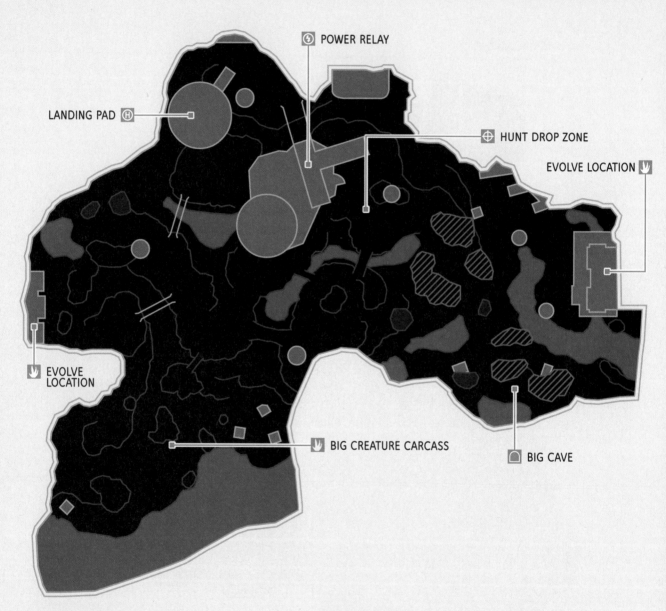

The bohrium that makes Shear so valuable has environmentally catastrophic effects when mined and brought to the surface, where it can directly interact with the planet's magnetic field.

The powerful plasma storms that accompany bohrium mining can be prevented through the use of PITRE's synoptic effector technology, also known as weather control towers.

Like many of the megastructures on Shear, the weather control towers are self-maintaining and self-repairing, allowing the massive, complex tower to run smoothly with a crew of only a few dozen.

Weather Control is highlighted by the weather control towers like the PITRE model SE-402. A big cave in the southeast side keeps Hank from using his annoying Orbital Barrage and gives Goliath a great location from which to pummel some Hunters. Extrasolar Research Institute has facilities on the two far sides, with each having a good location for the Monster to evolve. The Power Relay is located on the central structure. It is relatively open from all sides, with the surrounding equipment giving the Hunters nice perches to sit and wait.

NEW CALICO

Potential Map Effect with Hunter Win: Armored Turrets
Potential Map Effect with Monster Win: Armored Minions

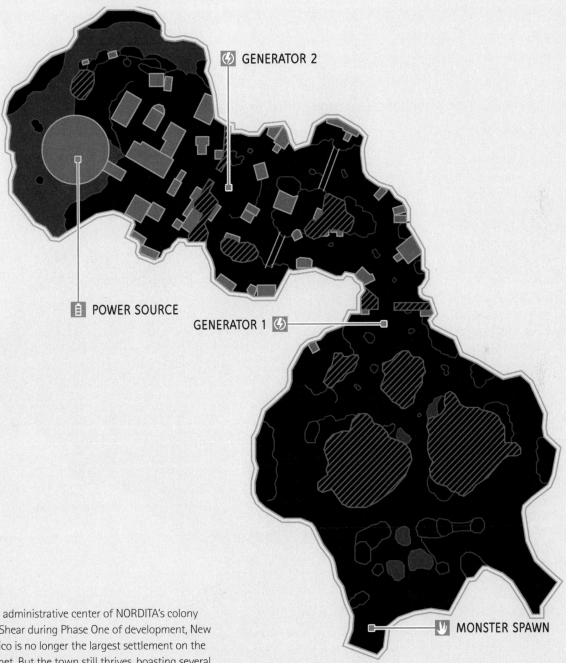

GENERATOR 2

POWER SOURCE

GENERATOR 1

MONSTER SPAWN

The administrative center of NORDITA's colony on Shear during Phase One of development, New Calico is no longer the largest settlement on the planet. But the town still thrives, boasting several bars, saloons, taverns, and churches. All the comforts of civilization!

Monsters start out in the far south side of the map, with three lanes of entry to the first generator. Protect them all with traps as the Monsters make their initial push, and put more out whenever the opportunity arises. After the first generator has been taken care of, the comforts of town living can be seen as the Monsters move through the right or left path. The power source sits on a circular platform not too far from the second generator. A bridge leading to the power source should be littered with traps whenever minions are incoming. If possible, avoid taking the fight to the ground level, as the minions continue to eat away at the objective above.

ICE BIOME

Creature Inhabitants: Basking Cephaladon, Blitzleopard, Crowbill Sloth, Glaciopod, Mammoth Bird, Obsidian Grub, Reaver, Spotter, Steamadon Trapjaw, Tyrant

AVIARY

Potential Map Effect with Hunter Win: Cargo Ship, Clear Skies, Scent Masking, Medbays

Potential Map Effect with Monster Win: Second Monster, Carnivorous Plants, Hostile Wildlife, Mutated Plants

Mapping recent speciation on Shear, the ERI installed a paleobotany observatory. This huge domed structure is built under a glacier that thaws out the millennia-old ice, allowing the seeds frozen below to bloom and blossom and grow again for the first time in millions of years.

This window into the ancient ecology of Shear attracts more than just scientists. Birds whose ancient migration patterns once carried them over this area have returned, giving the scientists an opportunity to study both the dangerous Batrays and the less threatening Phantoms.

The Aviary map is very unique, as it has two distinct environments. In the middle is the aviary, which is very green, with Phantoms flying high above. Through tight tunnels on the northeast and south, a frigid ice setting offers a whole new look, with a different selection of wildlife. With three distinct zones, the Hunters can eliminate each as they search for the Monster, but numerous tunnels allow the beast to slip in and out of each unnoticed. Split up the team if necessary, and keep an eye out for scattered birds, as that can drastically reduce the search area. The narrow tunnels are great locations for any traps. The Power Relay is smack dab in the middle of the aviary, wide open on all sides.

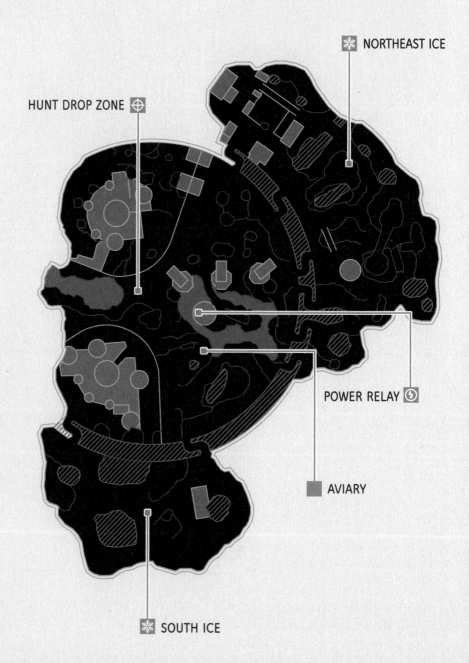

NORTHEAST ICE

HUNT DROP ZONE

POWER RELAY

AVIARY

SOUTH ICE

DISTILLERY

Potential Map Effect with Hunter Win: Birds, Medbays, Fair Weather

Potential Map Effect with Monster Win: Phantoms, Mutated Plants, Storms

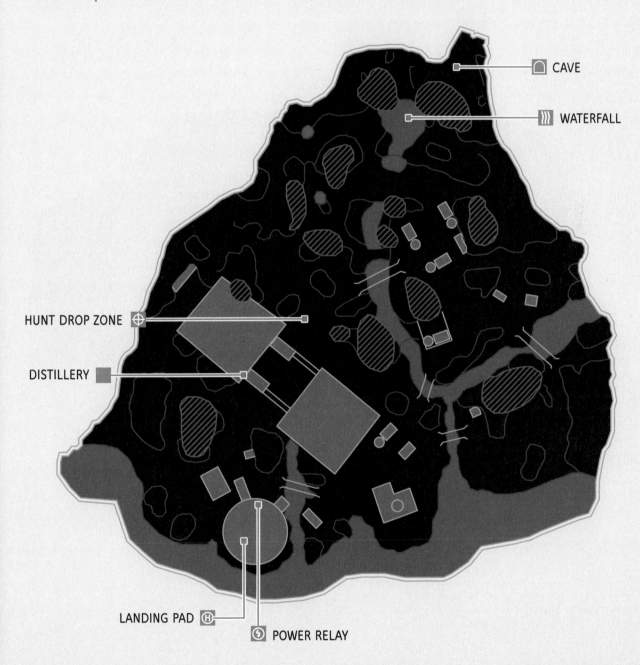

CAVE

WATERFALL

HUNT DROP ZONE

DISTILLERY

LANDING PAD

POWER RELAY

Entrepreneurial independent businessmen set up shop here in an abandoned chemical factory to make illegal...er, *authentic* simulated scent-masking chemicals. Because their product is many times cheaper than the stuff the Corps sells to the colonists, the colonists are not motivated to rat them out.

A huge distillery that stretches from the west to the south offers an indoor area that a Monster can easily get lost in. The far north is an all-natural environment, with a cave that offers some isolation. Plenty of water through the middle and south can confuse Hunters as the Monster moves between the zones. Mostly surrounded by water, the Power Relay is located on a landing pad in the far south. The area is fairly wide open, but there are plenty of equipment and structures to hide behind.

MEDLAB

Potential Map Effect with Hunter Win: Birds, Scent Masking, Clear Skies

Potential Map Effect with Monster Win: Phantoms, Hostile Wildlife, Carnivorous Plants

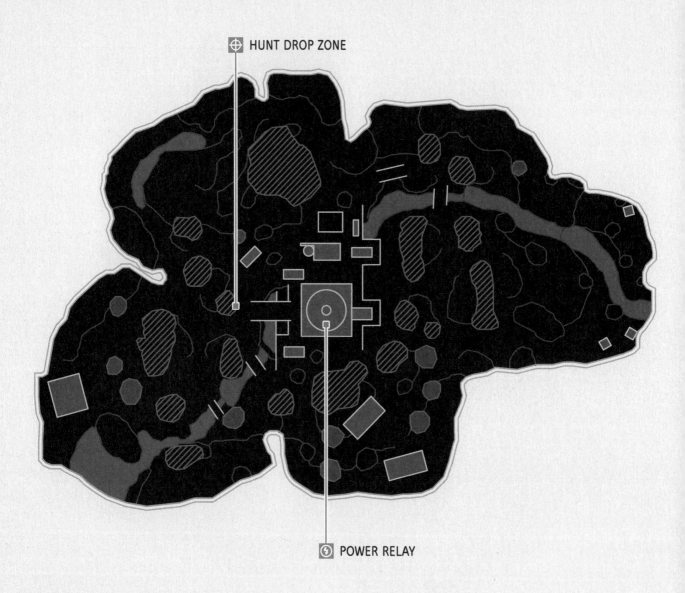

The refinery where SALVERON industries manufactures Generyst™, this facility is fitted with a special rocket capable of remote-deploying the company's patented remote-healing pods.

This is where Salveron's Medbays are produced, which is a possible map effect for the next map in Evacuation. The main facility sits in the middle of MedLab, with a mostly natural environment around the outsides. Watch out for the Steamadons on the west side, as they obscure your view with their steam. The Power Relay is located atop the central structure on a small circular platform. It is open from all sides, allowing Hunters to knock a Monster off from afar.

KING'S FORT

Potential Map Effect with Hunter Win: Armored Turrets

Potential Map Effect with Monster Win: Armored Minions

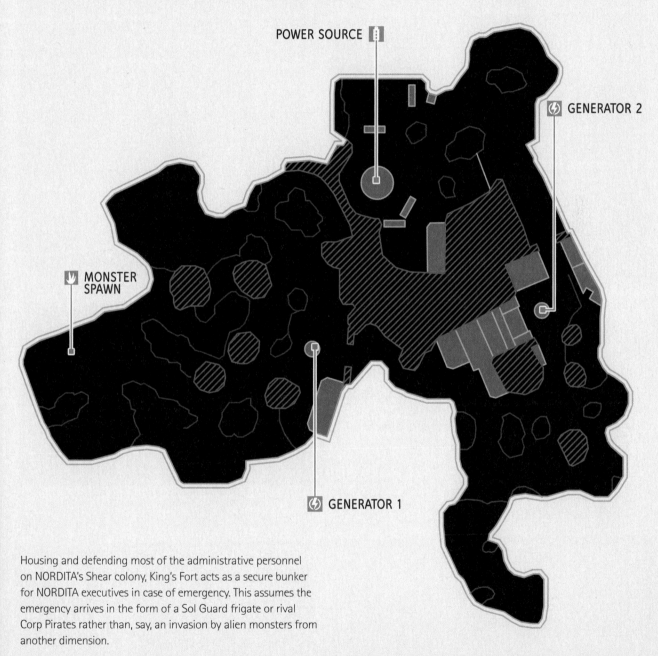

POWER SOURCE

GENERATOR 2

MONSTER SPAWN

GENERATOR 1

Housing and defending most of the administrative personnel on NORDITA's Shear colony, King's Fort acts as a secure bunker for NORDITA executives in case of emergency. This assumes the emergency arrives in the form of a Sol Guard frigate or rival Corp Pirates rather than, say, an invasion by alien monsters from another dimension.

King's Fort is the Defend map in the ice biome. Three lanes give the Monsters access to the first generator, which is fairly open to long-distance attacks. A tunnel that opens up once the first objective is destroyed contains a couple Glaciopods that should be removed quickly so the Monster does not receive too much free armor. Two paths lead to the second generator, though the left requires some climbing. To the far southeast, the Monster can spend some time feeding if necessary. Just beyond the second generator, the Monsters must pass through a narrow corridor before wrapping around to the power source in the middle of the map. It rests on the ground, with no upper or lower level. Traps should not only be placed along the incoming paths, but also around the temporary NORDITA facilities on the south side. Minions will often climb over them to avoid the main entry points.

MAP EFFECTS

☾ WRAITH TRAP

The Fusion Plant explosion caused severe radiation leakage, resulting in radioactive clouds in the area that are dangerous to Hunters.

DAY 4: RESCUE

The third and final group of Survivors is always the largest and most important group.

During a game of Evacuation, as the Hunters attempt to save the colonists of Shear from the rampaging Monsters, map effects are added to each round. If the Hunters win, a map effect from the Favors Hunters list below is added to the next round, and vice versa.

In Defend mode, map effects only appear during Evacuation. If the Hunters win the fourth day, the Armored Turrets map effect is added in the next game of Defend. Armored Minions is in effect if the Monsters win the fourth day.

All but the Defend mode map effects can be added to a Custom game in Multiplayer and Solo, but only one can be selected at a time.

SALVERON INDUSTRIES
DEFEND

FAVORS HUNTERS

The following map effects favor the Hunters, meaning that they gain an advantage in the game.

ARMORED TURRETS

Maps: Colonial Water & Power, King's Fort, New Calico, Salveron Industries

Only found in Defend mode, this map effect adds armor to the turrets, making them tougher for the Monster and its minions to destroy. This map effect only happens in the final round of Evacuation if the Hunters won the previous game.

ATTACK DRONES

Maps: The Dam, Wraith Trap

Attack drones released by EbonStar patrol the map to spot and attack the Monster. These floating turrets pursue the Monster, making pests of themselves. They are easily destroyed, but not until they've dealt a little damage and wasted the Monster's time.

BIRDS

Maps: Distillery, MedLab, Refueling Tower, Weather Control

More birds make it easier to find the Monster. Scattered birds are always a huge help for the Hunters, as they reveal the Monster's location. Adding more of these guys around the map allows the team to pinpoint the beast's position with a little more ease.

CARGO SHIP

Maps: Aviary, Fusion Plant, Rendering Plant, Weather Control, Wraith Trap

A cargo ship patrols the map and helps the Hunters spot the Monster. You can see the cargo ship patrolling the skies above, and every now and then, it tags the Monster. As you search the wilderness, look out for the red icon to appear. Obviously, tracking the Monster becomes less of a priority, so take this into account when selecting a character.

CLEAR SKIES

Maps: Aviary, Fusion Plant, MedLab, Refueling Plant

Clear skies force predators into hiding and make Monsters easier to see. The big thing here is that nocturnal predators do not bother the Hunters. This includes some of the tougher wildlife the team must deal with.

COLONISTS

Maps: Barracks, Refueling Tower, The Dam, Wraith Trap

Two colonists join the Hunters as they fight the Monster. These people are not nearly as powerful as the EbonStar soldier who joins the team with the EbonStar Ally map effect. These guys can be protected, but they aren't worth going too much out of the way for. Still, they are a nice distraction for the Monster.

EBONSTAR ALLY

Maps: Orbital Drill, Rendering Plant, The Dam

After the Hunters help defend the Barracks, an EbonStar ally joins the team to fight the Monsters. This soldier is quite a bit tougher than the colonists.

FAIR WEATHER

Maps: Armory, Barracks, Distillery, Orbital Drill, Rendering Plant, The Dam, Weather Control, Wraith Trap

Experience natural lighting, with no adverse weather effects.

FORCEFIELD

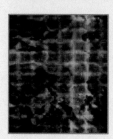

Maps: Armory, Barracks, Rendering Plant, Wraith Trap

Forcefield walls limit the available space in which the Monster can run and hide. A tall blue wall runs across the map, drastically reducing its size. Access the in-game map to see exactly where it is positioned. With less space for the Monster to hide in, the Hunters have an easier time finding it.

MEDBAYS

Maps: Aviary, Distillery, Weather Control

Medbays, deployed by the MedLab, allow Hunters to heal and remove strikes. Open the in-game map for the locations of each Medbay, which the plus icons indicate. Step into the bay, and let it heal you. While you're standing inside, strikes are also removed.

SCENT MASKING

Maps: Aviary, MedLab

Scent masking inhibits the Monster's ability to smell. This is a great map effect for the Hunters, since it allows them to sneak up on their target much more easily.

SENTRY GUNS

Maps: Refueling Tower, Weather Control, Wraith Trap

Sentry guns, scattered around the map, defend areas against Monster attacks. These turrets are marked on the map. Although the Monster can destroy them, use these to the team's advantage by flushing the enemy toward them.

SPACE LASER

Maps: Barracks, Rendering Plant

A laser from space periodically fires at the Monster, severely damaging it. When playing as the Monster, watch for incoming laser strikes, and dodge out of the way to avoid taking damage.

TELEPORT GATES

Maps: Armory, Fusion Plant, Refueling Tower, Rendering Plant, The Dam

Teleport Gates allow Hunters to teleport to a central location. Take a peek at the map to see where the gates are placed. Stepping inside one sends the Hunter to a pad located in the middle of the map. All gates lead to the same spot.

With good planning and timing, you can trap the Monster around one of the distant Teleport Gates and slip out through the device. In Nest or Rescue mode, the team can continue taking care of the objectives without fear of the Monster until the Mobile Arena comes down.

FAVORS MONSTERS

The following map effects favor the Monsters, meaning that they gain an advantage in the game.

ARMORED MINIONS

Maps: Colonial Water & Power, King's Fort, New Calico, Salveron Industries

Only found in Defend mode, this map effect gives the Monster minions extra armor, making them tougher for the Hunters to take down. This map effect only happens in the final round of Evacuation if the Monsters won the previous game.

CANYON STRIDERS

Maps: Barracks, Orbital Drill, Refueling Tower, The Dam, Wraith Trap

Additional Canyon Striders provide more food for the Monster. These guys are extremely easy to kill and grant two bars of energy, making the Monster's feeding much more efficient.

CARNIVOROUS PLANTS

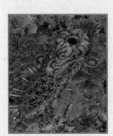

Maps: Aviary, MedLab, Refueling Tower

Additional carnivorous plants make environments more dangerous for Hunters. Watch your step when playing as a Hunter. These plants are a nuisance for the entire team, so take them out whenever you see them lying in wait.

EBONSTAR CORPSES

Maps: Orbital Drill, Rendering Plant, The Dam

EbonStar corpses provide more food for the Monster. Slain EbonStar workers lie around the environment, which make for easy feeding for the Monster.

EMP

Maps: The Dam, Wraith Trap

EMP blasts temporarily cancel and shut down Hunter abilities. Watch out for a yellowish circle to appear on the ground. This indicates an incoming EMP strike. If caught inside the blast, a Hunter loses his or her class ability. A blue electric aura signifies that the Hunter has been hit. The class ability icon in the lower-right corner of the HUD is obscured.

FALLING SATELLITE

Maps: Barracks, Rendering Plant

A satellite is destroyed, sending pieces to the ground. Hunters who are caught underneath one are damaged. Watch out for incoming parts, and dodge to the side to avoid impact.

HOSTILE WILDLIFE

Maps: Aviary, MedLab

Chemicals from the destroyed ship contaminated the waterways, causing local wildlife to act dangerous and hostile to Hunters. If the wildlife on Shear weren't tough enough to avoid already, now they all attack the Hunters with even more aggression. Have your weapon prepared as you move through the environment.

MAN-EATING EELS

Maps: Armory, Barracks, Rendering Plant, Wraith Trap

Flooded areas with man-eating eels make environments more dangerous for Hunters. Steer clear of water, as these eels quickly eat away at a Hunter's health. Monsters are unaffected by them, so use that to your advantage.

MUTATED PLANTS

Maps: Aviary, Distillery, Weather Control

Mutated plants allow the Monster to restore health when eating them. Carnivorous plants not only devour Hunters who pass by, but they now provide Monsters with a health boost. It is even more important now that Hunters destroy these plants whenever they find one.

PHANTOMS

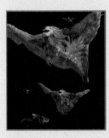

Maps: Distillery, MedLab, Refueling Tower, Weather Control

Phantoms create more hostile encounters for the Hunters. Watch out for the stingray-looking flying creatures, which swoop down and deal some decent damage to the Hunters. When nearing one, shoot it out of the sky.

RADIOACTIVE CLOUDS

Maps: Refueling Tower, Weather Control, Wraith Trap

Radioactive clouds damage Hunters in their vicinity. When playing as the Hunters, watch out for green, gaseous clouds around the environment, which eat away at a character's health as they walk through. There is no effect on the Monster, so use it to your advantage.

SECOND MONSTER

Maps: Aviary, Fusion Plant, Rendering Plant, Weather Control, Wraith Trap

A Monster minion follows the Monster and attacks Hunters. If you have played a game of Defend or Nest, you know what it is like to go up against the Monster and a minion. This enemy heads straight for the team, so be ready.

STORMS

Maps: Armory, Barracks, Distillery, Orbital Drill, Rendering Plant, The Dam, Weather Control, Wraith Trap

The weather becomes stormy with this map effect. The type of storms depends on the chosen map (for example, select an ice map, and you get snow). This map effect does tend to obscure vision a bit, making it a little tougher to spot the enemy.

TELEPORT RIFTS

Maps: Armory, Fusion Plant, Refueling Tower, Rendering Plant, The Dam

Teleport Rifts allow the Monster to teleport to different locations. Check out the map to find the location of the rift. Step inside, and be sent to a different location—either near or far. This is great for getting far away from the Hunters at the start of the round.

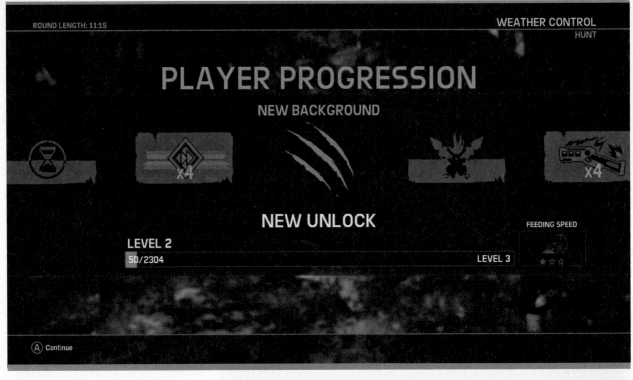

XP earned from Accolades and Awards go toward a player's progression in the game. Once enough XP is collected, the player's level is increased by one. Each increase in level gives the player another Perk, up to the maximum level of 40.

You can improve each of the Hunter's non-class specific loadout items and all of the Monster abilities by completing specific requirements. Progress toward each one is displayed after each game as the Character Mastery.

PLAYER PROGRESSION

LEVEL	XP REQUIRED	PERK UNLOCKED
2	1800	Quick Switch 1
3	4104	Feeding Speed 1
4	6592	Jet Pack Recharge 1
5	9279	Damage Bonus 1
6	12181	Smell Range 1
7	15315	Reload Speed 1
8	18700	Damage Resistance 1
9	22356	Cooldown Reduction 1
10	26304	Capacity Increase 1
11	30568	Movement Speed 1
12	35173	Stamina Increase 1
13	40147	Health Regeneration 1
14	45519	Armor Regeneration 1
15	51321	Quick Switch 2
16	57587	Feeding Speed 2
17	64354	Jet Pack Recharge 2
18	71662	Damage Bonus 2
19	79555	Smell Range 2
20	88079	Reload Speed 2
21	97285	Damage Resistance 2

LEVEL	XP REQUIRED	PERK UNLOCKED
22	107228	Cooldown Reduction 2
23	117966	Capacity Increase 2
24	129563	Movement Speed 2
25	142088	Stamina Increase 2
26	155615	Health Regeneration 2
27	170224	Armor Regeneration 2
28	186002	Quick Switch 3
29	203042	Feeding Speed 3
30	221445	Jet Pack Recharge 3
31	241321	Damage Bonus 3
32	262787	Smell Range 3
33	285970	Reload Speed 3
34	311008	Damage Resistance 3
35	338049	Cooldown Reduction 3
36	367253	Capacity Increase 3
37	398793	Movement Speed 3
38	432856	Stamina Increase 3
39	469644	Health Regeneration 3
40	509376	Armor Regeneration 3

CHARACTER MASTERY

Use the following lists of Character Mastery requirements as a quick reference to power up all Hunters and Monsters. The tables include the type of Buff earned and tier unlocks.

HUNTERS

ABE'S CHARACTER MASTERY

	TIER 1 REQUIREMENTS		TIER 2 REQUIREMENTS		TIER 3 REQUIREMENTS	
	REQUIREMENT	BUFF	REQUIREMENT	BUFF	REQUIREMENT	BUFF
CUSTOM SHOTGUN	Do 14,000 damage	Damage increase	Do 29,000 damage to the Monster	Damage increase	Do 12,000 headshot damage to the Monster	Damage increase
STASIS GRENADES	Slow the Monster 130 times	Radius increase	Slow the Monster for 800 seconds	Radius increase	Keep the Monster slowed for 3 seconds 160 times	Radius increase
TRACKING DART PISTOL	Dart the Monster 15 different times	Duration increase	Dart the Monster for 3,000 seconds	Duration increase	Dart the Monster from 30 meters 60 times	Duration increase
UNLOCKED	Badge Foreground		Badge Foreground		Abe Elite Skin, Badge Foreground	

BUCKET'S CHARACTER MASTERY

	TIER 1 REQUIREMENTS		TIER 2 REQUIREMENTS		TIER 3 REQUIREMENTS	
	REQUIREMENT	BUFF	REQUIREMENT	BUFF	REQUIREMENT	BUFF
GUIDED MISSILE LAUNCHER	Do 9,000 damage	Damage increase	Do 25,000 damage to the Monster	Damage increase	Get 390 direct hits to the Monster	Damage increase
SENTRY GUNS	Do 15,000 damage	Range increase	Do 20,000 damage to the Monster	Range increase	Have 3 Sentry Guns firing at once 30 times	Range increase
UAV	Cover 3,000 meters in Hunt or Rescue	Tracker duration increase	Find the Monster 30 times in Hunt or Rescue	Tracker duration increase	Find 25 Stage 1 Monsters in Hunt or Rescue	Tracker duration increase
UNLOCKED	Cabot		Badge Foreground		Bucket Elite Skin, Badge Foreground	

CABOT'S CHARACTER MASTERY

	TIER 1 REQUIREMENTS		TIER 2 REQUIREMENTS		TIER 3 REQUIREMENTS	
	REQUIREMENT	BUFF	REQUIREMENT	BUFF	REQUIREMENT	BUFF
RAIL CANNON	Do 12,000 damage	Damage increase	Do 34,000 damage to the Monster	Damage increase	Do 26,000 headshot damage to the Monster	Damage increase
DAMAGE AMPLIFIER	Amplify 9,000 damage	Energy pool increase	Amplify 24,000 damage to the Monster	Energy pool increase	Amplify 54 damage in a single use 250 times	Energy pool increase
DUST TAGGING	Reveal 70 creatures	Radius increase	Reveal the Monster 60 times	Radius increase	Reveal the Stage 1 Monster 25 times	Radius increase
UNLOCKED	Badge Foreground		Badge Foreground		Cabot Elite Skin, Badge Foreground	

CAIRA'S CHARACTER MASTERY

	TIER 1 REQUIREMENTS		TIER 2 REQUIREMENTS		TIER 3 REQUIREMENTS	
	REQUIREMENT	BUFF	REQUIREMENT	BUFF	REQUIREMENT	BUFF
NAPALM GRENADE LAUNCHER	Do 3,300 damage	Range increase	Do 4,000 damage to the Monster	Range increase	Get 170 direct hits on the Monster	Range increase
HEALING GRENADE LAUNCHER	Heal 32,000 damage	Range increase on area of effect burst	Revive 15 teammates	Range increase on area of effect burst	Heal multiple teammates 900 times	Range increase on area of effect burst
ACCELERATION FIELD	Cover 2,200 meters using Acceleration Field	Duration increase	Give teammates a boost 74 times	Duration increase	Cover 50 meters with teammates in a single match 100 times	Duration increase
UNLOCKED	Badge Foreground		Badge Foreground		Caira Elite Skin, Badge Foreground	

GRIFFIN'S CHARACTER MASTERY

	TIER 1 REQUIREMENTS		TIER 2 REQUIREMENTS		TIER 3 REQUIREMENTS	
	REQUIREMENT	BUFF	REQUIREMENT	BUFF	REQUIREMENT	BUFF
GAUSS SMG	Do 10,000 damage	Damage increase	Do 14,000 damage to Monsters	Damage increase	Do 8,000 headshot damage to Monster	Damage increase
HARPOON GUN	Hold Monster for one second 14 times	Range increase	Hold Monster for 115 seconds	Range increase	Harpoon the Monster in mid-air 80 times	Range increase
SOUND SPIKES	Plant 15 spikes at least 50 meters apart	Range increase	Reveal Monster 120 times	Range increase	Reveal a Stage 1 Monster 20 times in Hunt mode	Range increase
UNLOCKED	Abe		Badge Foreground		Griffin Elite Skin, Badge Foreground	

HANK'S CHARACTER MASTERY

	TIER 1 REQUIREMENTS		TIER 2 REQUIREMENTS		TIER 3 REQUIREMENTS	
	REQUIREMENT	BUFF	REQUIREMENT	BUFF	REQUIREMENT	BUFF
LASER CUTTER	Do 6,000 damage	Damage increase	Do 20,000 damage to Monsters	Damage increase	Do 5,000 headshot damage	Damage increase
SHIELD PROJECTOR	Shield teammates from damage 20 times	Capacity increase	Shield 35,000 damage	Capacity increase	Prevent 30 teammates from beccoming incapped	Capacity increase
ORBITAL BARRAGE	Do 6,600 damage	Damage increase	Do 24,000 damage to the Monster	Damage increase	Damage the Monster 30 times from a distance greater than 50 meters	Damage increase
UNLOCKED	Bucket		Badge Foreground		Hank Elite Skin, Badge Foreground	

HYDE'S CHARACTER MASTERY

	TIER 1 REQUIREMENTS		TIER 2 REQUIREMENTS		TIER 3 REQUIREMENTS	
	REQUIREMENT	BUFF	REQUIREMENT	BUFF	REQUIREMENT	BUFF
FLAMETHROWER	Do 20,000 damage	Range increase	Do 50,000 damage to the Monster	Range increase	Do 50,000 residual burn damage	Range increase
MINIGUN	Do 4,500 damage	Accuracy increase	Do 15,000 damage to the Monster	Accuracy increase	Do 3,000 headshot damage to the Monster	Accuracy increase
TOXIC GRENADES	Do 11,000 damage	Damage increase	Do 32,000 damage to the Monster	Damage increase	Do 100 damage to Monster with a single Toxic Grenade 250 times	Damage increase
UNLOCKED	Parnell		Badge Foreground		Hyde Elite Skin, Badge Foreground	

LAZARUS' CHARACTER MASTERY

	TIER 1 REQUIREMENTS		TIER 2 REQUIREMENTS		TIER 3 REQUIREMENTS	
	REQUIREMENT	BUFF	REQUIREMENT	BUFF	REQUIREMENT	BUFF
SILENCED SNIPER RIFLE	Place 200 targets on the Monster	Damage increase	Teammates must do 270 damage by hitting Lazarus's targets on the Monster	Damage increase	Place 150 headshot targets on the Monster	Damage increase
LAZARUS DEVICE	Use the Lazarus Device 4 times	Recharge rate increase	Use the Lazarus Device 28 times on teammates	Recharge rate increase	Use the Lazarus Device on 3 teammates in single match 25 times	Recharge rate increase
PERSONAL CLOAK	Cloak revive 7 creatures with the Lazarus Device	Duration increase	Cloak revive 22 teammates with the Lazarus Device	Duration increase	Cloak revive 3 teammates in a single match 25 times with the Lazarus Device	Duration increase
UNLOCKED	Caira		Badge Foreground		Lazarus Elite Skin, Badge Foreground	

MAGGIE'S CHARACTER MASTERY

	TIER 1 REQUIREMENTS		TIER 2 REQUIREMENTS		TIER 3 REQUIREMENTS	
	REQUIREMENT	BUFF	REQUIREMENT	BUFF	REQUIREMENT	BUFF
MACHINE PISTOL	Do 8,000 damage	Damage increase	Do 21,000 damage to the Monster	Damage increase	Do 12,000 headshot damage to the Monster	Damage increase
HARPOON TRAPS	Harpoon the Monster 40 times	Range increase	Harpoon the Monster at least 8 times in 14 different matches	Range increase	Catch Monster in two traps 50 times	Range increase
PET TRAPJAW	Follow Daisy for 2,600 meters	Health increase for Daisy	Revive 10 teammates with Daisy	Health increase for Daisy	Revive 2 teammates in a single match 30 times with Daisy	Health increase for Daisy
UNLOCKED	Griffin		Badge Foreground		Maggie Elite Skin, Badge Foreground	

MARKOV'S CHARACTER MASTERY

	TIER 1 REQUIREMENTS		TIER 2 REQUIREMENTS		TIER 3 REQUIREMENTS	
	REQUIREMENT	BUFF	REQUIREMENT	BUFF	REQUIREMENT	BUFF
LIGHTNING GUN	Do 24,000 damage	Range increase	Do 84,000 damage to the Monster	Range increase	Do 23,000 chained damage	Range increase
ASSAULT RIFLE	Do 4,000 damage	Accuracy increase	Do 18,000 damage to the Monster	Accuracy increase	Do 10,000 headshot damage to the Monster	Accuracy increase
ARC MINES	Do 8,000 damage	Damage increase	Do 50,000 damage to the Monster	Damage increase	Damage the Monster with 2 Arc Mines without taking damage 60 times	Damage increase
UNLOCKED	Hyde		Badge Foreground		Markov Elite Skin, Badge Foreground	

PARNELL'S CHARACTER MASTERY

	TIER 1 REQUIREMENTS		TIER 2 REQUIREMENTS		TIER 3 REQUIREMENTS	
	REQUIREMENT	BUFF	REQUIREMENT	BUFF	REQUIREMENT	BUFF
COMBAT SHOTGUN	Do 19,000 damage	Damage increase	Do 75,000 damage to the Monster	Damage increase	Do 31,000 headshot damage to the Monster	Damage increase
MULTIFIRE ROCKET LAUNCHER	Do 32,000 damage	Damage increase	Do 64,000 damage to the Monster	Damage increase	Get 900 direct hits to the Monster	Damage increase
SUPER SOLDIER	Do 17,000 damage using Super Soldier	Duration increase	Do 58,000 damage to the Monster using Super Soldier	Duration increase	Do 20,000 headshot damage using Super Soldier	Duration increase
UNLOCKED	Badge Foreground		Badge Foreground		Parnell Elite Skin, Badge Foreground	

VAL'S CHARACTER MASTERY

	TIER 1 REQUIREMENTS		TIER 2 REQUIREMENTS		TIER 3 REQUIREMENTS	
	REQUIREMENT	BUFF	REQUIREMENT	BUFF	REQUIREMENT	BUFF
ARMOR-PIERCING SNIPER RIFLE	Place 12 targets on the Monster	Damage increase	Enable teammates to deal 12,000 bonus damage to the Monster	Damage increase	Place 30 headshot targets on the Monster	Damage increase
MEDGUN	Heal 16,000 damage	Capacity increase	Revive 12 teammates with MedGun	Capacity increase	Heal 40 teammates before they're incapped	Capacity increase
TRANQUILIZER GUN	Tranquilize the Monster 14 different times	Duration increase	Tranquilize the Monster for 400 seconds	Duration increase	Tranquilize the Monster from 100 meters away or more 60 times	Duration increase
UNLOCKED	Lazarus		Badge Foreground		Val Elite Skin, Badge Foreground	

MONSTERS

GOLIATH'S CHARACTER MASTERY

	STAGE 1		STAGE 2		STAGE 3	
	REQUIREMENT	BUFF	REQUIREMENT	BUFF	REQUIREMENT	BUFF
ROCK THROW	Do 12,000 damage	Damage increase	Damage multiple targets 35 times	Damage increase	Hit mid-air Hunters 150 times	Damage increase
LEAP SMASH	Do 12,000 damage	Range increase	Damage multiple targets 50 times	Range increase	Hit Hunters from 20 meters 50 times	Range increase
FIRE BREATH	Do 12,000 damage	Range increase	Damage multiple targets 175 times	Range increase	Do 80,000 damage to mid-air Hunters	Range increase
CHARGE	Do 8,000 damage	Duration increase	Damage multiple targets 50 times	Duration increase	Damage Multiple Hunters 100 times	Duration increase
UNLOCKED	Kraken		Badge Foreground		Goliath Elite Skin, Badge Foreground	

KRAKEN'S CHARACTER MASTERY

	STAGE 1		STAGE 2		STAGE 3	
	REQUIREMENT	BUFF	REQUIREMENT	BUFF	REQUIREMENT	BUFF
LIGHTNING STRIKE	Do 20,000 damage	Damage increase	Damage multiple targets 50 times	Damage increase	Do damage to multiple Hunters 80 times	Damage increase
BANSHEE MINES	Do 27,000 damage	Damage increase	Do 80,000 damage to Hunters	Damage increase	Do damage to multiple Hunters 60 times	Damage increase
AFTERSHOCK	Do 15,000 damage	Damage increase	Damage multiple targets 40 times	Damage increase	Damage multiple Hunters 60 times	Damage increase
VORTEX	Do 30,000 damage	Blast speed increase	Do damage to multiple Hunters 80 times	Blast speed increase	Knock back 360 mid-air Hunters	Blast speed increase
UNLOCKED	Wraith		Badge Foreground		Kraken Elite Skin, Badge Foreground	

WRAITH'S CHARACTER MASTERY

	STAGE 1		STAGE 2		STAGE 3	
	REQUIREMENT	BONUS	REQUIREMENT	BONUS	REQUIREMENT	BONUS
WARP BLAST	Do 30,000 damage	Damage increase	Damage multiple targets 90 times	Damage increase	Damage multiple Hunters 15 times	Damage increase
ABDUCTION	Abduct 35 targets	Range increase	Abduct 45 mid-air Hunters	Range increase	Abduct Hunters from team 225 times	Range increase
DECOY	Do 12,500 damage with Decoy	Damage increase	Do 32,000 damage to Hunters with Decoy	Damage increase	Stealth pounce 30 times while invisible	Damage increase
SUPERNOVA	Do 34,500 damage while Supernova is active	Duration increase	Do 125,000 damage to Hunters while Supernova is active	Duration increase	Damage using abilities 70 times while Supernova is active	Duration increase
UNLOCKED	Badge Foreground		Badge Foreground		Wraith Elite Skin, Badge Foreground	

As you complete certain objectives throughout a match, you earn Medals and Awards. After each game, XP is given to the players for each one received. You can check current progress toward the five tiers of each Accolade in your Profile.

AWARDS

ICON	AVAILABLE TO	AWARD	MODE	REQUIREMENT	XP EARNED
	HUNTER	Cryptozoologist	Any	Kill 10 wildlife.	50
	HUNTER	Liberator	Any	Rescue a grappled Hunter.	100
	HUNTER	Egg Beater	Nest	Deal 300 damage to eggs.	50
	HUNTER	Minion Masher	Any with a minion	Deal 4,000 damage to minions.	50
	HUNTER	Helping Hand	Rescue	Pick up two survivors.	50
	HUNTER	Evacuation Award	Evacuation	Complete an Evacuation campaign.	Varies
	MONSTER	Evacuation Award	Evacuation	Complete an Evacuation campaign.	Varies
	HUNTER—ASSAULT	Self-Defense	Any	Absorb 800 damage with the Personal Shield.	50
	HUNTER—MARKOV	Lighten Up	Any	Dish out 2,000 damage to the Monster with the Lightning Gun.	50

ICON	AVAILABLE TO	AWARD	MODE	REQUIREMENT	XP EARNED
	HUNTER—MARKOV	Bullet Time	Any	Deal 2,000 damage to the Monster with the Assault Rifle.	150
	HUNTER—MARKOV	Tesla Coiled	Any	Deal 1,000 damage to the Monster with the Arc Mine.	75
	HUNTER—HYDE	Flame Broiled	Any	Deal 2,000 damage to the Monster with the Flamethrower.	50
	HUNTER—HYDE	RPS Beast	Any	Deal 2,000 damage to the Monster with the Minigun.	50
	HUNTER—HYDE	Noxious	Any	Deal 1,000 damage with the Toxic Grenade.	50
	HUNTER—PARNELL	Street Sweeper	Any	Deal 2,000 damage to the Monster with the Combat Shotgun.	50
	HUNTER—PARNELL	Going Nuclear	Any	Deal 2,000 damage to the Monster with the Multifire Rocket Launcher.	50
	HUNTER—PARNELL	Overpowered	Any	Deal 3,500 damage while using Super Soldier.	50
	HUNTER—TRAPPER	Thunderdome!	Any	Absorb 800 damage with the Personal Shield.	100
	HUNTER—MAGGIE	Hand Cannon	Any	Deal 2,000 damage to the Monster with the Machine Pistol.	50
	HUNTER—MAGGIE	Tripped Up	Any	Harpoon the Monster three times with the Harpoon Traps.	50
	HUNTER—MAGGIE	Good Girl	Any	Follow Daisy for 500 meters.	50
	HUNTER—GRIFFIN	Close Quarters	Any	Deal 2,000 damage to the Monster with the Gauss SMG.	50
	HUNTER—GRIFFIN	Tug O' War	Any	Harpoon the Monster three times with the Harpoon Gun. It must hold the Monster.	50
	HUNTER—GRIFFIN	Uncovered	Any	Reveal the Monster two times with Sound Spikes.	50
	HUNTER—ABE	Boomstick	Any	Deal 2,000 damage to the Monster with the Custom Shotgun.	50
	HUNTER—ABE	Slow and Steady	Any	Slow the monster three times with Abe's Stasis Grenades.	50
	HUNTER—ABE	Stick and Blink	Any	Mark the Monster with Abe's Tracking Dart twice.	50
	HUNTER—MEDIC	Medic!	Any	Heal two Hunters at once with the Healing Burst.	100

ICON	AVAILABLE TO	AWARD	MODE	REQUIREMENT	XP EARNED
	HUNTER—VAL	Sure Shot	Any	Mark the Monster two times with the Armor-Piercing Sniper Rifle.	100
	HUNTER—VAL	Quick Fix	Any	Heal the Hunters for 1,000 health with the Medgun.	50
	HUNTER—VAL	Sleepy Time	Any	Shoot the Monster two times with the Tranquilizer Gun.	50
	HUNTER—LAZARUS	Silent and Deadly	Any	Mark the Monster four times with the Silenced Sniper Rifle.	50
	HUNTER—LAZARUS	Revivified	Any	Revivify two Hunters with the Lazarus Device.	100
	HUNTER—LAZARUS	Friendly Ghost	Any	Revive or revivify multiple Hunters while using Personal Cloak.	50
	HUNTER—CAIRA	Scorched	Any	Deal 2,000 damage to the Monster with the Napalm Grenade Launcher.	50
	HUNTER—CAIRA	Healthsplosion	Any	Heal a teammate for 1,000 HP with the Healing Grenade Launcher.	50
	HUNTER—CAIRA	Speedy	Any	Over 500 meters with Adrenaline Field.	50
	HUNTER—SUPPORT	Now You See Me	Any	Cloak two Hunters at once with the Cloaking Field.	100
	HUNTER—HANK	Laser Show	Any	Deal 2,000 damage to the Monster with the Laser Cutter.	50
	HUNTER—HANK	Protector	Any	Shield the Hunters for 2,000 damage with the Shield Projector.	50
	HUNTER—HANK	Duck and Cover	Any	Deal 2,000 damage to the Monster with Orbital Barrage.	50
	HUNTER—BUCKET	Steady Hand	Any	Deal 2,000 damage to the Monster with the Guided Missile Launcher.	50
	HUNTER—BUCKET	Set and Forget	Any	Deal 2,000 damage to the Monster with the Sentry Guns.	50
	HUNTER—BUCKET	Hide and Seek	Any	Reveal the Monster two times with the UAV.	100
	HUNTER—CABOT	Hypersonic	Any	Deal 2,000 damage to the Monster with the Rail Cannon.	50
	HUNTER—CABOT	Amped Up	Any	Provide 1,000 damage amplification.	50
	HUNTER—CABOT	Tag and Bag	Any	Reveal the Monster two times with Dust Tagging.	100

ICON	AVAILABLE TO	AWARD	MODE	REQUIREMENT	XP EARNED
	MONSTER	Hatchery	Nest	Hatch two eggs.	50
	MONSTER	Survivor Slayer	Rescue	Kill two survivors.	50
	MONSTER	Turret Tamer	Defend	Destroy three turrets.	50
	MONSTER	Hit the Lights	Defend	Destroy one generator.	50
	MONSTER	DNR	Any	Incapacitate two Hunters.	50
	MONSTER	Bulletproof	Any	Evolve without losing any health.	100
	MONSTER	It's Evolution	Any	Evolve to Stage 3.	150
	MONSTER—GOLIATH	Barbaric	Any	Deal 2,000 damage to Hunters with Rock Throw.	50
	MONSTER—GOLIATH	Air Strike	Any	Deal 2,000 damage to Hunters with Leap Smash.	50
	MONSTER—GOLIATH	Fire Starter	Any	Deal 2,000 damage to Hunters with Fire Breath.	50
	MONSTER—GOLIATH	Charger	Any	Deal 2,000 damage to Hunters with Charge attack.	50
	MONSTER—KRAKEN	Grounder	Any	Deal 2,000 damage to Hunters with Lightning Strike.	50
	MONSTER—KRAKEN	Screeching Halt	Any	Hit three Hunters with Banshee Mines.	50
	MONSTER—KRAKEN	Daisy Chained	Any	Deal 1,000 damage to Hunters with Aftershock.	50
	MONSTER—KRAKEN	Elementalist	Any	Knock down three Hunters with Vortex.	50
	MONSTER—WRAITH	Kamikaze	Any	Deal 1,000 damage to Hunters with Warp Blast.	50
	MONSTER—WRAITH	Sneak Attack	Any	Abduct two Hunters.	50
	MONSTER—WRAITH	Body Double	Any	Decoy delivers 500 damage to Hunters.	50
	MONSTER—WRAITH	Voided	Any	Deal 1,000 damage to Hunters while in Supernova.	50

ACCOLADES: GENERAL MEDALS

ACCOLADE	REQUIREMENT	TIER 1 #/XP	TIER 2 #/XP	TIER 3 #/XP	TIER 4 #/XP	TIER 5 #/XP
ACID ACE	Win # matches on acid maps.	10/100	25/200	50/300	100/400	250/500
AND THE WINNER IS...	Get # Awards.	25/300	100/500	250/700	1000/900	2500/1100
BIG PERK HUNTER	Get # elite wildlife Perks.	10/100	25/200	50/300	100/400	250/500
BLITZKRIEGED	Kill # Blitzleopards.	25/100	100/300	250/500	500/700	1000/900
CLEVER GIRL	Kill # Canyon Striders.	25/100	100/300	250/500	500/700	1000/900
COLD KILLER	Win # matches on ice maps.	10/100	25/200	50/300	100/400	250/500
DESERT DESTROYER	Win # matches on desert maps.	10/100	25/200	50/300	100/400	250/500
ELECTRIFIED	Kill # Mammoth Birds.	25/100	100/300	250/500	500/700	1000/900
FOREST FIGHTER	Win # matches on forest maps.	10/100	25/200	50/300	100/400	250/500
GREEN MACHINE	Kill # carnivorous plants.	25/100	100/300	250/500	500/700	1000/900
HARD SHELLED	Kill # Dune Beetles.	25/100	100/300	250/500	500/700	1000/900
HARMLESS	Kill # Marsh Striders.	25/100	100/300	250/500	500/700	1000/900
HUNTER GOLD	Complete the Hunter tutorial under #.	15:00/50	8:00/100	6:00/150	N/A	N/A
IRONED OUT	Kill # Steamadons.	25/100	100/300	250/500	500/700	1000/900
IT'S A TRAPJAW!	Kill # Trapjaws.	25/100	100/300	250/500	500/700	1000/900
MAP MAVEN	Win # matches on any map.	10/100	25/300	50/500	100/700	250/900

ACCOLADE	REQUIREMENT	TIER 1 #/XP	TIER 2 #/XP	TIER 3 #/XP	TIER 4 #/XP	TIER 5 #/XP
MARATHONER	Run # meters.	1000/100	5000/200	10000/300	20000/400	42195/500
MIDDAY SNACK	Kill # Obsidian Grubs.	25/100	100/300	250/500	500/700	1000/900
MONSTER GOLD	Complete the Monster tutorial under #.	15:00/50	8:00/100	6:00/150	N/A	N/A
OH, THE HUMANITY!	Kill # wildlife.	25/500	100/1000	250/1500	500/2000	1000/2500
ONE LAYER AT A TIME	Kill # Armadons.	25/100	100/300	250/500	500/700	1000/900
PACKS A PUNCH	Kill # Crowbill Sloths.	25/100	100/300	250/500	500/700	1000/900
PHANTOM ZONED	Kill # Phantoms.	25/100	100/300	250/500	500/700	1000/900
REAVER RAMPAGE	Kill # Reavers.	25/100	100/300	250/500	500/700	1000/900
SILENT BUT DEADLY	Kill # Megamouths.	25/100	100/300	250/500	500/700	1000/900
SPOTTER SWATTER	Kill # Spotters.	25/100	100/300	250/500	500/700	1000/900
SQUISHY	Kill # Glaciopods.	25/100	100/300	250/500	500/700	1000/900
SUN KILLER	Kill # Basking Cephaladons.	25/100	100/300	250/500	500/700	1000/900
THE BIGGER THEY ARE	Kill # Nomads.	25/100	100/300	250/500	500/700	1000/900
TYRANNICAL	Kill # Tyrants.	25/100	100/300	250/500	500/700	1000/900
VENOMOUS	Kill # Venomhounds.	25/100	100/300	250/500	500/700	1000/900

ACCOLADES: GAME MODE

ACCOLADE	GAME MODE	REQUIREMENT	TIER 1	TIER 2	TIER 3	TIER 4	TIER 5
			#/XP	#/XP	#/XP	#/XP	#/XP
DEFENDER	Defend	Win # matches in Defend.	10/100	25/200	50/300	100/400	250/500
CREEP KILLER	Defend as Hunters	Kill # Monster minions in Defend.	10/100	25/300	100/500	250/700	500/900
GOODBYE	Defend as Monster	Destroy # turrets in Defend.	5/100	10/300	50/500	100/700	250/900
TROPHY HUNTER	Hunt	Win # matches in Hunt.	10/100	25/200	50/300	100/400	250/500
TOO YOUNG TO DIE	Hunt as Hunters	Kill # Stage 1 Monsters in Hunt.	5/100	25/200	50/300	100/400	250/500
OBJECTIFIED	Hunt as Monster	Destroy # objectives in Hunt.	5/100	25/200	50/300	75/400	100/500
EGGOMANIAC	Nest	Win # matches in Nest.	10/100	25/200	50/300	100/400	250/500
MAYBE IT'S AN ANT HIVE?	Nest as Hunters	Destroy # eggs in Nest.	10/100	25/200	100/300	250/400	500/500
OMELETTE MAKER	Nest as Monster	Hatch # eggs in Nest.	10/100	25/200	100/300	250/400	500/500
RESCUER	Rescue	Win # matches in Rescue.	10/100	25/200	50/300	100/400	250/500
SAVIOR	Rescue as Hunters	Rescue # EbonStar in Rescue.	10/100	25/500	100/1000	250/1500	500/2000
FLATLINER	Rescue as Monster	Kill # EbonStar in Rescue.	10/100	25/300	100/600	250/900	500/1200

ACCOLADES: HUNTER

ACCOLADE	REQUIREMENT	TIER 1 #/XP	TIER 2 #/XP	TIER 3 #/XP	TIER 4 #/XP	TIER 5 #/XP
10 MILES HIGH	Jet Pack for # meters.	1000/1000	2500/2000	5000/3000	10000/4000	16093/5000
BOOM, HEADSHOT!	Get # headshots.	10/100	50/300	100/500	250/700	500/900
CRADLE TO GRAVE	Deal # damage to evolving Monsters.	250/250	500/500	1000/1000	2500/2500	5000/5000
FREESTYLE CHAMPION	Swim # meters.	25/500	100/1000	250/1500	750/2000	1500/2500
GO, GO, GO!	Use a dropship 260 times.	10/100	25/200	50/300	100/400	250/500
STAY CLASSY	Use a class ability # times.	10/100	50/300	100/500	250/700	500/900
THE ASSAULT	Get # Assault Awards.	25/100	100/200	250/300	500/400	1000/500
THE MEDIC	Get # Medic Awards.	25/100	100/200	250/300	500/400	1000/500
THE SUPPORT	Get # Support Awards.	25/100	100/200	250/300	500/400	1000/500
THE TRAPPER	Get # Trapper Awards.	25/100	100/200	250/300	500/400	1000/500
WAYPOINT WIZARD	Mark # Monsters using the Waypoint tool.	5/100	25/300	50/500	100/700	250/900

ACCOLADES: MONSTER

ACCOLADE	REQUIREMENT	TIER 1 #/XP	TIER 2 #/XP	TIER 3 #/XP	TIER 4 #/XP	TIER 5 #/XP
ALL MEAT DIET	Eat # wildlife.	25/100	100/300	250/500	500/700	1000/900
BLOODTHIRSTY	Incapacitate # Hunters.	10/100	25/200	100/300	250/400	500/500
BULLET SPONGE	Absorb # damage using armor.	2500/250	10000/500	25000/1000	50000/2500	100000/5000
OSMOLOGIST	Use Smell # times.	10/100	50/300	100/500	250/700	500/900
STOP WRIGGLING!	Eat # Hunters.	1/100	#VALUE!	50/300	100/400	200/500
SUPER SNEAKY	Sneak # meters.	25/1000	100/2000	250/3000	1000/4000	2000/5000
WALL CRAWLER	Climb # meters.	100/1000	250/2000	1000/3000	2500/4000	10000/5000
THE MONSTER	Get # Monster Awards.	25/100	100/200	250/300	500/400	1000/500

BADGES

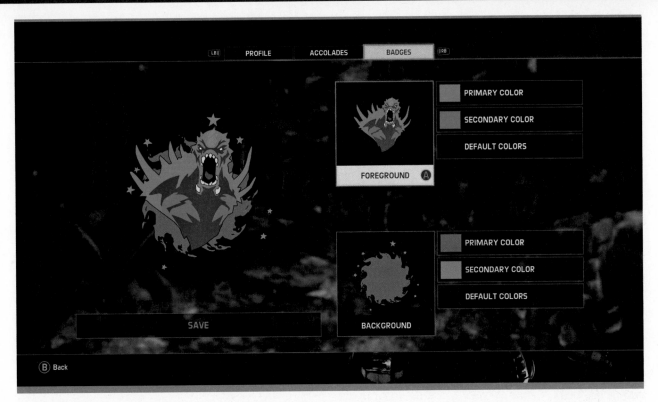

Your Badge is your personal identifier. You unlock various foregrounds and backgrounds throughout each Hunter and Monster's Character Mastery, which you can then use to customize the Badge. This is accessed in your Profile. There, you can select the two graphics and adjust the colors to your liking. Refer to the following tables for information about how to unlock each Badge piece.

FOREGROUNDS

ARMADON

BADGE PIECE	HOW TO UNLOCK
	Unlock Maggie
	Complete Tier 2 of Maggie's Character Mastery
	Complete Tier 1 of Maggie's Character Mastery
	Complete Tier 3 of Maggie's Character Mastery
	Can be obtained through the Evolve Companion App

BLITZLEOPARD

BADGE PIECE	HOW TO UNLOCK
	Unlock Abe
	Complete Tier 1 of Abe's Character Mastery
	Complete Tier 2 of Abe's Character Mastery
	Complete Tier 3 of Abe's Character Mastery
	Can be obtained through the Evolve Companion App

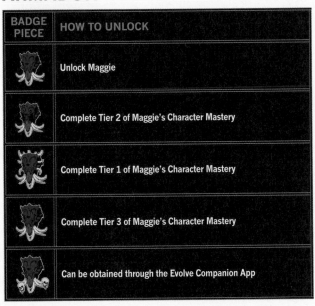

BUCKET

BADGE PIECE	HOW TO UNLOCK
	Unlock Bucket
	Complete Tier 1 of Bucket's Character Mastery
	Complete Tier 2 of Bucket's Character Mastery
	Complete Tier 3 of Bucket's Character Mastery
	Can be obtained through the Evolve Companion App

DINO

BADGE PIECE	HOW TO UNLOCK
	Unlock Hank
	Complete Tier 2 of Hank's Character Mastery
	Complete Tier 1 of Hank's Character Mastery
	Complete Tier 3 of Hank's Character Mastery
	Can be obtained through the Evolve Companion App

DRAGON

BADGE PIECE	HOW TO UNLOCK
	Unlock Parnell
	Complete Tier 1 of Parnell's Character Mastery
	Complete Tier 3 of Parnell's Character Mastery
	Complete Tier 2 of Parnell's Character Mastery
	Can be obtained through the Evolve Companion App

GOLIATH

BADGE PIECE	HOW TO UNLOCK
	Unlock Goliath
	Complete Tier 2 of Goliath's Character Mastery
	Complete Tier 3 of Goliath's Character Mastery
	Complete Tier 1 of Goliath's Character Mastery
	Earn a Gold on the Monster Tutorial
	Can be obtained through the Evolve Companion App

KRAKEN

BADGE PIECE	HOW TO UNLOCK
	Unlock Kraken
	Complete Tier 2 of Kraken's Character Mastery
	Complete Tier 3 of Kraken's Character Mastery
	Complete Tier 1 of Kraken's Character Mastery
	Reach Level 32
	Can be obtained through the Evolve Companion App

LEVIATHAN

BADGE PIECE	HOW TO UNLOCK
	Unlock Markov
	Complete Tier 1 of Markov's Character Mastery
	Complete Tier 2 of Markov's Character Mastery
	Complete Tier 3 of Markov's Character Mastery
	Can be obtained through the Evolve Companion App

TYRANT

BADGE PIECE	HOW TO UNLOCK
	Unlock Griffin
	Complete Tier 3 of Griffin's Character Mastery
	Complete Tier 1 of Griffin's Character Mastery
	Complete Tier 2 of Griffin's Character Mastery
	Can be obtained through the Evolve Companion App

PHOENIX

BADGE PIECE	HOW TO UNLOCK
	Unlock Cabot
	Complete Tier 1 of Cabot's Character Mastery
	Complete Tier 2 of Cabot's Character Mastery
	Complete Tier 3 of Cabot's Character Mastery
	Can be obtained through the Evolve Companion App

VALKYRIE

BADGE PIECE	HOW TO UNLOCK
	Unlock Val
	Complete Tier 3 of Val's Character Mastery
	Complete Tier 1 of Val's Character Mastery
	Complete Tier 2 of Val's Character Mastery
	Can be obtained through the Evolve Companion App

SALAMANDER

BADGE PIECE	HOW TO UNLOCK
	Unlock Caira
	Complete Tier 2 of Caira's Character Mastery
	Complete Tier 1 of Caira's Character Mastery
	Complete Tier 3 of Caira's Character Mastery
	Can be obtained through the Evolve Companion App

WARRIOR

BADGE PIECE	HOW TO UNLOCK
	Complete Monster Elite Mastery
	Complete Assault Elite Mastery
	Complete Support Elite Mastery
	Complete Trapper Elite Mastery
	Can be obtained through the Evolve Companion App

WEREWOLF

BADGE PIECE	HOW TO UNLOCK
	Unlock Hyde
	Complete Tier 1 of Hyde's Character
	Complete Tier 2 of Hyde's Character Mastery
	Complete Tier 3 of Hyde's Character Mastery
	Can be obtained through the Evolve Companion App

ZOMBIE

BADGE PIECE	HOW TO UNLOCK
	Unlock Lazarus
	Complete Tier 1 of Lazarus' Character Mastery
	Complete Tier 2 of Lazarus' Character Mastery
	Complete Tier 3 of Lazarus' Character Mastery
	Can be obtained through the Evolve Companion App

WRAITH

BADGE PIECE	HOW TO UNLOCK
	Unlock Wraith
	Complete Tier 2 of Wraith's Character Mastery
	Complete Tier 3 of Wraith's Character Mastery
	Complete Tier 1 of Wraith's Character Mastery
	New Calico
	Can be obtained through the Evolve Companion App

BACKGROUNDS

ARROWHEAD

BADGE PIECE	HOW TO UNLOCK
	Reach Level 4
	Reach Level 19
	Reach Level 34
	Colonial Water & Power

BANNER

BADGE PIECE	HOW TO UNLOCK
	Medic Elite Mastery
	Earn Bronze on Hunter Tutorial
	Earn Silver on Hunter Tutorial
	Earn Gold on Hunter Tutorial

CIRCLE

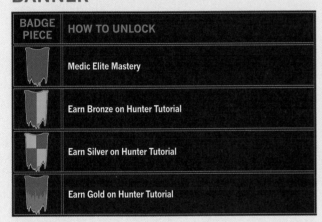

BADGE PIECE	HOW TO UNLOCK
	Unlocked by default
	Unlocked by default
	Unlocked by default
	Unlocked by default

CRESCENT

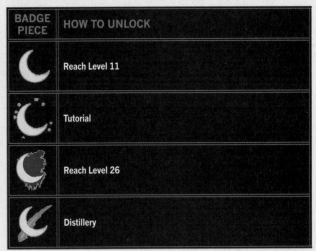

BADGE PIECE	HOW TO UNLOCK
	Reach Level 11
	Tutorial
	Reach Level 26
	Distillery

DIAMOND

BADGE PIECE	HOW TO UNLOCK
	Reach Level 15
	Reach Level 30
	Rendering Plant
	Defend

DIAMOND 2

BADGE PIECE	HOW TO UNLOCK
	Reach Level 13
	Reach Level 28
	Nest
	Medlab

HEART

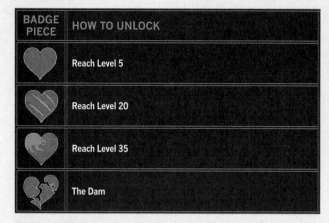

BADGE PIECE	HOW TO UNLOCK
	Reach Level 5
	Reach Level 20
	Reach Level 35
	The Dam

MOUNTAINS

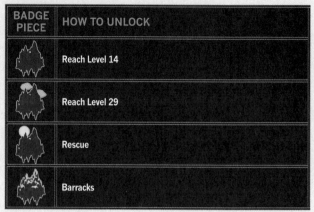

BADGE PIECE	HOW TO UNLOCK
	Reach Level 14
	Reach Level 29
	Rescue
	Barracks

JUNGLE

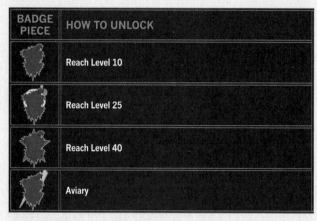

BADGE PIECE	HOW TO UNLOCK
	Reach Level 10
	Reach Level 25
	Reach Level 40
	Aviary

OCTAGON

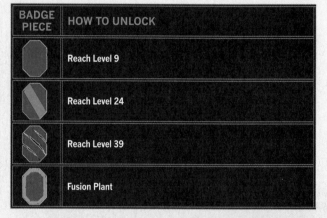

BADGE PIECE	HOW TO UNLOCK
	Reach Level 9
	Reach Level 24
	Reach Level 39
	Fusion Plant

MOONS

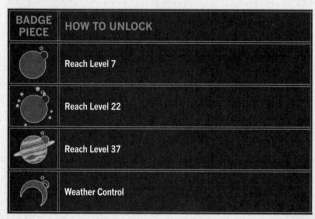

BADGE PIECE	HOW TO UNLOCK
	Reach Level 7
	Reach Level 22
	Reach Level 37
	Weather Control

SHIELD

BADGE PIECE	HOW TO UNLOCK
	Reach Level 6
	Reach Level 21
	Reach Level 36
	Armory

SKULLS

BADGE PIECE	HOW TO UNLOCK
	Reach Level 8
	Reach Level 23
	Reach Level 38
	Refueling Tower

SUPERNOVA

BADGE PIECE	HOW TO UNLOCK
	Reach Level 12
	Hunt
	Wraith Trap
	Reach Level 27

SLASHES

BADGE PIECE	HOW TO UNLOCK
	Reach Level 2
	Earn a Silver on the Monster Tutorial
	Earn a Bronze on the Monster Tutorial
	Reach Level 17

TRIUNE

BADGE PIECE	HOW TO UNLOCK
	Reach Level 3
	Reach Level 18
	Reach Level 33
	King's Fort

STAR

BADGE PIECE	HOW TO UNLOCK
	Reach Level 17
	Reach Level 31
	Salveron Ind.
	Orbital Drill

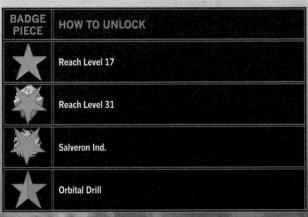

The Achievements/Trophies for *Evolve* are fairly straightforward. There are no real secrets, just a whole lot of gameplay.

AS THE MONSTER

CARDBOARD TIER

XBOX ONE GAMER SCORE	10
PLAYSTATION 4 TROPHY	Bronze
DESCRIPTION	Complete the Monster tutorial.

Simply play through Goliath's Monster tutorial in Solo.

TEACHER'S PET

XBOX ONE GAMER SCORE	20
PLAYSTATION 4 TROPHY	Bronze
DESCRIPTION	Earn Gold in the Monster tutorial.

Complete the Monster tutorial in under six minutes to earn this one.

COUNTER STRIKE

XBOX ONE GAMER SCORE	5
PLAYSTATION 4 TROPHY	Bronze
DESCRIPTION	Attack a Hunter within 15 seconds of them deploying in Hunt.

As the Monster, find the dropship within 30 seconds of the start, and wait for the Hunters to touch down. Simply attack them at this point to earn this one. If you know their drop point, you can place a mine or other damaging trap and still flee the area.

LEFT FOR DEAD

XBOX ONE GAMER SCORE	5
PLAYSTATION 4 TROPHY	Bronze
DESCRIPTION	Incapacitate a Hunter and leave them to bleed out.

As the Gamer Score points suggest, this is an easy reward to obtain. It is bound to happen as you play the game. Knock a Hunter out, and then camp the body, keeping the rest of the team from healing or reviving the character.

EVOLUTION MANIA!

XBOX ONE GAMER SCORE	5
PLAYSTATION 4 TROPHY	Bronze
DESCRIPTION	Evolve to Stage 3 as a Monster 25 times.

Reach Stage 3 as the Monster 25 times. To reach the ultimate stage, flee from battle when you start losing health and/or avoid the Hunters altogether.

GOTCHA!

XBOX ONE GAMER SCORE	5
PLAYSTATION 4 TROPHY	Bronze
DESCRIPTION	Sneak pounce the final living Hunter to end a match.

With one Hunter remaining in the game, sneak around until you are near them, and then pounce. There is no getting out of your grasp, so it is game over. However, a timely dropship may spoil this one. Use Wraith for the best results, as her Decoy ability can help you get the jump on the Hunter.

GET OFF MY PLANET

XBOX ONE GAMER SCORE	25
PLAYSTATION 4 TROPHY	Bronze
DESCRIPTION	Win Evacuation as a Monster.

As the Monster, destroy the ship in the Defend stage of Evacuation.

UNBEATABLE

XBOX ONE GAMER SCORE	20
PLAYSTATION 4 TROPHY	Bronze
DESCRIPTION	Win a match as a Monster without doing damage to the Hunters until Stage 3.

Use the huge environment and stealth to avoid the Hunters until you are able to devour enough wildlife and evolve to Stage 3. Then, take them down with your improved power and abilities. This is made tougher since the Hunters will not have any strikes against them.

DARWINISM

XBOX ONE GAMER SCORE	30
PLAYSTATION 4 TROPHY	Silver
DESCRIPTION	Win a match without losing any health as a Monster.

This is a tough one, though probably best achieved with Wraith. Stay out of sight, and sneak pounce each Hunter. Be careful, though, as a nearby Hunter will fire at you once they notice you have a teammate. As with a few of the other rewards, this one is much easier with cooperative friends.

MUD MONSTER

XBOX ONE GAMER SCORE	20
PLAYSTATION 4 TROPHY	Bronze
DESCRIPTION	Win a match having spent most of your time in Sneak.

This is a great match for Wraith, as she excels at stealth. Use Sneak and the Pounce ability to eliminate the Hunters one by one. As long as you are sneaking more than walking or running, you earn this Achievement/Trophy.

MASSACRE

XBOX ONE GAMER SCORE	20
PLAYSTATION 4 TROPHY	Bronze
DESCRIPTION	Kill an entire Hunter team as a Stage 1 Monster.

You are definitely outmatched when facing the Hunters at Stage 1, but it can be done. Use the tougher Goliath or Kraken if you plan to go up against the entire group. You can also use Wraith if you manage to isolate each of the characters. Completing the Monster's Character Mastery gives a nice boost to the beast's abilities. Play Solo and change the difficulty to Favors Monster if you are having trouble getting this one. If all else fails, go up against four friends, and take turns throwing the game as the Hunters.

NINJA TIME!

XBOX ONE GAMER SCORE	5
PLAYSTATION 4 TROPHY	Bronze
DESCRIPTION	Kill a Hunter without taking any damage.

This one simply requires a Monster to take down a Hunter without taking any damage. This is best done with a Sneak Pounce, and Wraith is the best at this maneuver. Isolate a Hunter as they attempt to hunt you down. Throw out a Decoy to distract them, and then pounce. Without a teammate around, he or she is an easy kill.

THE MONSTER

XBOX ONE GAMER SCORE	30
PLAYSTATION 4 TROPHY	Silver
DESCRIPTION	Reach elite status for a Monster.

Fully complete Character Mastery with any Monster. Use all of the Monster's abilities to complete the requirements for all three tiers.

THREE OF A KIND

XBOX ONE GAMER SCORE	90
PLAYSTATION 4 TROPHY	Gold
DESCRIPTION	Reach elite status on all Monsters.

Complete Character Mastery with all three Monsters. Play as all three beasts, and use their four abilities to complete all three tiers of requirements.

AS THE HUNTERS

BASIC TRAINING

XBOX ONE GAMER SCORE	10
PLAYSTATION 4 TROPHY	Bronze
DESCRIPTION	Complete the Hunter's tutorial.

Simply play through Markov's Hunter tutorial in Solo.

GOT A GOLD STAR

XBOX ONE GAMER SCORE	20
PLAYSTATION 4 TROPHY	Bronze
DESCRIPTION	Earn Gold in the Hunter tutorial.

Complete Markov's Hunter tutorial within six minutes to earn this one.

HOTSWAPAHOLIC

XBOX ONE GAMER SCORE	5
PLAYSTATION 4 TROPHY	Bronze
DESCRIPTION	Do damage with every class in a match.

Jump into Solo, and play as the Hunters. Swap between all four classes, using their weapons to damage the Monster or Shear creatures.

I LIVE...REDUX

XBOX ONE GAMER SCORE	5
PLAYSTATION 4 TROPHY	Bronze
DESCRIPTION	Incapacitate, hotswap, and revive yourself.

In a Solo game or a Custom game with an open slot, once a Monster knocks you out, swap to another Hunter and revive your character.

HELPING HAND

XBOX ONE GAMER SCORE	10
PLAYSTATION 4 TROPHY	Bronze
DESCRIPTION	Revive 25 incapacitated Hunters.

When a fellow Hunter gets knocked down, move nearby, and hold the Reload button to get him or her back up. This is easier said than done when a Monster is constantly trying to prevent you from doing so. You earn this reward once you have revived 25 Hunters in total.

DEATH TO TYRANNY

XBOX ONE GAMER SCORE	5
PLAYSTATION 4 TROPHY	Bronze
DESCRIPTION	Rescue a teammate from a Tyrant.

It is bound to happen some time. As the group of Hunters searches the environment for the Monster, a Tyrant jumps out of the water and snatches a teammate. Shoot the creature to free your comrade.

DEATH FROM ABOVE

XBOX ONE GAMER SCORE	10
PLAYSTATION 4 TROPHY	Bronze
DESCRIPTION	Kill the Monster while in mid-air.

As the Monster nears death, jump around and only attack when in the air. There are skills that must be used on the ground.

SQUERLY

XBOX ONE GAMER SCORE	25
PLAYSTATION 4 TROPHY	Bronze
DESCRIPTION	Achieve 95% or higher accuracy in a match.

Stick to the more accurate weaponry during a match, and limit your shots throughout. Avoid the more erratic automatic rifles and shotguns, and use the zoom when firing for improved accuracy.

EQUAL OPPORTUNITY HUNTERS

XBOX ONE GAMER SCORE	5
PLAYSTATION 4 TROPHY	Bronze
DESCRIPTION	Win a match with half of the team as the opposite sex.

Win any game of Evolve as the Hunters with Maggie as your Trapper and Val or Caira as the Medic. When you play Solo, the Hunter team defaults to the first characters, so as long as you select a female character or play as Assault or Support, you earn this reward.

CLASSLESS

XBOX ONE GAMER SCORE	25
PLAYSTATION 4 TROPHY	Bronze
DESCRIPTION	Win a match without using your class ability.

Win any match without using your class ability. Play as a Hunter, and do not deploy your fourth skill. If you play the Trapper, this means there is no Mobile Arena to trap the Monster in. The simplest choice may be a Support Hunter, who cannot use his Cloaking Field.

COCKROACH

XBOX ONE GAMER SCORE	30
PLAYSTATION 4 TROPHY	Bronze
DESCRIPTION	Kill the Monster while incapacitated.

This requires a Monster to have very low health, as your handgun does little damage. Get knocked out by your foe, and hope that it leaves you alone. Quickly fire your weapon at the beast. Having a Medic keep you in the down-but-not-out state can help give you the time needed to fire the kill shot.

WITH OUR POWERS COMBINED

XBOX ONE GAMER SCORE	25
PLAYSTATION 4 TROPHY	Bronze
DESCRIPTION	Win Evacuation as a Hunter.

Jump into a game of Evacuation in Solo or Multiplayer, and keep the Monsters from destroying the ship in the Defend stage.

PREMADE

XBOX ONE GAMER SCORE	20
PLAYSTATION 4 TROPHY	Bronze
DESCRIPTION	Win a round of Hunt while in a party of four players.

Go online and party with three other players. Enter a Multiplayer Hunt match, and win the game.

INCONCEIVABLE

XBOX ONE GAMER SCORE	15
PLAYSTATION 4 TROPHY	Bronze
DESCRIPTION	Kill the Monster without taking any damage.

This is a tough one, since you never know when the Monster is going to come after you. Select a Hunter who can perform their role away from the action. Typically, Support is last on the priority list, and they can all take care of most of their tasks from a high perch.

MANO A MONSTER

XBOX ONE GAMER SCORE	20
PLAYSTATION 4 TROPHY	Bronze
DESCRIPTION	Kill a Stage 3 Monster while being the only Hunter alive.

This requires getting the Stage 3 Monster down to low health and being the final Hunter alive. Taking the beast down at this point really depends on how much health is left, but it may help to be the Assault Hunter. Otherwise, Hank's Orbital Barrage is a good skill to finish off a hurting foe.

THE HUNTER

XBOX ONE GAMER SCORE	30
PLAYSTATION 4 TROPHY	Silver
DESCRIPTION	Reach elite status for a Hunter.

Fully complete Character Mastery with any Hunter. Use all of a Hunter's non-class specific loadout items to complete the requirements for all three tiers.

12-SIDED DIE

XBOX ONE GAMER SCORE	90
PLAYSTATION 4 TROPHY	Gold
DESCRIPTION	Reach elite status on all Hunters.

These two Achievements/Trophies take the preceding three a step further. Complete Character Mastery with all 12 Hunters. This requires you to use every character and their skills. There is a reason this trophy is Gold; it takes a long time to achieve.

AS EITHER MONSTER OR HUNTER

WILDLIFE GENOCIDIST

XBOX ONE GAMER SCORE	10
PLAYSTATION 4 TROPHY	Bronze
DESCRIPTION	Kill 1,390 wildlife.

Simply take out the wildlife as a Monster or Hunter. It may take a while to rack up 1,390 kills, but eventually, you will get there.

TASTE OF SHEAR

XBOX ONE GAMER SCORE	25
PLAYSTATION 4 TROPHY	Bronze
DESCRIPTION	Kill one of each creature on Shear.

There are 20 different species of wildlife on the planet Shear. Kill one of each type to earn this reward. Refer to the Wildlife chapter for a full list of creatures.

#SHEARPROBLEMS

XBOX ONE GAMER SCORE	5
PLAYSTATION 4 TROPHY	Bronze
DESCRIPTION	Destroy 100 objects.

There are many objects around Shear, both natural and manmade, that you can demolish. You can take down these objects easily as a behemoth Monster, but it is also possible to destroy trees and other items with your Hunter weapons. Tally 100 objects destroyed to earn this reward.

BEAT THEM ALL

XBOX ONE GAMER SCORE	10
PLAYSTATION 4 TROPHY	Bronze
DESCRIPTION	Win a match in all online game modes.

This one must be done in Multiplayer. Go online, and win a match in Hunt, Nest, Rescue, and Defend as either a Hunter or Monster.

IF IT BLEEDS

XBOX ONE GAMER SCORE	15
PLAYSTATION 4 TROPHY	Bronze
DESCRIPTION	Win 25 matches in Hunt.

Tally 25 wins in Hunt mode with the Hunters or Monster in either Solo or Multiplayer.

KNOCK-KNOCK

XBOX ONE GAMER SCORE	15
PLAYSTATION 4 TROPHY	Bronze
DESCRIPTION	Win 25 matches in Defend.

Tally 25 wins in Defend mode with the Hunters or Monster in either Solo or Multiplayer.

WE'RE NOT ASSASSINS

XBOX ONE GAMER SCORE	15
PLAYSTATION 4 TROPHY	Bronze
DESCRIPTION	Win 25 matches in Rescue.

Tally 25 wins in Rescue mode with the Hunters or Monster in either Solo or Multiplayer.

PAYBACK TIME

XBOX ONE GAMER SCORE	15
PLAYSTATION 4 TROPHY	Bronze
DESCRIPTION	Win 25 matches in Nest.

Tally 25 wins in Nest mode with the Hunters or Monster in either Solo or Multiplayer.

NATURAL SELECTION

XBOX ONE GAMER SCORE	20
PLAYSTATION 4 TROPHY	Bronze
DESCRIPTION	Complete an entire Evacuation campaign without dying.

In a game of Evacuation, last all five days without dying once as the Monster or a Hunter. It is possible to lose a round without dying.

BONE JOCKEY

XBOX ONE GAMER SCORE	10
PLAYSTATION 4 TROPHY	Bronze
DESCRIPTION	Win a match while having spent most of the time in the air.

This requires that you spend more time in the air than on the ground and win a game. The easiest way to earn this is with the Kraken. Simply remain in the air for as long as possible, and be sure to win the game.

VEGAN POLICE

XBOX ONE GAMER SCORE	20
PLAYSTATION 4 TROPHY	Bronze
DESCRIPTION	Win a match without killing any creatures.

A Monster needs creatures to give them armor and to evolve. Hunters can easily go a game without killing any wildlife; they can even nab a Buff from a Monster's prey. This one is possible with either side, but playing as a Hunter and not shooting at any creatures is the simplest method.

INVINCIBLE

XBOX ONE GAMER SCORE	25
PLAYSTATION 4 TROPHY	Bronze
DESCRIPTION	Win a match in under 2:05 minutes.

This goes well with Massacre. Take your Stage 1 Monster straight to the Hunters. You are outmatched, but with some skilled play and a little luck, the other team may go down within 2:05. Winning the fight within this time may be easier as the Hunters, but that requires finding it immediately. Just like Massacre, this Achievement/Trophy is easily obtained with cooperative players on the other side.

Try this rush tactic. As Kraken, feed on any nearby wildlife to build up your armor, but get ready to meet up with the Hunters at their drop point. Look for the dropship overhead, and throw down some Banshee Mines just below. As they near the ground, unload an upgraded Lightning Strike directly on top of the group. If things seem to be going well, stick around and continue pummeling the humans. This gives little time to increase your armor, so keep an eye on your health.

You can also earn this reward as the Hunters. Team up Caira and Maggie to give Daisy a speed boost, and quickly find the Monster at Stage 1. Take it down quickly with team play.

COLLECT THEM ALL!

XBOX ONE GAMER SCORE	30
PLAYSTATION 4 TROPHY	Silver
DESCRIPTION	Unlock all the Hunters and Monsters.

Completing the first tier requirements for the following Hunters and Monsters unlocks the corresponding characters. Once the entire second column is available, you earn Collect Them All!

COMPLETING TIER 1 CHARACTER MASTERY REQUIREMENTS FOR...	UNLOCKS...
Markov	Hyde
Hyde	Parnell
Maggie	Griffin
Griffin	Abe
Val	Lazarus
Lazarus	Caira
Hank	Bucket
Bucket	Cabot
Goliath	Kraken
Kraken	Wraith

APEX PREDATOR

XBOX ONE GAMER SCORE	85
PLAYSTATION 4 TROPHY	Gold
DESCRIPTION	Achieve Rank 40.

The maximum level in Evolve is 40. At this point, all three-star Perks have been unlocked. This trophy is Gold for a reason, as it takes a long time to achieve.

AWARD ADDICTION

XBOX ONE GAMER SCORE	20
PLAYSTATION 4 TROPHY	Bronze
DESCRIPTION	Obtain 25 unique Awards.

There are a number of Awards that you can earn as you play a game of Evolve. Some are unique to the side you play, and others can only be won in certain modes. Rack up 25 unique ones to get this Achievement/Trophy.

INSTANT ARTIST

XBOX ONE GAMER SCORE	5
PLAYSTATION 4 TROPHY	Bronze
DESCRIPTION	Create a Badge in the Profile Badge creator.

Simply go to Badge within the Profile screen, and modify the Foreground, Background, or colors of your Badge. Save the result to earn this reward.

STRATEGIST

XBOX ONE GAMER SCORE	30
PLAYSTATION 4 TROPHY	Silver
DESCRIPTION	Watch all Basic and Advanced Tutorial Videos.

Select Video Gallery from the Extras menu, and watch all of the Basic and Advanced Tutorial Videos. This may take some time to go through, but you may learn some valuable strategies as you do so.

THANK YOU

XBOX ONE GAMER SCORE	5
PLAYSTATION 4 TROPHY	Bronze
DESCRIPTION	Watch the credits all the way through the end.

Simply select Credits from the Extras menu, and watch them all the way to the end.

EVOLVE PLATINUM TROPHY

XBOX ONE GAMER SCORE	N/A
PLAYSTATION 4 TROPHY	Platinum
DESCRIPTION	Obtain all other trophies.

As with most games, the Platinum Trophy is a tough one. Earn all 50 trophies.

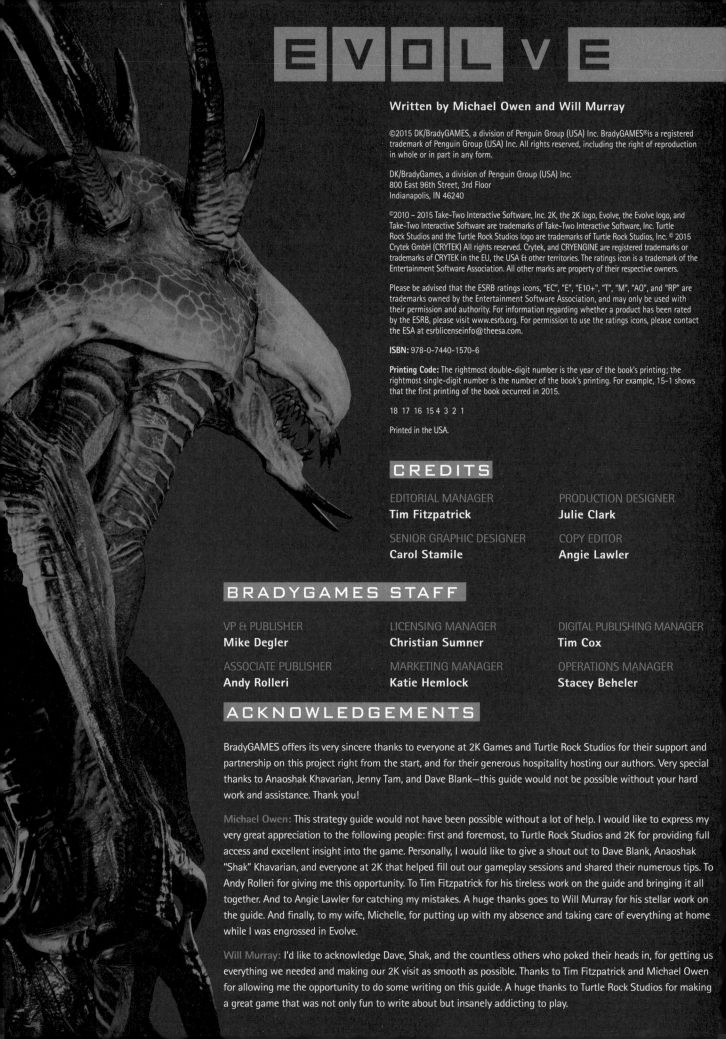

EVOLVE

Written by Michael Owen and Will Murray

DK/BradyGames, a division of Penguin Group (USA) Inc.
800 East 96th Street, 3rd Floor
Indianapolis, IN 46240

ISBN: 978-0-7440-1570-6

Printing Code: The rightmost double-digit number is the year of the book's printing; the rightmost single-digit number is the number of the book's printing. For example, 15-1 shows that the first printing of the book occurred in 2015.

18 17 16 15 4 3 2 1

Printed in the USA.

CREDITS

EDITORIAL MANAGER
Tim Fitzpatrick

SENIOR GRAPHIC DESIGNER
Carol Stamile

PRODUCTION DESIGNER
Julie Clark

COPY EDITOR
Angie Lawler

BRADYGAMES STAFF

VP & PUBLISHER
Mike Degler

ASSOCIATE PUBLISHER
Andy Rolleri

LICENSING MANAGER
Christian Sumner

MARKETING MANAGER
Katie Hemlock

DIGITAL PUBLISHING MANAGER
Tim Cox

OPERATIONS MANAGER
Stacey Beheler

ACKNOWLEDGEMENTS

BradyGAMES offers its very sincere thanks to everyone at 2K Games and Turtle Rock Studios for their support and partnership on this project right from the start, and for their generous hospitality hosting our authors. Very special thanks to Anaoshak Khavarian, Jenny Tam, and Dave Blank—this guide would not be possible without your hard work and assistance. Thank you!

Michael Owen: This strategy guide would not have been possible without a lot of help. I would like to express my very great appreciation to the following people: first and foremost, to Turtle Rock Studios and 2K for providing full access and excellent insight into the game. Personally, I would like to give a shout out to Dave Blank, Anaoshak "Shak" Khavarian, and everyone at 2K that helped fill out our gameplay sessions and shared their numerous tips. To Andy Rolleri for giving me this opportunity. To Tim Fitzpatrick for his tireless work on the guide and bringing it all together. And to Angie Lawler for catching my mistakes. A huge thanks goes to Will Murray for his stellar work on the guide. And finally, to my wife, Michelle, for putting up with my absence and taking care of everything at home while I was engrossed in Evolve.

Will Murray: I'd like to acknowledge Dave, Shak, and the countless others who poked their heads in, for getting us everything we needed and making our 2K visit as smooth as possible. Thanks to Tim Fitzpatrick and Michael Owen for allowing me the opportunity to do some writing on this guide. A huge thanks to Turtle Rock Studios for making a great game that was not only fun to write about but insanely addicting to play.

EVOLVE

FREE EGUIDE

Go to www.primagames.com/code and enter this unique code to access your FREE eGuide!

y4s9-4rqf-5ukk-dg4e

www.primagames.com   www.2k.com   www.evolvegame.com